Latina/o Stars in U.S. Eyes

Latina/o Stars in U.S. Eyes

The Making and Meanings of Film and TV Stardom

MARY C. BELTRÁN

UNIVERSITY OF ILLINOIS PRESS

Urbana and Chicago

Library of Congress Cataloging-in-Publication Data
Beltrán, Mary.
Latina/o stars in U.S. eyes: the making and meanings of film
and TV stardom / Mary C. Beltrán.
p.   cm.
Includes index.
ISBN 978-0-252-03454-1 (cloth: alk. paper) —
ISBN 978-0-252-07651-0 (pbk.: alk. paper)
1. Hispanic Americans in motion pictures. 2. Hispanic Americans
on television. 3. Hispanic American motion picture actors and
actresses—Biography. 4. Hispanic American television actors
and actresses—Biography.
I. Title.
PN1995.9.H47B45   2009
791.4302'8092368073—dc22   2008037941
[B]

Contents

Acknowledgments

A book project such as this one takes years to complete; there are a great many people who helped me bring it to fruition. I was lucky to be guided in my early research by Charles Ramírez Berg and John "JD" Downing, both of whom were instrumental in sharing their expertise and offering sage advice that informed the approach of this book. Charles in particular provided inspiration to this project, given his impassioned and incisive teaching and research on Latina and Latino representation and creative authorship in Hollywood and independent film and media. I will always be grateful for Charles and JD's support, mentorship, and friendship. I also want to thank Federico Subervi for his early mentoring, Janet Staiger for her early guidance and inspiration, and S. Craig Watkins, Thomas Schatz, and Gigi Durham for their helpful suggestions on early drafts of several book chapters.

Since I have joined the faculty at the University of Wisconsin–Madison, I have been fortunate to have joined a community of extremely supportive colleagues as I continued to develop this project. I have especially benefited from the support and mentorship of Michael Curtin, Michele Hilmes, Vance Kepley, Norma Saldivar, Julie D'Acci, and Camille Guerin-Gonzales. I also want to thank the undergraduate and graduate students with whom I work for making the UW a home where I have been inspired and encouraged to do this work. My research also has been supported by grants from the University of Wisconsin–Madison Graduate School and the UW System's Institute on Race and Ethnicity. In addition, the UCLA Chicano Studies Research Center provided helpful administrative support while I was a visiting scholar in the summer of 2005. In recent years, several colleagues outside the

UW also have provided feedback on manuscript chapters or have supported my research more generally. These colleagues, to whom I send my warm appreciation, include Frances Aparicio, Chon Noriega, Diane Negra, Clara Rodríguez, Catherine Benamou, Angharad Valdivia, Curtis Marez, Camilla Fojas, Chris Holmlund, Yeidy Rivero, Yvonne Tasker, George Lipsitz, and Shanti Kurmar.

With respect to the nuts-and-bolts work of the research and writing of this manuscript, I want to thank the library staff of several archives that provided their expert assistance. This list includes Steve Wilson of the Harry Ransom Center for the Humanities at the University of Texas at Austin; Barbara Hall, Kathy Krueger, and the entire staff of the Reading Room of the Margaret Herrick Library of the Academy of Motion Picture Arts and Sciences in Los Angeles; Sona Basmadjian of the David L. Wolper Center for the Study of the Documentary at the USC Library of Cinema Arts; the staff of the UCLA Film & Television Archive; and the staff of the Museum of Television and Radio (now the Paley Center for Media) in Los Angeles. I also want to thank Sreya Mitra, my research assistant in the summer of 2007, who provided invaluable assistance in some of the final research for this manuscript. At the University of Illinois Press, I also would like to thank Joan Catapano for believing in this project when it was far from completion, and Breanne Ertmer and Beth Gianfagna for shepherding the manuscript along the various stages of publication. Finally, I thank Karen Verde for her meticulous editing of the final manuscript.

I also have members of the "Latinowood" community to thank for sharing their insights with me early in my research. I extend my appreciation to Bel Hernandez, editor and publisher of *Latin Heat* trade journal, my home base during my early field research, who was instrumental in introducing me to Latina/o media industry professionals and helping me gain an insiders' view of the industry. Thanks also to the many individuals who shared their thoughts with me. These individuals include Bonnie Abounza, Rosemary Alderete, Nancy de Los Santos, Ken Diaz, Moctesuma Esparza, Bel Hernandez, Bob Morones, Santiago Pozo, Susan Racho, Luis Reyes, Monica Rivas, Monalee Seshilling, Sandy Varga, Jerry Velasco, Susana Zepeda, and Pedro Zamora.

Speaking of "Latinowood," I also must thank the celebrated actors—both those who are no longer with us and those who continue to make important contributions to U.S. films, television, and popular culture—who are the subject of this study. Their hard work, perseverance, tremendous talent, and poise throughout their careers have made a Latinowood possible. Thank you, Dolores Del Rio, Desi Arnaz, Rita Moreno, Freddie Prinze, Edward James

Olmos, Jennifer Lopez, Jessica Alba, and Rosario Dawson. I made a decision early in the research on this project not to try to interview those stars profiled who are still living, primarily because I wished to focus instead on the promotion these stars received, and stories about their lives that were widely circulated. But I of course kick myself now for not having attempted to interview Rita Moreno, Edward James Olmos, and the other, younger actors studied here. An excuse for a second book! I attempted to relate the details of these actors' lives as truthfully as possible; I apologize in advance for any errors to this effect.

Finally, I wish to thank my family and friends who have inspired and encouraged me throughout this project. My parents, Veronica Beltrán Caudle and Rodney Caudle, are my role models and champions; it has been especially fun to work on a project that could include watching movies and gossiping about stars with them. My brothers, Don and David, sister Anita, and their families have also been strong supports who always encouraged me to complete this unwieldy project.

I also am grateful to my friends and partners over the years; their support has made a huge difference as I have made the sometimes-bumpy journey in the last decade from social worker to graduate student to university professor. Amber Feldman and Lee Sparks in particular fed my spirit during the difficult days of graduate school. And I am grateful to my supportive *comadres* and *compadres:* Becky Lentz, Carmen Cruz, Jane Park, Sharon Ross, Alice Chu Johnson, Julie Dowling, Brian Ritzel, Yeidy Rivero, Alnisa Allgood, Lisa Nakamura, Peter Streicher, Chris Garlough, Amy Singer, and many other wonderful folks who have been there as my friends, sounding boards, and cheering squad when I have needed it most. Thanks also to Mrako Fenster, for the barley soup and the many other good things that we have shared.

Latina and Latino Stars in U.S. Eyes

This is a book about Latina and Latino stardom, but even more it is about the U.S. entertainment media's imagining of Latina/os.[1] In the case studies that follow, I interrogate the dynamics of star production and promotion for a handful of film and entertainment television stars since the silent film era and what we can learn from them about the evolution of Latina/o and national identities in the American imagination (or "U.S. eyes"), as filtered through Hollywood film and star promotion. More specifically, I ask, how have Latina/o opportunities and star images reflected or challenged the shifting status of Latina/os in relation to racial, class, and gendered notions, and notions of citizenship and national identity? And given that sociohistorical and film and television industry contexts have established radically different openings and opportunities for Latina/o actors at distinct junctures, what can Latina/o stardom teach us about these periods in Hollywood and in U.S. social life?

When I began this project in 1998, it seemed, on the surface at least, that Latina/os had reached a level of visibility, popularity, and status in English-language film, television, and popular culture that was unprecedented. Ricky Martin was shaking his bon-bon for television audiences, and "J.Lo," then known only as Jennifer Lopez, was drawing the spotlight with her acting achievements and celebrated body. While few Latina/os could be found on network television at the time, Hollywood films included a growing roster of well-known Latina/o and Latin American stars, including Lopez, Salma Hayek, Benicio del Toro, and Jimmy Smits. Indeed, along with the fact that Latina/os were soon to surpass African Americans as the largest nonwhite group in the United States, mainstream news sources were also trumpeting the news that Latina/os were becoming increasingly visible and influential in popular culture. In a "Latin USA" cover issue, *Newsweek* announced the rise of "Generation Ñ," while *New York* magazine, renamed *Nueva York* for its own special issue, heralded the recent "Latino explosion" in cultural life, sports, and politics.[2] Yet the success and grand-scale promotion of such performers as Lopez and Martin was not the complete picture; the actual behind-the-scenes scenarios and star promotion texts often did not match the optimism or the hype regarding a late-1990s "Latin Wave." As I discuss in more detail in chapter 6, hints of contradiction and marginalization could easily be discerned, whether in promotional texts that emphasized the curvaceous bodies and supposed innate sensual earthiness of these performers or in discussion of U.S.-born Latina/os as "crossover" stars.

I offer this quick glimpse of a recent moment in Latina/o media representation as a way to demonstrate both the complexity of this research topic and the importance of pursuing it through in-depth, historically contextualized study. Latina/o images in the U.S. entertainment media have been nothing if not ambivalent, reflecting the shifting and equally ambivalent racial and social status of Mexican Americans and other Latina/os in this country in the last century. For example, in more recent years it has become more likely that we may witness Latina/o actors portraying richly textured characters, such as that of college-bound teen Ana Garcia, played by America Ferrera (now of *Ugly Betty* fame) in *Real Women Have Curves* (2002). But my students still tell me, overwhelmingly, that they feel that negative and stereotypical images continue to be more the norm than the exception. And they know all too well the age-old stereotypes, given useful labels by Charles Ramírez Berg and others: the Latin lover, the bandido/cholo, the harlot or spitfire, and so on.[3] These sorts of one-dimensional images continue to be seen and to carry weight today, even as some Latina/o actors and media professionals are experiencing greater opportunity.

The exploration of Latina/o opportunity and stardom promises to be informative far beyond the study of media representation, moreover. This is because such images have power. As Richard Dyer most famously has argued and other scholars have since documented, media representation and stardom in particular provides important and telling clues regarding the sociopolitical status of a people within a society, as well as playing a role in relations between various groups.[4] Not only have they provided images to non-Latinos of who and what Latina/os might be, but over the decades they have provided images to people of Latin descent that can affect how we see ourselves and what we can make of our lives.

To provide parameters and focus to my research on this complex topic, I structure my study several ways. First, I look at questions regarding the evolving racial status of Latina/os through the lens of film and television stardom, with the understanding that it is a forum through which ethnic notions and racial borders are reinforced, challenged, and otherwise made meaningful.[5] Given this understanding, a great deal can be learned regarding the media construction of Latinidad (what I term "Hollywood Latinidad" to describe the industries' construction of a collective, imagined "Latin-ness" through media products and star publicity) from exploring the careers and media texts produced in relation to popular Latino and Latina stars in previous eras and today. It also can teach us a great deal about Latinidad as defined by Frances Aparicio and Susan Chávez Silverman, referring to Latina/o identity formation through lived experience by Latina/os themselves. They refine the term as "Latinidades" to refer to this dynamic in relation to the diverse communities and identities that comprise Latina/o identities in the United States and transnationally.[6] Thus, both Hollywood Latinidad and its potential influence on Latinidades are the focus of this book.

My study is not encyclopedic, however. It does not aim to address the experiences of all Latina/o stars or to document the entire careers of the stars that serve as case studies. Rather, I further structured this book by situating my case studies within transitional moments in media and U.S. social history and what can be gleaned from them with respect to Latina/o representation and stardom. In this evolution there have been important junctures in media history with respect to Latina/o opportunity and representation; for instance, they include the transition from silent to sound film in the late 1920s, the 1970s era of "socially relevant" television, and the period when the first Latino-directed feature films reached national audiences in the 1980s. In addition, sociopolitical developments that had an equally influential impact and which I address in the chapters that follow include the Great Depression, World War II, and the rise of Chicano and Puerto Rican media activism targeting U.S. television networks and film studies. These periods and events offered new, although not necessarily better, opportunities to Latina/o performers, times and spaces in which popular notions of Latinidad and how Latina/os should be represented in the entertainment media were brought to attention or called into question.

Structuring the chapters in this way provides an abbreviated overview of the historical evolution of Latina/o representation and stardom in Hollywood film and U.S. entertainment television, major components of what I term Hollywood Latinidad. I build here on the work of Ana M. López, who aptly described Hollywood as a cultural ethnographer, figuratively creating race and ethnicity through its cinematic representations of various groups.[7] As López illustrates in her work on Latina stars of the "Good Neighbor" era, such images are embedded within and reflect the ideology and material realities of their social and historical moment.

To this end, *Latina/o Stars in U.S. Eyes: The Making and Meanings of Film and TV Stardom* explores the evolution of Latina/o and American identities as evidenced in transitional moments in U.S. media history and Latina/os who became stars in these moments. Chapter 1 is centered on Mexican actress Dolores Del Rio, whose Hollywood film career from 1925 through the early 1940s spanned the transition from silent to sound film. Chapter 2 then examines the career of Cuban musician, actor, and television executive Desi Arnaz, who, after appearing in "Good Neighbor" films in the 1940s, became an extremely popular television actor in and executive producer of the 1950s hit series *I Love Lucy*. Chapter 3 surveys the early decades (1950s and 1960s) of the film career of Puerto Rican performer Rita Moreno, who witnessed the breakdown of the studio system and the rise of independent film companies. The attention in chapter 4 turns to Puerto Rican and German Hungarian actor Freddie Prinze, who quickly rose to stardom in the title role of NBC's *Chico and the Man* (1974–78), but not without intense controversy and complaints from Chicano media activists and other viewers. Chapter 5 then shifts the focus to Mexican American actor Edward James Olmos, who became a symbol of Latino filmmaking in the 1980s. In chapter 6, the focus is Nuyorican actress, singer, and franchise head Jennifer Lopez, who rose to mainstream stardom amidst the growth of Latina/o media production and the news media's discursive construction of "crossover" stardom in the late 1990s. Finally, in chapter 7, I investigate the impact of millennial trends that have emphasized mixed-race heritage and ethnically ambiguous characters on Latina/o opportunity and stardom through an exploration of the career of actress Jessica Alba and comparison to her contemporary, Rosario Dawson.

Readers may wonder at some of these choices. While some of these actors may never have reached major star status, each exemplified success for a performer of Latina/o heritage in his or her respective historical juncture and media era. Their diversity with respect to gender, nationality, training, class background, appearance, and career entrée also allows for exploration of questions regarding the conflation and at times privileging of particular Latina/o groups in Latina/o representation and star promotion, the diversity and disparity of opportunities experienced by Latina/o actors over the decades, and the impact of increasingly pan-Latino identities today. The inclusion of both film and television stars also allows for comparative analysis of the opportunities and limitations afforded by each media industry at different historical junctures, shedding greater light on the complex evolution of Latina/o stardom and of the Hollywood media industry's more general imagining of Latinidad.

Stardom and the American Imaginary

> The stakes here are about more than entertainment. They're about who we allow to dance inside our imaginations and why.
> —Kristal Brent Zook, *Color by Fox: The Fox Network and the Revolution in Black Television* (New York: Oxford University Press, 1999), 64

As scholars such as Richard Dyer, George Lipsitz, and Ella Shohat and Robert Stam have well documented, media representations play a powerful role in American and global social relations.[8] We can look to the entertainment media as one of the most important places where "ideas, myths, fictions, ideologies, and social models are produced, displayed, negotiated, and contested," as Alberto Sandoval-Sánchez has argued,[9] and stars are the heroes and heroines that populate and invigorate this landscape. In this regard, stardom operates on a national and increasingly global scale as a powerful social force. Stars—or the lack of stars from particular groups in a society— "teach" notions of identity and leadership to citizens from all walks of life, including lessons regarding the meaning of gender, class, race, and ethnicity in a particular time and place. For example, stars' public images have long assisted in the reification and reinforcement of U.S. racial categories and particularly in the construction and celebration of whiteness. In this regard, whiteness traditionally has been likened to such qualities as purity, beauty, and integrity—and perhaps more important, to the various privileges and rights inherent to American citizenship and identity.[10] Scholars have documented the reinforcement of such notions of whiteness, to list just a few examples, in relation to stardom associated with vaudeville theater performances and early Hollywood film.[11]

I should note here that I use terms such as "whiteness" and the more general "race" with the understanding that racial categories are not biological constructs, but rather categories that have been constructed socially, as described by Michael Omi and Howard Winant and others.[12] More specifically, race historically has been constructed in relation to a black-white binary in the United States. As Neil Foley points out, such a binary was made possible only because "the United States . . . repudiated the idea of racial hybridity for most of its history"; as a result, the United States has had "no cultural or legal context for understanding the racial place of mestizo peoples" such as Latina/os.[13] Unsurprisingly, there is continuing confusion regarding the status of Mexican Americans and other Latina/os as racialized citizens, and whether we should be considered a separate race or an ethnic group even today.[14]

Moreover, studies have documented the importance of film and media stars as role models and as influential in the establishment of self-image and social attitudes toward other groups.[15] We learn from such role models what sort of a life we can hope for, literally what to aspire to, as well as what to think of others and to expect others will think of us. Will others think we're smart, capable, trustworthy, and attractive, or unintelligent, untrustworthy, and/or unattractive? These are powerful messages that can play determining roles in the futures of all young people and in social relations between ethnic groups. A greater understanding of the construction and marketing of stars from nondominant ethnic and racial groups, such as Latina/os within the context of the United States, therefore can reveal a great deal about the prevailing racial attitudes and social relations of a time and place.

And what is stardom? Scholars such as Christine Gledhill define film and television stars as actors who become the object of public fascination to the extent that their lives off-screen are as interesting to fans as their performances.[16] I would add that the opportunity for an actor to attain star status generally comes with being cast in psychologically compelling lead roles, as well as through being given "star treatment" publicity in the entertainment media. When we consider stardom from this perspective, the odds appear stacked against Latina/os in many respects. Although the number of Latina/o television and film roles has increased in the last decade, there are still few Hispanic characters that are well-developed protagonists around which stories revolve. In the realm of television representation, studies have documented that Latina/o characters have only recently increased from 2 to 6 percent of all prime-time roles,[17] even while the Latina/o population has grown to 15 percent of the U.S. population. Those characters that do appear typically are in minor rather than starring roles.

This lack of visibility and substance in film and TV story worlds dovetails with the relative dearth of Latino and Latina stars, when you consider that opportunity to attain star status typically emerges from being cast in well-developed lead roles. While studios, networks, production companies, and related industries spend millions each year to create and promote stars that will appeal to the widest possible audience, Latina/os still are seldom the object of such promotion. Given how few Latina/o images are circulating in the popular imagination, these images, of both performers and characters, arguably hold more importance and are more heavily judged, given that they carry what James Baldwin, Kobena Mercer, and others have termed a "burden of representation."[18]

It is an especially useful time to explore the meaning and significance of these dynamics in popular culture. The burden of representation experienced by Latino and Latina stars can be seen as growing heavier as they represent an increasing population. In this respect, the proportion of Latina/os in the United States has more than tripled, from 4.5 percent of the population in the 1960s to an estimated 15 percent in 2008, while Latina/os comprise one in five U.S. youth today.[19] Scholars are just beginning to critically examine the impact of this population shift on the media landscape and on U.S. social life and identity.

Perhaps as an early reflection of these shifts, the rising status of a handful of Latinos and Latinas in U.S. film and television also makes the topic of Latina/o stardom particularly timely. Actors such as Jennifer Lopez, Benicio del Toro, America Ferrera, and George Lopez have gained critical recognition and status in the last decade, while Latina/o filmmakers and producers are successfully launching films and television series, signs of an increasingly visible and powerful "Latinowood"[20] within the historically white media production and star system. Should the success of these individuals be taken as a sign of improvements for Latina/os in Hollywood with respect to opportunity, creative agency, or star promotion? While this has yet to be determined, Latino and Latina stars likely will have increasing visibility and impact.

The Racial Riddle and Other Twists of Latina/o Stardom

The first wave of scholars to study Latina/o stardom have laid an important foundation on which I build here; they include but are not limited to Charles Ramírez Berg, Ana M. López, Chon Noriega, Clara E. Rodríguez, Angharad Valdivia, and Gary Keller.[21] For one, Latina/o film and television representation rests heavily on notions of appearance and race that have dictated a bifurcation of opportunity for Latina/o actors: those who might be potential stars, and those who will only be cast in minor and character roles, regardless of talent. In fact, over the last century most Latina/o stars have had fair skin and European phenotypic features (body type, facial features, hair type, etc.). Antonio Ríos-Bustamante and Clara E. Rodríguez, for example, have documented how casting opportunities in the first decades of U.S. film were dependent on how closely Latina/o performers embodied such "white" beauty and body ideals.[22] Interviews that I conducted with Latina/o actors and media professionals as part of my research confirmed that this sort of typing has diminished only slightly. The unwritten rules of Hollywood casting generally include the necessity for Latina/o star hopefuls to have light tan skin and European rather than indigenous features, the ability to speak English well and without an "undesirable" accent, and that they be of medium to tall height, with a slim build.

In addition, Rodríguez points out that fair-skinned, blonde, and blue-eyed Latino actors and actresses, like those of darker coloring, typically are not considered for Latina/o roles; by Hollywood standards they do not have what she terms the preferred "Latin look."[23] These norms have broadened slightly in recent years, however, as a handful of Latina/o actors of darker skin tones and more indigenous phenotypic features are finding acting opportunities. Actress Rosario Dawson, who is of Puerto Rican, Afro-Cuban, Irish, and Native American descent, and comedian and actor George Lopez, who is Mexican American, are two illustrations of this trend.

Complicating the process of racialization that Latina/o actors experience is the phenomenon of cultural racialization. As scholars such as Rosaura Sanchez explain, cultural racialization describes the dynamics by which Mexican Americans in the United States have been categorized as nonwhite based on such factors as language, accent, cultural practices, and class differences, rather than appearance.[24] Similarly, Latina/o actors have been categorized (as, for example, "Latin," "Hispanic," or "ethnic") based on class-related associations related to such factors as family background, accent, comportment, and body language, as much as appearance. For example, as Alicia Rodríguez-Estrada documents, Mexican-born, fair-skinned actress Lupe Vélez experienced more intense racialization in Hollywood in the late 1920s than fellow Mexican Dolores Del Rio, at least in part because of her perceived working-class background.[25] These dynamics are of no minor importance; given the equation of whiteness with citizenship and all of its attendant rights in the United States, whether Latina and Latino stars have been constructed as white, nonwhite, or indeterminate, citizens or foreigners at various junctures arguably has had a profound impact not only on film, television, and star images but also on public attitudes, and thus on social institutions and legislation that made a difference in the lives of U.S. Latina/os.

In addition, it has been argued that when it comes to Latina/o actors, some are perceived to be more appealing by film and television casting agents and producers than others, with nationality and other elements of ancestry factoring in to these dynamics. As I note in chapter 1, for example, Dolores Del

Rio's promotion in the late 1920s showcased her Spanish ancestry and to an extent downplayed her Mexican nationality. More recently, Spanish actors Antonio Banderas and Penelope Cruz have been among the most heavily hyped Latina/o stars, despite the fact that many U.S. Latinos do not include Spaniards in their definition of Latina/o identity because of their European status. Angharad Valdivia has aptly documented this privileging of Spanish nationality in Hollywood's version of Latinidad.[26] Actors who have already become stars in Latin American countries also have often been privileged over "home-grown" Latina/os by casting directors, as my interviews in the industry bore out. Mexican Americans in particular have been underrepresented among Latina/o stars, despite the fact that they are the largest Latina/o group in the United States, comprising 58.5 percent of the Latina/o population in recent years.

The climate of a particular social era also necessarily has an influence. The status of Latina/os in the racial hierarchy of the United States—and thus within the realm of popular entertainment—has evolved in relation to historical and social developments. As scholars of Latina/o history have documented, Latina/os have been considered "maybe, sometimes white" based on what is most politically useful to those in power at particular junctures.[27] In turn, Latina/o actors have faced greater or lesser opportunity in Hollywood during various periods. Eras in which Latin cultures are the object of interest among mainstream Americans and in which a "Latin look" has been considered particularly beautiful have brought about peaks in opportunity. A case in point is the substantially more welcoming and open star system that some Latina/os encountered in the last years of silent cinema in the mid- to late 1920s. In this period, a rage for the foreign and cosmopolitan, including the popularity of Spanish fantasy heritage mythology, contributed to audience interest in stars considered Latin lovers, as I address in chapter 1. Similarly, President Franklin D. Roosevelt's Good Neighbor policy of the late 1940s prompted increased interest in Latino and Latina performers with musical abilities. Desi Arnaz, the subject of chapter 2, found openings in Hollywood film and U.S. television because of this trend. Even such "Latin explosions" have often typically involved ambivalent media representation and star promotion, however.

Finding opportunities to be cast in roles is only one element of Latina/o representation and stardom, moreover. "Hollywood often . . . capitalize[s] on the economic possibilities of difference," as Joanne Hershfield argues,[28] and the star images constructed for nonwhite stars historically have capitalized to some extent on the employment of stereotypical associations—both those considered "positive" and "negative"—held by whites of nonwhites and white ethnic groups.[29] Such has often been the case in the marketing of Latina/o stars. These promotional tendencies have included ambivalent and contradictory discourses regarding race, ethnicity, and difference as considered relevant for promoting Latina and Latino star hopefuls; typically through deliberate measures by media producers, publicists, management personnel, and actors themselves in hopes of adding to the potential star's unique appeal.

For example, in time periods when Latina/os have been promoted as stars, the utilization of "tropicalist" tropes, neocolonialist associations with Latin America as always involving "heat, violence, passion, and spice,"[30] has often flavored their promotion to U.S. audiences. It has been argued by Frances Aparicio and Susana Chávez-Silverman that such associations always imply Euro-American superiority, even while purportedly celebrating Latin America.[31] With respect to Latina/o stars, a tropicalist slant on their promotion has often resulted in stars being referred to as "fiery" and "hot" and given such labels as "spitfires" and "pepperpots." While these tendencies are perhaps most associated with Carmen Miranda and Latin musicals of the Good Neighbor film cycle, they have long been intrinsic to Hollywood Latinidad, to the extent that they are seldom noticed or questioned. For example, Rita Moreno was photographed inside a life-size firecracker in 1954 without comment, while almost fifty years later, Ricky Martin was showcased on the cover of *Entertainment Weekly* under the headline "Caliente!"[32]

Such associations have often been extended to the Latino and particularly the Latina star body. The image of the curvaceous, hypersexualized Latina star is an entrenched trope of Latina cinematic representation. Although for actors of all ethnic backgrounds, "sex sells,"[33] Latina/o actors appear to have the most difficulty escaping publicity that labels them as exceptionally and innately sexy, or as having excessively sexy and/or voluptuous bodies. The media obsession with Jennifer Lopez's rear end in the late 1990s, a topic of chapter 6, serves as a vivid case in point; retrospective exploration of her predecessors' careers demonstrates that this is not a new phenomenon. Related notions of personality and social status also have been reinforced through such tropicalist discourses; Latina/o performers in this manner have been promoted to the non-Latino public primarily as passionate, inviting bodies with little intellectual or moral substance.

Latina/o Star Hopefuls: Behind the Scenes

Also important to consider are the corporate structures and climate behind the scenes in the film, television, and talent management industries that have an impact on actors being provided (or not being provided) opportunities to demonstrate whether they possess the intangible qualities that might support stardom. These include the challenges that actors face when they vie to secure agents and other management personnel, be cast in roles, and be promoted as stars. While a handful of Latina/o actors have achieved success, it is still extremely difficult for most to break into the industry or find substantial employment, as has been documented most recently in a 1999 Tomás Rivera Policy Institute (TRPI) study commissioned by the Screen Actors Guild.[34]

In this respect, stardom is a phenomenon that cannot be separated from its production, and in particular from the decisions on the part of executives to promote a would-be star. Scholars such as Gill Branston, Reba L. Chaisson, and Barry King attest to the "self-fulfilling prophecy," in Branston's words, inherent in the promotion of stars and hit films.[35] With respect to these dynamics, the long-term invisibility of Latina/os in the film, television, and promotion industries, particularly in executive circles, combined with a severe under-representation of Latina/os in writer and other creative positions, arguably plays into a Hollywood mind-set that seldom considers Latina/os worth the financial investment of star promotion.

In coming to a more nuanced understanding of the situation that Latina/o actors face, however, it is important to make a distinction between these actors and the Latina/o characters that populate film and television story worlds. Actors, of course, are limited only by Hollywood's and society's norms with respect to cross-cultural portrayal, while Latina/o characters can be and have been portrayed by actors of any racial or ethnic designation. As Sarah Berry points out, drawing on Shohat and Stam, a "racialized politics of casting" exists,[36] which has historically limited the acting opportunities for Latina/os and other actors deemed nonwhite. Charles Ramírez Berg describes this dynamic with respect to Hollywood narrative tradition: Hero and heroine roles have historically been the exclusive domain of the white actors and actresses, while Latina/os and other actors deemed nonwhite have typically been cast as villains, sidekicks, and temporary love interests.[37] While this paradigm is occasionally sidestepped today, there were very few exceptions in Hollywood's classical era and thus few opportunities for Latina/o actors to prove whether they might have star appeal. Conversely, cross-cultural portrayals by white actors in Latina/o roles have until recently been acceptable. More substantial, "star-making" Latina/o roles in fact were often played by Anglo actors during the classical Hollywood era. The role of Puerto Rican immigrant Maria in *West Side Story* (1961), played by Natalie Wood, and of Mexican revolutionary leader Emiliano Zapata, played by Marlon Brando in

Viva Zapata! (1952), are just two cases in point. Other Anglo actors who have played Latina/os in brownface over the decades include Charlton Heston, Bette Davis, Madonna, Paul Muni, and Marisa Tomei.

When Latina/o actors *have* portrayed Latina/o characters, their roles and star promotion have been influenced by age-old patterns in Latina/o representation. As I explain throughout the first chapters of this book, this has included such tendencies as the inaccurate conflation of disparate Latina/o cultures and the stereotypical representation of Latina/os as highly sexual, comic, subservient, and/or criminal. Ramírez Berg's description of Latina and Latino film roles as Latin lovers, bandidos, harlots, and clowns aptly describes the majority of such roles.[38] Valdivia, borrowing a term from Gayle Tuchman, describes such stereotypes and obstructions to being cast as active protagonists as an example of the "symbolic annihilation" that Latina/os have historically experienced in the mainstream media.[39] While some of these patterns are shifting, traces still remain in contemporary representations and star promotion.

This is not to say that Latina/os have been passive victims throughout the decades with respect to media representation and participation in the Hollywood industries, however. Mexican Americans and other Latina/os have protested denigrating news coverage and media representation in the United States since at least the early twentieth century, as José E. Limón has noted, with Latina/o media advocacy focused on the film studios and networks reaching a peak in the late 1960s and early 1970s.[40] They have also worked to become filmmakers, television producers, and other media professionals on both independent and mainstream projects and as such to gain creative agency over such representations. The dedication and hard work of Latina/o media activists and filmmakers, as I discuss in more detail in chapters 4 and 5, has profoundly influenced how Latina/os have come to be represented and possibilities that Latina/o actors now face in the mainstream media environment.

Organization of This Book

As noted earlier, this study analyzes the evolution of Latina/o film and television representation and its reflection of the broader social status of Latina/os, through the lens of mediated stardom. To do so, I draw on Ella Shohat's conception of "ethnicities-in-relation" in studying Latina/o stardom in relation to evolving notions of whiteness and national identity and to the social and industrial history and climate in which these dynamics of star production, promotion, and reception have been embedded.[41] In particular, I examine the individual and industrial choices and structures that have influenced opportunities for and orchestrated the career trajectories of individual Latina/o stars in U.S. media and social history.

This topic, however, introduced a number of research challenges. Stardom, as a multifaceted phenomenon that includes the production of media texts and star publicity texts, the performance of the public image by the celebrity, and critical and audience response, can be difficult to reconstruct and study. As Joshua Gamson notes, this is a subject that bridges the realms of both institutional and interpretive analysis, making it difficult to research adequately through a single research method.[42]

For this reason, I combined a number of methodological approaches in my research. These approaches included archival research at a number of locations around the country. These sites included the Margaret Herrick Library of the Academy of Motion Picture Arts and Sciences, the Paley Center for Media (formerly the Museum of Television and Radio in Los Angeles), the Harry Ransom Center for the Humanities at the University of Texas at Austin, the Cinema-Television Library at the University of Southern California, the UCLA Film and Television Archive, and the Center for Film and Television Research at the University of Wisconsin. At these archives I studied film, television, and star promotional materials, focusing in particular on promotional posters, publicity stills, film exhibitors' press books, studio-produced biographies, and magazine and newspaper articles about the stars in question and their peers. The Margaret Herrick Library at the Academy of Motion Picture Arts and Sciences, with its meticulous archive of star and film-related materials, proved to be a particular treasure trove in this regard.

My work also included study of critical and popular reception, such as evidenced in film and television reviews, box office figures, television ratings, and so on. In addition, I engaged in critical analysis of the stars' films and/or television episodes when available, viewing some at libraries and archives when they were not commercially available. Some of Del Rio's silent films, Moreno's B-films of the 1950s, and episodes of *Chico and the Man,* for example, were viewed at the Film and Television Archive of UCLA and the Museum of Television and Radio.

I also conducted interviews with Latina/o professionals working in the film and talent management industries (including producers, actors, writers, casting directors, and an agent) and engaged in participant observation work related to Latina/o star promotion activities in Los Angeles. Much of this work was made possible through an internship at the trade journal *Latin Heat* and by participating in events sponsored by Nosotros, a Latina/o actors' advocacy group in Los Angeles, in the summer of 2000. This fieldwork and the formal interviews and informal conversations that ensued provided a useful context for understanding the social climate in which Latina and Latino actors have worked in the last several decades and currently work within the film and other entertainment industries.

In chapter 1, "Latin Lovers and American Accents: Dolores Del Rio and Hollywood's Transition to Sound," I explore the opportunity experienced by a handful of Latino and Latina actors in the 1920s vogue for "Latin lovers" and the subsequent, dramatic changes in Hollywood's imagining of Latinidad after the transition to sound film and the economic downturn of the 1930s. In illustration, I survey the career and evolving star image of Mexican actress Dolores Del Rio (1905–83), whose U.S. film career roughly spanned the years 1925 to 1943. After her first hit film in 1926, at the peak of the late silent film era, Del Rio became a leading Hollywood star. She found her opportunities shifting by the early 1930s in relation to film industry notions of the American accent and the solidification of norms of American whiteness that marginalized Latina/os, however. Her post-sound publicity and film roles illustrate the de-evolution of Latina opportunity and the racialization of even light-skinned Latina/o actors in this period.

In chapter 2, "The Good Neighbor on Prime Time: Desi Arnaz and *I Love Lucy*," I survey Latina/o representation and racialization in the 1940s and 1950s as inflected in the career and star image of Cuban-born musician, actor, and later television producer Desi Arnaz (1917–86). Arnaz began as a singer and leader of Cuban bands in the United States and later embarked on a Hollywood career when he was enlisted as a performer in several Good Neighbor–flavored films in the 1940s. He is best known, however, as the first Latino television star, from his performance as Ricky Ricardo on the extremely popular television series *I Love Lucy* (1950–57), opposite his real-life wife, Lucille Ball. Arnaz also was the first Latino television executive, serving as the show's executive producer and president of Desilu Productions. Exploration of Arnaz's career and star promotion thus brings up a number of questions regarding Latino and Cuban identities and U.S. racial borders as expressed in the mediums of film and television in these decades.

This is followed by chapter 3, "A Fight for 'Dignity and Integrity': Rita Moreno in Hollywood's Postwar Era." I return to focus on the film industry, exploring Latina opportunity and star promotion during the 1950s and 1960s. With respect to industrial shifts, this was a period that included the breakdown of the studio system and the growth of independent film production. Despite a growing awareness of racism in the United States, the film industry remained staunchly "all-American." The impact of these trends is examined in this study of Puerto Rican performer Rita Moreno's early film career. The actress experienced many obstacles during this period, in particular casting norms that dictated that Latinas be cast only in secondary, nonwhite roles— whether Latina, Asian, American Indian, or other ethnic variety—even after her talent was officially recognized with an Oscar win in 1962 for *West Side Story.* I conclude with consideration of a theater and film role that Moreno portrayed in the 1970s, that of Googie Gomez in *The Ritz,* and the question that it raises regarding the importance of Latina and Latino authorship in the construction of both Latina/o cinematic characters and star images.

In chapter 4, "The Burden of Playing Chico: Freddie Prinze and Latino Stardom in Television's Era of 'Relevance,'" I examine shifts in Latina/o representation and stardom in the 1970s, described by scholars as network television's era of "social relevance," as the presence of Chicano and Puerto Rican media activists began to be felt. *Chico and the Man,* which aired on NBC from 1974 to 1978, offered the first Latino lead role since *I Love Lucy,* as well as being the only "socially relevant" series with a Latino in a starring role. Starring Puerto Rican and German Hungarian actor Freddie Prinze as Francisco "Chico" Rodriguez, *Chico and the Man* focused on the *Odd Couple* pairing of an older white garage owner and Chico, the young Mexican American man who worked and lived with him. Prinze's character, notably, was the subject of ongoing debate and negotiation among the producers, the network, and Chicana/o and other viewers; such dynamics are revealing regarding network and national notions of Mexican American, Latino, and American ethnic identities in the 1970s. In this chapter I analyze Freddie Prinze's promotion as a star before his suicide in 1977 in light of the negotiations that took place on the series.

In chapter 5, "The Face of the 'Decade': Edward James Olmos and Latino Films of the 1980s," I focus on shifts in Hollywood's construction of Latinidad as Latina/o filmmakers began to have an impact on a national level. While not the full-blown "Decade of the Hispanic" trumpeted by the mainstream news media, it was a period in which the first Chicano and Latino-helmed feature films reached national audiences, often to critical and popular acclaim; these films included *El Norte* (1983), *Zoot Suit* (1981), *The Ballad of Gregorio Cortez* (1982), and *Stand and Deliver* (1988). Interestingly, in the press coverage that ensued about the new Latina/o filmmakers and films, Mexican American actor Edward James Olmos was promoted as the primary star and as a symbol of Latina/o visibility in U.S. popular culture. I study Olmos's 1980s career and star promotion in relation to the rise of Latina/o feature filmmaking and the shifting status and voice of Chicana/os and other Latina/os in other respects in U.S. culture.

In chapter 6, "Crossing Over the Latina Body: Jennifer Lopez and the 1990s 'Latin Wave,'" I document 1990s shifts in Latina/o opportunity, media representation, and star promotion in relation to the career and star image of Nuyorican actress, singer, and media mogul Jennifer Lopez during her rise to mainstream stardom. A number of social and industrial developments provided openings that were instrumental to Lopez's success, including the growth and a rising awareness of the Latina/o audience and increased Latina/o and African American media production. An illustration of these developments but also of the continued strength of traditional tropes that have long colored Latina/o star promotion, Lopez was introduced to U.S. and global audiences in highly body-focused promotional texts, a phenomenon that I explore. I conclude by reflecting briefly on Lopez's subsequent status in Hollywood and the upper-class associations and ethnic flexibility that later came to dominate her image, as well as on her re-emphasis on Latina/o-focused projects in more recent years.

Finally, in chapter 7, "Ethnic Ambiguity in the Era of *Dark Angels*: Jessica Alba and Mixed Latina/o Trends," I address the question of Latino and Latina stars of mixed ethnicity. Although in the past mixed-race stars of partial Hispanic descent typically shrouded some aspect of their mixed heritage (Anthony Quinn and Raquel Welch are two well-known examples of stars who were "closeted" in this way), currently such actors are more often "out" about their mixed ancestry. In the post-millennial era, they also happen to be among the most successful Latina/o stars. What are the implications with respect to historical and contemporary notions of Latinidad in Hollywood and the United States, when many of today's Latino and Latina stars, such as Freddie Prinze Jr., Salma Hayek, and Benjamin Bratt, are of partial Hispanic descent? Through exploration of the careers of mixed Latina actors Jessica Alba and Rosario Dawson, I speculate on the significance of the contemporary broadening of notions of Latina/o identity as constructed by the Hollywood media industries, by Latina/o and other media professionals, and by audiences themselves.

1

Latin Lovers and American Accents

Dolores Del Rio and Hollywood's
Transition to Sound

Going to the local cineplex or turning on the television with the hope of finding Latina and Latino actors featured in starring roles can be a more heartening experience these days than it was just a few decades ago. Today we might happen upon a variety of actors of Latina/o and Latin American descent, among them America Ferrera, Benicio del Toro, Rosario Dawson, Michelle Rodriguez, or Diego Luna, to name a few, playing film and television characters that are richly textured and not predicated on the old standby stereotypes. Celebrity publicity venues such as entertainment news shows and supermarket tabloids also heavily feature Latina/o icons: Jennifer Lopez, Wilmer Valderrama, and Eva Longoria Parker, among others, have made regular appearances in recent years. It's a shift from what was the norm even two decades ago, when Latina/o actors more typically struggled with extremely limited roles and casting opportunities.

Taking this historical survey of Latina/o participation in Hollywood film back even further reveals that the 1990s' "Latin Explosion" was only the most recent wave of Latina/o global stardom, however. There was another era, now often forgotten, in which Latino and Latina actors were hired for their perceived box office potential, viewed as especially attractive and trendy, and promoted as international stars. In the mid- to late 1920s, known as the Golden Age of U.S. silent film, a number of actors of Latina/o descent were among the top stars at their respective studios and in the film industry more generally. This first "Latin invasion," as the film fan magazine *Photoplay* described the influx of Hispanic actors in 1927, provided opportunities for a handful of actors that has only recently been matched.[1] Actors from Mexico in particular, such as Ramon Novarro, Dolores Del Rio, Gilbert Roland, and Lupe Vélez, the popular "Latin lovers" of this period, possessed star status that is only beginning to be equaled today by the most popular Latina/os working in film and television.

The reign of the Latin lovers was cut short by a number of industrial and social developments, however, among them the transition to "talkies" in the last years of the decade. The conversion to sound was to have a profound impact. Aside from prompting a shift in popular film genres and acting styles, producers and industry executives had to make decisions regarding what the American accent should sound like. In this re-imagining of cinematic story worlds, actors with Hispanic accents, even those of the most exalted status, had fewer and less lucrative prospects, as I explore in this chapter. It is no coincidence that American social life also underwent a major upheaval in this decade because of the onset of the Great Depression in 1929. In this period of widespread unemployment and poverty, Mexican Americans found themselves increasingly scapegoated and racialized as nonwhite, dynamics that also were reflected in how Latinidad came to be defined in film representations and star promotion.

In this chapter, I explore the representational shifts of the late 1920s and early 1930s, when these social and industry shifts took place. I focus in particular on the case study of the career of Mexican-born actress Dolores Del Rio as an especially telling illustration of the rise and fall of opportunity that Latina/o stars experienced in this period. What social and industrial conditions allowed these actors to become some of Hollywood's top stars in the late silent film era? And how did sound film and the new status of Latina/os in the 1930s alter the likelihood of Latina/o success and stardom in the American imagination?

Described as the "leader of the Latin invasion" by popular film fan magazine *Photoplay*, Dolores Del Rio was the most successful Latina actress in Hollywood within a few years of her arrival in Los Angeles in 1925.[2] At the peak of her success, she starred in a number of critical and box office hits, including the silent films *What Price Glory?* (1926), *The Loves of Carmen* (1927), and *Resurrection* (1927), and the early sound film *Ramona* (1928). She also was among the top money earners in Hollywood at her career peak, signing a $5 million, multifilm contract with United Artists in 1928. Dolores Del Rio's career underwent major changes with the industrial and social shifts of the 1930s, however. Although she continued working, she found that the lead roles she had been offered in the late 1920s were no longer in her purview after the industry's conversion to sound film and notions of star appeal had shifted to privilege "all-American" stars over those of Latina/o or Latin American descent.

The work of Joanne Hershfield and Ana M. López on Dolores Del Rio provides a helpful jumping-off point from which to begin this work.[3] Both have studied Del Rio as a star; Hershfield in particular has done so with a focus on Del Rio's Hollywood films. My unique contribution in this respect lies in my focus on the work that went into the construction of Del Rio's public image and the impact of the broader social landscape on the opportunity that she experienced. Such a focus promises to glean new information about the relationships of Latina/o stardom both to the evolving status of Latina/os in the country and to the film industry in particular.

The 1920s and Hollywood's First "Latin Wave"

The 1920s were a unique period for U.S. popular culture. In this era of suffragists, flappers, and tensions over immigration, the social norms of masculinity, femininity, and whiteness were met with challenge, and at times, revision. Such tensions played a role in the popularity among many Americans of fashions, art forms, and performers deemed foreign, cosmopolitan, sexually transgressive, or culturally taboo. For example, the tango, jazz music, Harlem dance clubs, and more skin-baring fashions for women became popular in this time period. Influenced in part by the influx of films imported from such countries as Germany and France, as well as by the relative prosperity of the times, Americans appeared to be looking outside the United States and particularly to Europe for direction with regard to sophisticated culture and lifestyle.[4]

These national cultural trends included a romanticization of the Spanish colonial history of California and Mexico, as scholars such as Carey McWilliams and John R. Chávez have described.[5] There also was a rising interest in Latin American cultural forms in the realm of popular entertainment. Broadway had begun to turn to Latin America for inspiration with respect to narratives and music in the 1910s,[6] while a number of songs that borrowed rhythms and words from Latin music became popular with the general public in the next decade. The tango also came into vogue as social dancing became a popular pastime in the 1920s.

These trends were particularly felt in the growing film industry. Along with the importation of films, directors, actors, and other creative personnel from Europe and elsewhere were emigrating to the United States and taking leading roles at the major studios, becoming some of the most popular and influential players within the industry. Foreign names and faces proliferated in the American star system by the 1920s, with such actors as Pola Negri, Rudolph Valentino, Emil Jannings, and home-grown American vamp Theda Bara (the stage name and later legal name of Theodosia Goodman) filling the pages of *Photoplay, Motion Picture World,* and other film fan magazines. In line with the sensibilities of the times, these stars typically were promoted in a manner that emphasized their wealth, glamour, and flamboyant lifestyles.

With respect to film genres, melodramas set in exotic locales and populated with passionate and romantic characters were extremely popular with U.S. moviegoers. As film scholars such as Alexander Walker, Richard Kozarski, and Robert Sklar have documented and surveys of popular films prior to the conversion to sound reveal, 1920s films often capitalized on public curiosity with the foreign and the wealth and tastes of the upper class.[7] Films such as *The Mark of Zorro* (1920) and *The Sheik* (1921) were national sensations that prompted the production of other melodramas set in exotic locales, a trend that continued throughout much of the decade.

The popular acting style in these Great Lover roles in the silent films of the day was broad and passionate, emphasizing the display and expressiveness of actors' bodies. As Sklar asserts, "[T]he alternative to traditional American behavior that movie audiences most clearly demanded [during the silent film era] was passionate behavior."[8] The Latina/o actors and actresses who were successful in this era arguably were made stars by film audiences who not only appreciated their aesthetic appearance, but also were responding to their effective physical expression of emotion on the screen. It should be noted that these actors typically were not portraying Latina/o characters, however. As Dolores Del Rio once commented regarding her silent film career, "I tried to interest my producers in stories about Mexico. I wanted to play a Mexican. But they preferred me to play a French woman or Polynesian."[9]

Rudolph Valentino's popularity played no small part in these trends. Public passion for the Italian actor considered the first Latin lover blossomed with *The Sheik* and *The Four Horsemen of the Apocalypse,* both released in 1921, and the star's popularity only seemed to grow with his unexpected death in 1926. The Valentino craze demonstrated the appeal of mysterious ethnic Others as romantic figures to U.S. audiences in this period, encouraging studios to incorporate this type in their films.[10] Actresses who fell within the Latin lover category also were popular, at least in part because of American audiences' fascination with how they "temporarily blurred the boundaries of gender, ethnicity, and race," according to Matthew Bernstein.[11] (Perhaps not coincidentally, in this period notions of whiteness itself were shifting as immigrants of southern and eastern European descent were beginning to be viewed as white Americans.) Regardless of the reasons for their appeal, the Valentino phenomenon prompted a positive disposition toward employing actors in the Latin lover tradition. Erotic androgyny (on the part of men), an air of mystery, and a darkly handsome appearance became lucrative traits for actors and actresses to possess, and a number were employed expressly because of this. This group included several actors born in Mexico, including Ramon Novarro, Dolores Del Rio (who happened to be his second cousin),[12] Lupe Vélez, and Gilbert Roland, all of whom secured contracts at the major studios in the 1920s. Some non-Latina/o actors even acquired Latina/o-sounding names to capitalize on the vogue, the best-known example being that of Austrian Jewish actor Jacob Krantz, who changed his name to Ricardo Cortez in the early 1920s to better exploit his Valentino-like looks. Notably, in this era of silent film it didn't matter whether these actors spoke English or spoke it well; it was their looks and expressiveness that were key to their acting and appeal as stars.

Latina/o heritage and culture were not simplistically viewed as positive within the landscape of U.S. popular culture of the period, however. This can be seen in how the promotion of successful Latina/o stars typically performed a function of distancing them from more "ethnic" Latina/os living in the United States, Mexico, or Latin America. Gaylyn Studlar, in her exploration of Spanish actor Antonio Moreno's career in the late 1910s (when Spanish heritage was not yet firmly associated with whiteness), describes a process by which Moreno was promoted to the status of the "right kind of ethnic" in star promotion texts.[13] For Mexican actors such as Ramon Novarro and Dolores Del Rio, negotiation that defined them as acceptable "Latins" or foreigners without association with the Mexican or Mexican American working class also arguably was necessary.

Not coincidentally, outside Hollywood, tensions were beginning to mount regarding the status of Mexicans and Mexican Americans in the United States, particularly with respect to Mexicans who had emigrated in response to the need for laborers. During this period, "nativists" argued for the superiority of Anglo-Saxons and called for English-only laws and other covenants to deny Mexican Americans full citizenship rights. In contrast, Southwestern employers asserted their desire for unrestricted immigration so that they might hire Mexican laborers. These tensions came to a head in debates over such topics as "Americanization" programs and the segregated schooling of Mexican American children, reflecting the society's ambivalence regarding the cultural citizenship of Mexican Americans in this era.[14]

Another telling illustration of the disassociation of Latina/os from a white American mainstream in the 1920s could be found in the broader popular culture. In early cosmetics industry promotions, for example, light-skinned, Anglo women were foregrounded as the most beautiful, even while images of Latinas and other ambiguously ethnic women were at times used to promote particular products, reflecting the foundational belief that "the true American face was still a white face," Kathy Peiss argues.[15] The status of a light-skinned Latina star was unclear in relation to these national norms, her look considered beautiful but never fully American and always racially nebulous.

Del Rio's Journey: From Mexico to Hollywood Star

This was the historical and industrial context in which Dolores Del Rio achieved success in Hollywood. Her entrance into the star system in the mid-1920s serves as a vivid illustration of how the vogue for the foreign and exotic in U.S. popular culture created an opening for some Latina/os to establish careers, play leading roles in popular films, and become international stars, while her Hollywood career as a whole illustrates the subsequent reversals and shifts that took place in opportunity and star promotion in the next decade.

Given the emphasis on Dolores Del Rio's family background in her early star image, certain facts are well known. According to biographical sources, Del Rio was born Maria Dolores Asúnsolo, in Durango, Mexico, on August 3, 1905. She grew up in a wealthy family of Spanish-Basque heritage; her father was a bank president and landowner. Del Rio (then Asúnsolo) attended school at the Convent of St. Joseph in Mexico City, where she reportedly was allowed to speak only French and also learned several other languages. When her family traveled to Europe, she studied dance; she later became known as one of the finest tango dancers among the Mexican elite. At age sixteen, she married wealthy businessman and philanthropist Jaime Martinez del Rio; after embarking on an extended honeymoon in Europe, they settled into a privileged life in Mexico City. Known as one of the best dancers in the city, Dolores would at times perform the tango or other Latin dances at society and charity functions.

It was at such an event that Del Rio met American film director Edwin Carewe. The story has it that Carewe, in Mexico with his fiancé to get married, saw Del Rio dance at a party and was immediately impressed by her. The Carewes and Del Rios struck up a friendship, and Carewe urged the Mexican couple to come to Hollywood so Dolores could try her hand at film acting and Jaime at screenwriting. ("He told me I was the female Valentino," Del Rio said in an interview published in the *San Francisco Chronicle* in 1981.)[16] The Del Rios finally relented in 1925; Dolores del Rio, whose last name was soon Anglicized with a capital "D" as Del Rio, was twenty at the time. She was quoted in a Mexican newspaper as saying that she hoped to be able to present an image of the sophisticated Mexicana that was missing in Hollywood film at the time. "It is my dearest wish to make fans realize their [Mexicans'] real beauty, their wonder, their greatness as a people. The vast majority seem to regard Mexicans as a race of bandits, or laborers, dirty, unkempt, and un-educated. My ambition is to show the best that's in my nation."[17]

Edwin Carewe subsequently was the first and most influential shaper of Dolores Del Rio's star image in Hollywood. At the time that Del Rio consented to work with him, he had a multipicture deal with First National and was a popular director with other studios. Carewe placed Del Rio under contract and acted as her manager, guiding the refinement of her public image, and most important, cast and directed her in many of her first films. Moreover, he was often mentioned alongside Del Rio in early news items introducing the young starlet. As such, he can be viewed as her "patron" in the mainstream American mass media, providing an association with his own success in the industry that arguably boosted Del Rio's status when she was still a rela-tive unknown, as well as offering her film roles and other opportunities for public exposure. Given the mixed attitudes toward Mexicans in the country at the time, Carewe's patronage also contributed to promoting the starlet as an acceptable ethnic. This arguably helped offset obstacles she might have faced as a Mexican, despite her fair appearance, Spanish ancestry, and her family's obvious wealth and status in Mexico.

Del Rio's film career began in 1925 with a bit role in Carewe's "jazz baby" romance, *Joanna*. Much of this role ended up on the cutting room floor, but roles in four more films followed in 1926. These included small roles in Carewe's society drama *High Steppers,* the lead in the crime caper *Pals First,* and a role in a Universal Pictures comedy. Unfortunately, these films are not archived; information on Del Rio's roles in them can only be gleaned from publicity stills that have been preserved and critical reviews. Her first reviews were not so positive, however. In response to her role in *Pals First, Variety,* referring to Del Rio as a "Latin actress" and "Edwin Carewe discov-ery," described her performance as lackluster.[18] In particular, the reviewer took umbrage with Del Rio's "Latin" appearance. Critics' opinions quickly turned around with Del Rio's fourth film role in 1926, however. In Fox Film's

comedic World War I tale *What Price Glory?* (the first Del Rio film I was able
to screen), Del Rio portrayed Charmaine, a flirtatious French innkeeper's
daughter caught in a love triangle between two American officers. The role,
capitalizing on Del Rio's exuberance and expressive body as an actress, is
that of a vivacious, free-spirited woman who can't help but share herself pas-
sionately with both men. A critic for *Variety* predicted that the film would
be a big success, based in no small part on Del Rio's perceived sex appeal:
"[S]he registers like a house afire. It is no wonder she had the whole army
after her!"[19] The film in fact proved to be a huge hit. The song "Charmaine"
also was extremely popular with audiences, who were able to buy the sheet
music in theater lobbies; over a million copies were reportedly sold.[20]

Meanwhile, Dolores Del Rio was introduced to the American public
through promotional efforts. Harry D. Wilson, Del Rio's high-profile publicist, targeted magazines and newspapers with introductory feature stories
and photographs that capitalized on the more positive stereotypes of high-
class Mexicans and proactively avoided the landmines of stereotypes that
assumed all Mexicans were laborers or banditos. While constructed as a sophisticated and fashionable lady, Del Rio's Mexican nationality never ceased
to figure in to this resulting publicity in interesting ways. She was typically
described as a Mexican (or just as often, Spanish or Castilian) beauty; notably,
associations were not made with Mexican Americans, however. *Photoplay,*
for example, dubbed Del Rio "The Daughter of the Dons" and a "perfect
Latin type" in an early article.[21] Del Rio's image was made more palatable,
additionally, through steady mentions of her family's wealth and references
to her presumed strict morality, very likely aided by associations with her
Catholicism and convent education. As Wilson trumpeted in his first biography of Del Rio, which we can surmise was disseminated widely to the
press: "This is the first time in film history that a Mexican girl has risen to
the highest rung of filmdom's ladder. Mexico justly rejoices in her achievements and her tremendous success. . . . Her social standing in Los Angeles
and Hollywood is one of the highest and her friends cannot be counted in
numbers. She is active in society and welfare work and spends many hours
of her spare time in helping worthy causes."[22] Similarly, pains were taken to
underscore that Del Rio had pursued acting as a leisure activity and had never
needed to engage in such unseemly behavior as training or alteration of her
physical appearance on the path to becoming an actress, well in line with
the construction of upper-class, white femininity in this era. For example,
Photoplay offered this description of Del Rio's entree into film acting: "She
was rich. She was happily married. She had everything she wanted. Dolores

Del Rio came to Hollywood seeking neither fame nor romance nor money. She went into the movies 'just for fun.' But the movies refuse to let her go, because she is one of the great discoveries of the year."[23]

Despite this narrative that was shared with the press, Del Rio's glamorous and fashionable image had in fact been crafted with the help of a fashion expert who coordinated a new, stylish wardrobe for the young actress. According to biographer Larry Carr, upon her arrival in Hollywood, Del Rio "bore little resemblance to the acknowledged beauty of world-wide fame she was to become. . . . Shy and reserved, she dressed conservatively and wore almost no makeup. The film colony found her 'interesting' and 'pretty in a foreign way,' but privately some thought her 'kind of dowdy' and 'too sedate.'"[24] In this era in which American women were challenging tradition and gender constraints through such fashion and beauty practices as bobbed hair and shorter hemlines, Del Rio's personal style was more aligned with an earlier era. Peggy Hamilton, a designer who had created clothes for popular film actress Gloria Swanson, was commissioned to design a high-fashion wardrobe more suitable for a young Hollywood star, according to Carr.[25] Meanwhile, countless publicity photographs were taken in which Del Rio is utilized as a fashion mannequin—initially in traditional Spanish garb such as lace dresses and shawls, but quickly in the latest American and French couture. These apparently were disseminated to women's magazines and the feature sections of daily newspapers; as Charles Eckert documents, this began to be a standard promotional practice for many female stars by the late 1920s as ties were forged between the Hollywood film studios and fashion designers.[26] Hamilton also served to an extent in the capacity of what would be considered an agent or personal manager's role today, throwing large parties at which fan magazine writers and others in the press could meet Del Rio.

The result of these efforts was a rash of positive publicity for the young Dolores Del Rio, such that her name reportedly was widely known by 1927. She was even "confident enough to turn down a lead opposite Douglas Fairbanks, Snr, [sic] which gave her compatriot, Lupe Velez, her break [playing a feisty Argentinean girl] in *The Gaucho*" that year.[27] She instead appeared in two other films that became hits. One was a Carewe-helmed adaptation of Leo Tolstoy's *Resurrection,* a melodrama about a Russian peasant girl forced to turn to prostitution after an affair with a married man ends unhappily. *Resurrection* was quite successful, with Del Rio described as a "potent" box office draw in at least one of her reviews.[28]

Reviews for her other 1927 film, Raoul Walsh's *The Loves of Carmen,* based on Bizet's famous opera, were even more positive. Del Rio received strong praise for her portrayal of the amorous Spanish siren. "Sid.," writing for *Variety,* raved that *Loves* contained "plenty of hell, sex and box office" and that Del Rio in particular made an erotic splash in the film.[29] *Photoplay* also praised Del Rio's beauty and sexual appeal in its critique of her portrayal of "the raven-haired, olive-skinned sinuous-limbed Carmen."[30] Several critics made ethnic comparisons, suggesting that Del Rio was particularly suited to play Carmen, implying an innate ability to portray a character of fiery temperament. Despite this early stereotyping of Del Rio by critics, her rising popularity was undeniable. Analysis of the film's promotional materials bears out that they capitalized almost solely on Del Rio's name and image; the young actress was proving to be one of Hollywood's top female box office draws.

When Latin Lovers Could Speak

The end of the window of opportunity enjoyed by popular Latino and Latina actors such as Dolores Del Rio was already in sight in 1927, however, as film studios, some quickly and others more grudgingly, began to prepare for the impending conversion to sound film. Prompting and coinciding with shifting public tastes, this change was to have a far-reaching impact. Virtually overnight, an actor's voice became an integral part of his or her public image. Alexander Walker, in his survey of the transition, found that actors begin to be panned after their first talkies for a variety of complaints, for instance for having voices considered not "robust" enough, for lacking what was deemed to be the appropriate emotional register for a particular role or their star image, or for having a voice that appeared to indicate a lack of education or class.[31] A speaking style associated with middle-class status and lack of identifiable ethnicity came to be associated with desirable notions of American whiteness. Stars who didn't speak English fluently or who had foreign accents were taking crash courses in English and elocution in an attempt to save their careers.

Particularly important, film executives were wrestling with what an American accent should sound like. Notions of race and class played no small part in this process. Interestingly, British-inflected English was initially seized on as the most desirable, in part because precise enunciation was deemed necessary with the rudimentary early microphones. While soon dropped as the ideal, this initial preference and other cultural biases in the first years of sound had a profound impact on actors' careers. For example, director William C. Demille, in describing problems that got in the way of some actors' achieving the proper American accent, stated that "the rolling Western 'r' gives the lie to an otherwise excellent 'society' characterization."[32]

In a related shift, audience tastes were changing as well. By the 1930s, public interest in the foreign and cosmopolitan began to wane. In response to Depression-era economic shifts, marriage and family, thrift, "all-American" (typically, Anglo-Saxon and blonde) looks, chastity, and natural beauty were now privileged, in sharp contrast to the prior emphases of the flamboyant and cosmopolitan public tastes of the 1920s. In film, down-to-earth narratives of family life and contemporary adventure stories began to be emphasized over the exotic storylines of previous decades, while new, wise-cracking romantic leads such as those played by Clark Gable and Jean Harlow replaced the "great lover" characters formerly in vogue.[33] As *Photoplay, Motion Picture World,* and other film fan magazines began to report on sound films and the new crop of actors, it became apparent that many stars of the late silent period no longer had an obvious starring role to play.

Scholars disagree on how Latina/o actors and actresses were affected by these changes. It is difficult to accurately surmise, moreover, how audiences might have reacted to Spanish accents on screen. The filmographies of Latina/o actors of the period reveal, however, that they typically faced the end of their Hollywood careers or were relegated to roles that incorporated (and often exaggerated) their accents. The few options for maintaining a film career included taking roles in the Spanish-language versions of studio films, as Lupita Tovar, Antonio Moreno, and occasionally Lupe Vélez chose to do. Other actors found work portraying singers or dancers in the Latin musicals produced in the 1930s and 1940s as Latinidad was increasingly paired with music and dance, dynamics described by Ana M. López in discussion of the representational politics of such "Good Neighbor" films.[34] These were typically minor characters supporting white American lead characters, however, and thus were not star-making roles to the same degree as those played by the Latin lovers of late silent film. Carmen Miranda, perhaps the lone exception, made her living almost exclusively in such roles and became a major star.

Moreover, such performances arguably reinforced the cultural racialization of Mexican Americans and other Latina/os by emphasizing the "foreign" language, accent, and music of Latina/os and Latin Americans. As Curtis Marez notes, accent and sound became "important ideological weapon[s]" in U.S. race relations through such dynamics in this era.[35] Similarly, another of the few options for Latina/os in early Hollywood sound film was taking roles that exaggerated accents, and often exploited stereotypes, for laughs or suspense. For example, at the time of her suicide in 1944, Lupe Vélez was best known for the RKO *Mexican Spitfire* series, in which her character's fractured English played prominently for laughs. Similarly, Ramon Novarro, "to his eternal discomfort," found work in lower-tier studio Republic's film parodies of major studio films,[36] while Gilbert Roland was now often stuck in Latin gigolo roles such as he portrayed in Mae West's *She Done Him Wrong* (1933).

The social preoccupations of the times played a large part in the declining opportunities that Latina/o actors experienced. The Great Depression (called *La Crisis* in Spanish) in particular, which resulted in unprecedented, widespread unemployment and poverty, dampened American enthusiasm for foreign stars and fed the preoccupation with defining what it meant to be American. With its onset in 1929, previously contested attitudes toward Mexican Americans turned increasingly negative. The new patriotism often defined Mexican Americans, and by extension other Latina/os, as un-American and a threat to the nation. Such sentiment was promoted, for example, by President Herbert Hoover, who denounced Mexicans as "one of the causes of the Depression," established the first border patrol, and supported the deportation of hundreds of thousands of Mexicans (and at times by mistake, Mexican Americans) in the early 1930s.[37] Hollywood was in no way left out of the crisis. In Los Angeles, by now firmly established as the nation's movie-making capital, 41.6 percent of Angelenos were reported to be unemployed.[38] Mexican American neighborhoods in particular were hard hit by new barriers to employment and massive poverty that arose in relation to *La Crisis*. The Mexican American theater community, for example, was decimated by the joint devastation of the repatriation of talented actors, playwrights, and directors, and massive poverty and unemployment.[39] Such struggles further obstructed Mexican Americans and Mexicans from working in a creative capacity in the film industry.

Meanwhile, the film studios were facing difficulties on two fronts. First, film attendance dipped alarmingly in the early 1930s as Americans had less money to spend on leisure pursuits.[40] Second, various religious and civic groups, most notably the Catholic organization Legion of Decency, were calling for censorship of films because of what they deemed racy, un-American subject matter. In reaction, film producers began to enforce the Production Code, voluntary guidelines on acceptable film content, and to emphasize "Americanism" in films. Overall, Hollywood cinema became more conservative, patriotic, and white-centrist by the late 1930s.

The Production Code itself likely also played a part in the decreasing opportunities for Latina/o actors and actresses throughout this period. While it ostensibly banned defamation in the form of certain racial slurs, it also forbid the portrayal of "miscegenation," or sexual relations between people of different (typically interpreted as white and black) racial designations. These strictures left Latina/o actors and characters, defined variously in Hollywood and the nation at the time as both white and nonwhite, in hazy limbo. The casting of "ethnic" Latino men in romantic roles opposite Anglo actresses apparently became taboo, even while light-skinned Latinas were at times paired romantically with Anglo men, as Carlos E. Cortés asserts, reflecting continuing tensions and ambiguity regarding the racial and ethnic status of Latina/os in the United States.[41]

In relation to the many changes taking place in the country and in Hollywood, stars in the 1930s became what Walker terms "more 'democratic' and less 'divine,'" though the term *democratic* is a misnomer here with respect to race and ethnicity.[42] Family life, "all-American" looks, and down-to-earth personalities came to be emphasized in promotional efforts over the exotic images attached to many stars in the 1920s. In particular, studios were looking to hire what they considered the Boy or Girl Next Door. Although not actually spelled out, it was assumed that the folks next door were fair-skinned and of Western European extraction.

Given these various developments, Latina/o stardom in the mid- to late 1930s never matched the level of possibility that existed in the late silent film era. As Hispanic accents increasingly were coded as comic or threatening and always as un-American, and Latina/o actors were considered less desirable as romantic leads, Latina/o stars faced uncertainty in Hollywood; most were unable to maintain their star status over the course of the decade.

Dolores Del Rio and the Shift to Sound

As noted earlier, Dolores Del Rio weathered major changes in her career in relation to the conversion to talking film. Dewitt Bodeen asserts that even prior to the transitional years, Del Rio worked diligently on her English in preparation for the impending change.[43] Her stardom had yet to peak, however. The star's Hollywood career crested in 1928 with respect to the number of film projects in which she appeared and the variety of roles she played. She starred in six films in that year. Of these, two were silent films and four were sound films, a few of which included songs sung by the actors. Exploration of these films and Del Rio's career in these years reveals a great deal about the evolving status of Latina/os in Hollywood's new world of sound film.

Del Rio's silent films released in 1928 consisted of two produced and released by Fox Film, the Western *Gateway of the Moon,* in which the actress plays a "half-caste" Indian woman, and *No Other Woman,* a film that had almost been shelved permanently but was released after the success of *Loves of Carmen.* They received little attention; Del Rio had more success with the films with musical scores; in these she played a wide range of characters. These roles included a Jewish prospector's granddaughter in MGM's adventure film *The Trail of '98* (1928); a Russian woman who becomes a prostitute after being abandoned by her lover, the prince, in *The Red Dance* (1928); and an "untamable" Gypsy bear tamer who meets her match in Edwin Carewe's *Revenge* (1928). Del Rio also scored a resounding hit that year in the early sound film *Ramona* (1928), discussed further below.

A telling illustration of shifting public tastes can be found in reviews of *Revenge*, which offered Del Rio a flamboyant role as a fiercely independent woman that she appeared to take on with relish. Publicity for the film depicts Del Rio at the height of her star status; promotional stills and film posters are dominated by her image, highlighting her physicality and dark beauty. But despite the fact that *Revenge* was of the quality of many successful silent melodramas of earlier years in many respects, the film was rated "just fair" by *Variety*.

In spite of the busy year that Dolores Del Rio had in 1928, her status was rapidly shifting. As noted earlier, film actors were finding themselves on widely diverging paths at their studios while discussions took place among executives with respect to which of them were going to make the leap to talkies. For the most part, these meetings were held behind closed doors and were not recorded for the historical record. Allen R. Ellenberger, in his study of the career of Ramon Novarro, found documentation of one such meeting that took place at Novarro's studio, MGM. According to Frances Marion, a screenwriter also under contract with the studio at the time, an MGM executive had posed the all-important question regarding Novarro's prospects: "He can sing and play the guitar, but what about his accent?"[44] The answer was not recorded for posterity; what is known is that Lewis Stone, Lionel Barrymore, and Conrad Nagel were given the go-ahead for talkies, while Novarro was not. The distinction between different categories of sound films during the transitional period is also important to make here. Like Novarro, Del Rio, while appearing in early "soundies" (films with musical scores but no dialogue), also was not encouraged to quickly star in films with sound dialogue, or "talkies." In fact, even while she continued to be cast in studio films, Del Rio's accent ultimately brought about the waning of her status and casting possibilities as a Hollywood film actress as talkies became the norm.

This did not happen immediately, however. Another marker of Del Rio's status as one of the top stars in Hollywood before the transition was her inclusion on March 29, 1928, with the "[t]he most famous, the highest paid

Dolores Del Rio in a publicity photo for *Revenge* (1928), released by United Artists. Courtesy of the Academy of Motion Picture Arts and Sciences.

names in American motion pictures," a small group of successful actors under contract with United Artists, in a pioneering radio broadcast meant to "prove to millions of fans that their idols had voices . . . good enough to meet the challenge of the talkies."[45] Del Rio joined Mary Pickford, Douglas Fairbanks, Charlie Chaplin, D. W. Griffith, John Barrymore, Norma Talmadge, and Gloria Swanson in this endeavor and sang a song from *Ramona* as her contribution. Rumors that she had used a voice "doubler" on the broadcast spread in the newspapers in subsequent days, but they were soon quelled as false.

Ramona was a notable role for Del Rio in several respects. First, the film, featuring a Movietone musical score, marked Del Rio's singing debut. Second, it marked a distinct shift in the ethnic marking of the roles she began to be offered. The narrative, adapted from an 1884 novel by Helen Hunt Jackson, centers on a romance between a young Mexican woman (presumably of Spanish heritage, but later found to have American Indian blood) and an American Indian man played by Warner Baxter in brownface makeup, in the California of the romanticized mission era. A consistently popular story of racial mixing and misunderstanding, it had already been released in film version twice previously. It is striking that during this period in which Latina/o actors began to be racialized, Dolores Del Rio was chosen to star in this narrative that focused heavily on the crossing and confusion of U.S. racial boundaries on the part of its protagonist. Moreover, reviewers, in praising Del Rio's acting in the role, tended to confuse "'Indianness' with 'Mexicanness,'" as Hershfield points out.[46] *Photoplay,* for example, asserted that "there could have been no more fitting person to impersonate the Indian-blooded Ramona than the Mexican Dolores Del Rio."[47] Despite Del Rio's accent, which some found heavy, *Ramona* proved to be a success. The film's songs also were quite popular, particularly the title song.[48] Nonetheless, while the film may have solidified Del Rio's stardom, it may also have served as a symbolic marker of the Mexican-born actress's changing image in Hollywood as not sufficiently American.

Del Rio also starred the following year in the tearjerker *Evangeline* (1929), the last film in which she was directed by Carewe. The film, based on a poem by Henry Wadsworth Longfellow, focuses on the separation of the title character from her betrothed during the French Acadians' brutal expulsion from Nova Scotia by the British in 1755. Del Rio's accent is almost impossible to discern in the commercial DVD release of the film, given the dearth of dialogue; more notably, she sings two songs. Regarding the reception she received, the limitations that Latinas were beginning to face in Hollywood are immediately evident in publicity for the film. In a September 1929 *Vanity Fair* article while the film was in production, the magazine stated that, in

Dolores Del Rio with co-star Warner Baxter in *Ramona* (1928). Courtesy of the Academy of Motion Picture Arts and Sciences.

taking the role of the "Nordic heroine," Del Rio was undertaking a "hazardous" task, "for *Evangeline* is an American tradition, but one which Senora [*sic*] Del Rio's undoubted talent should make her understand."[49] Reviews of Del Rio's performance in the film were also mixed, and the film did not do well. *Film Daily* described Del Rio's voice as "small" but "charming," while according to *Variety*, Del Rio, "[t]he paprika Latina girl . . . has some good emotional sequences, but somehow doesn't seem to fit her role."[50]

In the meantime, Del Rio experienced some personal difficulties and rare bad publicity. Her separation and divorce from her husband Jaime Del Rio, and his later death from illness in Berlin in December 1928, put a momentary damper on her image. According to several accounts, she had been romantically involved with Edwin Carewe, who had divorced his wife, but Del Rio separated from him after the filming of *Evangeline*. In 1930, Carewe returned to his ex-wife and Del Rio married Cedric Gibbons, MGM's most successful art director.

Likely in an attempt to work her Spanish accent into a role, Del Rio's first talkie was in the role of a Spanish singer, Lita, who works at a French brothel but maintains her virtue in *The Bad One* (1930). She was not well received for her work in this picture. Ironically, Lita's awkward efforts to learn American slang in the film can be seen as an emblem of Del Rio's struggle to continue to be seen as a mainstream Hollywood star at the time. Her character's accent was criticized by *Variety*, which stated, "Lita's gradual efforts to simulate American slang are painfully self-conscious, rather than even suggestive of cuteness."[51] It is not possible to disentangle this critique from criticism of the increasing shallowness of Del Rio's roles, or from umbrage with Del Rio's own non-native accent.

The star broke her management contract with Edwin Carewe after this film and signed with Joseph Schenck at United Artists, then suffered what apparently was a nervous breakdown that kept her from fulfilling the contract. The United Artists contract was ultimately cancelled in 1931. While Del Rio never spoke directly about it, she later intimated that she was struggling with personal problems.[52] While she was away, further transformations were in motion in Hollywood. For one, the star system continued to evolve. Dominating the screen now were leading ladies of a different, more streetwise style, "screen ladies like Joan Crawford, Norma Shearer, Bette Davis, Ruth Chatterton and Jean Harlow, whose voices contributed so much to defining their roles as worldly women of the 1930s."[53] Del Rio was no longer in vogue as a dark beauty and was pigeonholed as a Latina (rather than American, or "white") actress at this time when Mexican, no matter how Spanish or wealthy, no longer easily translated as glamorous and cosmopolitan.

The 1930s brought decreasing options for Dolores Del Rio, although she was able to bank on her former stardom for a time. In 1931, Del Rio negotiated a new contract, this time with RKO Radio Pictures. Her subsequent roles and publicity increasingly were limited, however. The first of her films for RKO was *Girl of the Rio* (1932). Considering that this was a remake of *The Dove* (1927), which had been boycotted by the Mexican government for what it considered negative representations of Mexican characters, Del Rio's acceptance of this role is particularly telling of the constraints she now faced. Her role is that of a somewhat dimwitted cantina singer in a Mexican border town; the other Mexican characters (one given the embarrassing moniker of Señor Tostado) fare far worse. Del Rio appears to be struggling in the role, either with its apparent limitations or the subtler, talkie-style of acting, or both. Her actual accent is difficult to discern, as much of her character's dialogue calls for her to speak broken English (the character's trademark saying throughout is the awkward phrase, "You betcha your life!"). "Rush.," reviewing for *Variety,* ultimately panned Del Rio for what he or she called an "indifferent performance."[54]

The tactic of launching foreign actors' talkie careers in the roles of foreigners with imperfect English was in fact utilized many times in the early part of the decade. Greta Garbo's first talking role in *Anna Christie* (1930), promoted with the now-famous tag line, "Garbo talks!" is a prime example, while Ellenberger argues that Ramon Novarro also was confined to playing non-Americans.[55] This approach seems to have been more successful for Garbo than for Del Rio, Novarro, and other Latina/o actors, however, considering their subsequent career trajectories. Perhaps this was because Garbo was considered more easily definable as white and thus, even as a foreigner, was seen as closer to the American ideal.

By 1932, the industry had for the most part converted completely to talkies. Del Rio was still considered very much a star, with an image as a high-class, tasteful lady. Invitations to the parties that she and husband Cedric Gibbons threw were reportedly much coveted among Hollywood notables. She also continued to be lauded for her looks and figure throughout the 1930s. In just one such example, she was named the "most perfect feminine figure in Hollywood" in *Photoplay* in 1933.[56] Meanwhile, Del Rio was struggling to even be considered by casting directors for film leads. Her career was resuscitated somewhat by the splash she made in RKO's 1932 South Sea romance *Bird of Paradise,* in which she played the Polynesian island princess Luana. The film, which tells the story of Luana's forbidden love with Johnny, an American sailor, heavily exploits the titillation of a modern colonialist take on cross-cultural romance. As such, Del Rio's role offered her little to do other than lust for Johnny and speak in a gibberish meant to pass for a Polynesian language. The film advertising in turn emphasized the racy storyline, potential nudity, and sexual content. (One promotional poster showed a half-naked Del Rio, a flowery lei strategically placed on her torso, in a clinch with Joel McCrea, accompanied by the copy, "glamorous drama of lovers whose worlds were a million miles apart, but whose hearts throbbed together!" and "White man . . . native girl . . . two hearts in a flowery paradise!") Despite the praise the big-budget film received, it didn't earn enough to turn a profit.

In 1933, the star found she was now offered roles mainly in Latin musicals, her dancing ability again paying off. She acted in several for RKO and had a surprise hit in her first, *Flying Down to Rio* (1933). In this film she played a

Brazilian heiress, Belinha de Rezenda, who falls for an American bandleader. While Del Rio received positive reviews for her portrayal of the aristocratic Belinha, the role exemplified the Dark Lady motif that came to dominate her sound film career, as Charles Ramírez Berg has noted.[57] Del Rio was optimistic about the direction her career was taking, however, hoping the role meant her opportunities were on an upswing. As the actress noted to a journalist in later decades, "For the first time I was to play the part of a smart modern woman with plenty of music and comedy around me. I knew it was a sign I could play a sophisticated role. I was no longer little Luana or Ramona."[58]

Del Rio's optimism did not take her far, however. After the release of *Flying Down to Rio*, RKO chose not to renew her contract. Del Rio instead signed with Warner Bros. in 1934 and was cast in another string of Latin musicals. Her characters in fact seemed increasingly overshadowed by her dance costumes, whether ruffled, sequenced, or feathered. The first of these musicals and respective set of costumes for Warner Bros. was *Wonder Bar* (1934). In this film Del Rio played another Dark Lady character, in this case a Latin dancer, Inez, for whom three men (portrayed by Al Jolson, Dick Powell, and Ricardo Cortez) compete. Moreover, Inez has little agency or choice of her own within these dynamics. A still from the film of Del Rio as Inez dancing with co-star Ricardo Cortez illustrates how she often was utilized in these musicals more as a beautiful spectacle than a character with full agency or subjectivity, as David Ragan has commented.[59]

Still attempting to salvage her career, the following year Del Rio appeared in two more musicals, Warner Bros.' *In Caliente* (1935) and *I Live for Love* (1935). Del Rio garnered positive reviews, but critics' comments ultimately were far less effusive than those of years past. Such was the case in this review for *I Live for Love* from *Variety*: "Del Rio gives a nice performance and has been well photographed."[60] While Warner's remake of the historical sex farce *Madame Dubarry* (1934) had provided Del Rio with a potential change, a part in which she could actually show her acting range, it too proved a disappointment. It ultimately was cut drastically by the Hays Office, which administered the standards of the Production Code, because of perceived racy content, according to Del Rio.[61]

While Del Rio appeared in a few films in the late 1930s, her career was in noticeable decline. Audiences were looking for a radically different sort of star than had been the rage in her heyday. Dolores Del Rio herself is quoted as saying, "By the mid-1930s . . . there were a new set of fresh faces, and the really plum roles were going to actresses like Bette Davis or Katherine Hepburn or Barbara Stanwyck."[62] Following a few other films for Warner Bros.

Dolores Del Rio and Ricardo Cortez dancing in the musical *Wonder Bar* (1934). Courtesy of the Film Collection, Harry Ransom Humanities Research Center, The University of Texas at Austin.

that didn't register well with audiences, Del Rio and the studio had difficulties coming to an agreement during contract negotiations in 1936. Del Rio finally chose to sign with Columbia Pictures later that year. Del Rio made just one film, *Devil's Playground,* for Columbia. In this film she again played a Mexican dancer and femme fatale. She broke her contract, however, and signed with Twentieth Century-Fox in 1937. Her films for Twentieth Century-Fox included a role as herself in *Ali Baba Goes to Town* (1937), as a nightclub singer in the World War I espionage film *Lancer Spy* (1937), and as a French singer in the adventure drama *International Settlement* (1938).

By 1938 she was not able to land lead roles, according to Del Rio. Her personal life also was increasingly unstable. She had had an affair with Hollywood upstart Orson Welles in the late 1930s and divorced Cedric Gibbons as a result of it. Because of disappointment over a collaboration with Welles, *Journey into Fear* (1942), and the end of their relationship, Del Rio left Hollywood. She moved back to Mexico City, where she worked steadily in Mexican cinema, helping to usher in its Golden Age. Among her many accolades, she won the Mexican equivalent of an Academy Award for Best Actress, the Ariel, three times, for *Las Abandonadas* (1945), *Doña Perfecta* (1951), and *The Boy and the Fog* (1953). Her other Mexican films included the highly popular *Flor Silvestre* (1943), *Maria Candelaria* (1944), and *Bugambilia* (1945), all directed by Emilio Fernández. Dolores Del Rio was later married for a third time, to Lewis Riley in 1959. She made a few, brief forays back to Hollywood to act in such films as *Flaming Star* in 1960 and *Cheyenne Autumn* in 1964, and was cited both as a talented actress and a gracefully aging beauty. Dolores Del Rio died in Newport Beach, California, in 1983.

* * *

As I document in this chapter, the late silent film era of the mid- to late 1920s provided an opening for Latino and Latina stardom of a magnitude that only recently is beginning to be matched. This era provided unique opportunities for a number of light-skinned Latina/o actors, whose images were shaped in a manner that promoted them as acceptably foreign and thus unracialized stars to the American and global public. Such was the case for popular Mexican actress Dolores Del Rio. Developments in the film industry and sociopolitical changes of the 1930s changed the opportunities for and nature of stardom for Del Rio and other Latina/o stars and aspiring actors, however.

As a part of this evolution, Latina/o casting and star images underwent a dramatic shift. Increasingly, a racial politics of casting designated Latina/o actors and actresses as unacceptable for leading roles, particularly as unambiguously white characters, and limited their casting options in Hollywood films. As noted earlier, in the previous decade, Dolores Del Rio had been cast in roles that spanned a wide range of nationalities and character types. She found that the opportunity to play leads that were constructed as white was blocked after the transition to talking film, however, and she increasingly was cast only in Latina, Polynesian, or Spanish roles by the mid-1930s. Del Rio and other Latinas were offered more opportunities than nonwhite actresses of other ethnic and racial designations, however. For instance, their range of roles in this period stood in contrast to those of African American actresses such as Louise Beavers and Fredi Washington, who were confined to parts as maids and offered romantic lead roles only in black-cast films.

Latina/o actors and characters moreover were now consistently racialized when they were cast in white-dominant texts. Within the newly imagined (and, more important, aural) racial hierarchy of the star system and story worlds of sound film, Latina/os began to occupy a liminal, shadow space between the categories of whiteness and blackness, neither equated with blackness nor fully allowed into the privileged realm of whiteness. And when such differences didn't exist materially, they were produced. The voices and bodies even of light-skinned Latina and Latino stars came to be inscribed in a manner that distinctly set them apart from white actors, what might be termed a process of cultural racialization within Hollywood diegeses and in the realm of star promotion. In the case of Dolores Del Rio, these tendencies were tempered slightly, likely because of her elegant star image. Latinas also began to be set apart from white actresses in Hollywood films through their positioning as erotic others. As sexual Puritanism became a prominent aspect of the construction of white femininity in Depression-era Hollywood, the Latina star body in contrast was often coded as always comparatively more seductive. Role types such as the Dark Lady figure Del Rio portrayed in 1930s films increasingly became the norm for Latina actors.

Similar shifts were taking place in the sociopolitical landscape. During the years of early sound film, Olvera Street in downtown Los Angeles, once the heart of the Mexican American community, was restored to its turn-of-the-century quaintness as a tourist attraction. Mexican Americans in the city were not fooled into considering this a sign of growing equality, however: The restoration of Olvera Street took place in the same years that hundreds of thousands of Mexicans were forcefully deported and Mexican Americans continued to experience discrimination and segregation in the city and country at large. As George J. Sánchez notes: "The lesson [of the restoration of Olvera Street] was clear: Mexicans were to be assigned a place in the mythic past of Los Angeles—one that could be relegated to a quaint section of a city destined to delight tourists and antiquarians. Real Mexicans were out of sight and increasingly out of mind."[63] An argument can be made that the same thing was happening in the film industry and in Hollywood films themselves in these years. Most Latina/o actors, whether they had achieved a level of fame or were working to establish careers, found they had been racialized as non-American, with American now increasingly defined as fair, blonde, or redheaded in the eyes of film producers, and were increasingly limited to stereotyped roles in Hollywood story worlds that could be described as quaint at best.

2

The Good Neighbor on Prime Time

Desi Arnaz and I Love Lucy

My students these days were born in the late 1980s; they don't always know Latino and Latina actors whose careers peaked a few decades ago, Latina/os with promising careers in the 1970s and '80s such as Freddie Prinze, Maria Conchita Alonso, and Paul Rodriguez. It is all the more remarkable then that they do know of Cuban-born actor, musician, and producer Desi Arnaz. Even more intimately, they know Ricky Ricardo, the character he played on the popular television series *I Love Lucy* from 1951 to 1957 and in spin-off films and television texts in later years. If prompted, most could even imitate Ricky's most famous line, "Lucy, you've got some s'plaining to do!" The enduring popularity of this character and the series—which has been broadcast continuously in some form since the 1950s—underscores Arnaz's importance to an exploration of Hollywood stardom and its relationship to the evolving status of U.S. Latina/os, particularly given that Arnaz was a Cuban musician and actor who found success at a time when Latina/os seldom appeared in cinematic and televisual story worlds and performance spaces.

The late Desi Arnaz, born Desiderio Alberto Arnaz y de Acha in Santiago, Cuba, on March 2, 1917, established a career in U.S. music, theater, and film in the 1940s, the same decade in which Dolores Del Rio decided to leave the United States because of dwindling opportunities.[1] As noted, Arnaz went on to become a successful television star on the wildly popular *I Love Lucy* series in the 1950s, as well as executive producer of the series and an influential television executive as the president of Desilu Productions from 1951 to 1962. His career and public image as marketed to the American public thus provide a telling illustration of the evolution of Hollywood's imagining of Latinidad in the 1940s and 1950s, particularly as it was translated for the new medium of television in the latter decade, and its relationship to imagined notions of Cuban immigrants, Mexican Americans, and other Latina/os during World War II and its aftermath.

As noted in the previous chapter, the 1930s and '40s typically translated to constrained opportunities for Latino and Latina actors. In film story worlds, Latin accents overwhelmingly marked roles as comic or villainous; while a few actors were able to establish or maintain stardom, having a noticeable Hispanic accent almost always ensured that they would not be cast in lead roles in "A-list" films. The association of Hollywood Latinidad with dance and music also became further entrenched with the rise of Latin-themed musicals in the 1930s and '40s. This was compounded by shifts in U.S. global politics, among them a new emphasis on South America. In the years before and during World War II (which the United States participated in from 1941 to 1945), film studios aimed to support President Roosevelt's "Good Neighbor" policy and simultaneously sought new export markets in Latin America while European markets were closed. As scholars such as Ana M. López note, the opportunity afforded in the late 1920s to actors who could play sultry Latin lovers was now overshadowed by an interest in singers and dancers, particularly from South American countries, who could be featured in Latin-flavored, but ideologically U.S.-centric, musicals.[2] For some Latina/o performers, such as Carmen Miranda, from Brazil but of Portuguese descent, and the young Desi Arnaz, such musicals provided some opportunity, albeit with limitations that few were able to transcend with the ease and to the same personal benefit as Arnaz.

Other aspects of Hollywood Latinidad that existed previously come into high relief in this era as well. Films of the Good Neighbor variety typically conflated Latin American countries and cultural elements, a tendency that also describes aspects of Desi Arnaz's performance style.[3] As a young actor he played Latinos of a variety of nationalities, while as a musician and bandleader he was above all else a master showman, as Gustavo Pérez-Firmat notes, a "translation artist" for a primarily white American audience.[4] Despite the pan-Latina/o elements of Desi Arnaz's performance style, in order to understand him as a Cuban American star it is also necessary to view his career in the context of relations between the United States and Cuba. Politically friendly U.S.-Cuba relations in the 1950s allowed room for a Cuban star that loved America, a sentiment that Desi Arnaz often expressed. After the 1959 revolution that resulted in a Communist political regime in Cuba, such stardom might not have been possible.

As important to consider in relation to Desi Arnaz's evolving public image is how he as a Latino actor was promoted to the American public as one of the first stars of the emergent medium of television. The growth of commercial television to the status of a mass medium in the early 1950s created possibilities for a new type of national stardom. When *I Love Lucy* debuted on CBS stations on October 15, 1951, Desi Arnaz and Lucille Ball, along with their peers such as Milton Berle, George Burns, and Gertrude Berg, were among the first to experience it, and in large part, helped establish expectations of its parameters and impact. As Susan Murray notes in her study of early television stardom, it shared many similarities with radio stardom in that it engendered a feeling of intimacy related to such factors as appearing in American households and performers often creating unassuming personas similar to their own personalities.[5] Like other television stars of the period, Desi Arnaz and Lucille Ball also had a distinctly commercial role as television stars. They were expected to appear in advertising for their sponsor, Phillip Morris, and later sponsors, which included Proctor & Gamble and General Foods. In addition, the *I Love Lucy* series inspired a franchise of tie-in items; images of Arnaz and Ball as Lucy and Ricky Ricardo graced hundreds of products, many still collected today, that ran the gamut from dolls to aprons, and from pajama sets to Dixie cups.

Before this could be possible, however, Desi Arnaz had to convince both network executives and advertisers that he would appeal on a weekly basis to the mass American public that was considered the target television audience in these years. Meanwhile, white American social attitudes toward Mexican Americans and other U.S. Latina/os often leaned toward silent ambivalence at best in these decades, as discussed further in this chapter. Arnaz's career trajectory and the promotional texts that supported his stardom thus serve as important illustrations of the evolution of Hollywood Latinidad as constructed in 1940s films and 1950s television. How were Latina/os typically utilized in Good Neighbor–flavored musicals and in other films that featured Latina/os in the 1940s, and what sort of promotion did they receive? How did television producers (which included, in particular, Arnaz himself), advertisers, and publicists market Desi Arnaz as a potential American star? And how was Arnaz's star image as Cuban American, and—as I argue, both "Latin" and white—constructed?

Carrying out this analysis entails distinct challenges, not because of a dearth of research material, but rather because of an over-abundance. While Desi Arnaz appeared in only a handful of films in the 1940s, the original *I Love Lucy* series resulted in 180 episodes, 13 other hour-long episodes, a few tangentially related films, and the subsequent *Lucy-Desi Comedy Hour.*[6] Biographers and individuals who were part of the production of *I Love Lucy* also have written several books about the production of the series, Desilu Productions, and about Arnaz and Lucille Ball as a couple and as individuals. In the realm of academic writing, Gustavo Pérez-Firmat and Alberto Sandoval-Sánchez have considered Arnaz as a Cuban and Latino icon, while Susan Murray, Thomas Schatz, Mary Desjardins, Caren Kaplan, and others have conducted research on *I Love Lucy* in relation to television and film history.[7] In this distinct contribution, which builds on that work, particularly Pérez-Firmat's nuanced analysis of Desi Arnaz in relation to Cuban American identity, my focus is on Arnaz's star image in relation to the broader context of stardom and Hollywood Latinidad. In other words, I focus particularly on how Desi Arnaz was constructed and promoted as a Cuban, Latino, and American star by the film and television industries and how his stardom reflected or may have challenged the evolving status of Latina/os in the United States in the 1940s and '50s.

Latinidad for Non-Latinos: Desi as Bandleader

Desi Arnaz's stardom is best understood in light of not just his success in television but also his music and film career prior to *I Love Lucy* and the social trends and industry shifts of 1940s Hollywood. Arnaz, who began his career as a singer and bandleader, was cast as a performer in a handful of films in this decade, often Latin musicals and military dramas, and typically in small, supporting roles. Notably, despite the fact that not all were musicals, almost all capitalized on his musical talents in some form.

This period also illustrates Arnaz's considerable talent not only as a musician and bandleader, but also as an impresario. In these early years he both learned and demonstrated a particular talent for sharing Latin culture with American audiences in a manner they found both comfortable and appealing. Music scholar John Storm Roberts posits that Arnaz "knew relatively little about the music that he was popularizing," but that he and his performances helped to popularize Latin-flavored music. Some of the enduring hits from Arnaz's musical performances that were later incorporated into *I Love Lucy* episodes include "Cuban Pete," "Peanut Vendor," and "Babalú."[8] Cuban or Latino authenticity clearly is not the goal of such performances, which combine Cuban and other Latin rhythms with distinctly American malapropisms and humor. Regardless, or perhaps because of the cultural blending that was trademark to his style, Arnaz was extremely successful as a musical performer and bandleader. He would later apply these lessons to his appearances in film and subsequently television, as I explore further below.

According to biographers and Arnaz's autobiography (with the unassuming title *A Book*), Desiderio Arnaz was born to an illustrious, wealthy family of Spanish ancestry that lived in Cuba.[9] His relatives had held multiple positions of status: his great grandfather was appointed mayor of Santiago by the queen of Spain, while his father served as mayor in later years. The family's position changed with the Batista uprising in 1932, however. At that time the family homes were seized, and Arnaz's father, who had just been elected to the Cuban congress under former dictator Gerardo Machados's regime, was sent to prison. Arnaz and his mother fled to Miami, Florida, with few resources, and Arnaz began to work at a series of odd jobs to help support them. After six months in prison, his father was released and able to join them.

While still in his teens, Arnaz decided to pursue a career as a musician. He learned to play the guitar, he says in his autobiography, because it, and in particular the "tradition of the serenade," was a part of his culture.[10] Even at this early age, impressing young women was apparently a motivation for Arnaz, supporting Gustavo Pérez-Firmat's interpretation of Arnaz as embodying the Cuban notion of a *vivo* and in fact a *vividor*, or bon vivant who finds his head easily turned by romance.[11] While still in high school, he joined a Cuban rumba band, Sibony Septet, playing guitar and singing vocals. As Max Salazar and John Storm Roberts document, American audiences were demonstrating a rising interest in Latin and particularly Afro-Cuban music in this period.[12] Arnaz's work with this band eventually led to his meeting bandleader Xavier Cugat. Cugat invited him to join and sing with his band as soon as he completed high school, which he did six months later; this was to prove an important training ground for Arnaz. From Cugat, Arnaz learned how to appeal to U.S. audiences, as he has put it, "how the music should be played, how it should be presented, what the American people liked to dance to."[13] Arnaz quickly found success with audiences, and his numbers, such as "Para Vigo Me Voy" and "Quiereme Mucho," were very popular. His ability to get audiences up to learn Latin dances such as the rumba or the conga soon became one of Arnaz's trademarks. He became known for leading his audience in a conga line at the end of the night, which was very popular with his patrons.

Arnaz later formed his own band with musicians supplied by Cugat, named Desi Arnaz and his Xavier Cugat Orchestra. After some early struggles and an eventual break from Cugat, the newly named Desi Arnaz and His Orchestra found regular work in Miami. Broadway songwriter Lorenz Hart, impressed when he heard them play, brought the combo to become regular headliners at the La Conga nightclub in Manhattan. Known for his high energy, romantic allure, and for creating a dynamic and fun atmosphere for his audience, Arnaz quickly came to the attention of socialites, celebrity journalist Walter Winchell, who gave him plugs in his column, and purportedly even a famous madam who supported his career. His appeal quickly led, among other things, to offers to appear in a Broadway play and in films. This review by Malcolm Johnson for the *New York Sun* is typical of the type of publicity that he received at the time: "Desi Arnaz is a young man with a drum. He is a new type of Pied Piper who leads enthusiastic, uninhibited followers in the sinuous, serpentine conga dance every night at La Conga, the night club dedicated to torrid Cuban music and entertainment. Two or three times each night, Arnaz steps down from the bandstand, his tall, goat-skin drum slung across his shoulders, and begins beating out the wild, savage rhythm which lures dancers on to the floor and behind him in the conga line. Arnaz, a youthful, handsome Cuban (he is barely 22 years old), has headed his rhumba band at La Conga for two months now and is an established success."[14]

Also noted in the *New York Sun*'s review of Arnaz's popular club act, the young musician's popularity and success as a bandleader had led to his being cast in a 1939 "football musical," *Too Many Girls*, by Lorenz Hart and director George Abbott. Arnaz has claimed that this was because he fit a type distinct from the stereotypical Latino roles that was hard to find at the time.[15] Arnaz had an appearance and performance style likely seen as too sophisticated to play a standard Latin "bandido" or "buffoon" and too wholesome to portray the traditional Latin lover, which both hindered and helped him throughout his career. *Too Many Girls,* a romantic farce about a wealthy father of a coed who hires four football heroes to protect her without her knowledge, included Arnaz's role as Manuelito Lynch, a young Argentine considered the best football player in Latin America (yes, football, not *fútbol*). The musical offered Arnaz a chance to sing and dance as well as act. The producers, impressed with his performance, capitalized on his nightclub act when they incorporated "Babalú," an energetic musical number in which Arnaz would lead the entire cast in a conga line, always a sure audience pleaser. Despite its flimsy narrative, *Too Many Girls* and Desi Arnaz were a hit. When RKO Radio Pictures acquired the film rights, Arnaz was signed on to reprise his role. Contract players Richard Carlson and Lucille Ball were signed on, which soon enabled Desi Arnaz to meet his future wife.

The film version of *Too Many Girls* (1940) is troubling when considering Latina/o representation, to say the least, with the implausibility of the character of Manuelito the least of the problematic elements in the film. As both Pérez-Firmat and Sandoval-Sánchez note, the narrative characterizes Latina/o and Latin American cultures in a manner that is wildly inaccurate,[16] through such choices as casting Ann Miller as a young Mexican American coed named Pépe, and using set designs for the fictional New Mexico college campus that haphazardly mix American Indian, Latina/o, and college sports motifs, creating what Pérez-Firmat aptly termed a "multiculturalist's nightmare."[17] The "Babalú" number, in which Arnaz as Manuelito leads the cast in a conga to celebrate their football win, marks the culmination of such confusion, with Arnaz appearing remarkably comfortable presiding over it. Such incongruities were apparently lost on critics, moreover, as they found the film conventional but likely to do well because of its entertainment value. RKO marketed Arnaz as a Latin lover of the clean-cut variety; typical publicity photos showcased Arnaz with his conga drum, looking handsome, wholesome, and exuberant.

Some, but not all, of the critics were impressed. "Walt.," writing for *Variety*, commented that Desi Arnaz, "who is getting an extensive publicity buildup as the heartthrob from Cuba, has an intriguing film personality that might carry him far."[18] Bosley Crowther of the *New York Times* did not like Arnaz, however, calling him "a noisy, black-haired Latin whose face, unfortunately, lacks expression and whose performance is devoid of grace."[19] While the film didn't do tremendous business, audiences apparently were smitten with Arnaz, as many moviegoers wrote on comment cards after the film that they liked "the Mexican boy," "the Spanish actor," "the little Argentine fellow," and "the Cuban boy," calling Arnaz "darn good" and "excellent."[20] Such comments illustrate not only Arnaz's appeal but also how American audiences confused various Latina/o groups without compunction in these years.

What to Do with a Latin Heartthrob? Arnaz in Hollywood

The positive feedback that Desi Arnaz received in *Too Many Girls* had a major impact on Arnaz's career, however, as it resulted in Arnaz being signed by RKO to a two-year, three-picture contract, which would be fulfilled with roles in *Father Takes a Wife* (1941), the comedy *Four Jacks and a Jill* (1942), and the war film *The Navy Comes Through* (1942). Making a small attempt to promote him as a dashing young star, RKO also disseminated publicity photographs of Arnaz in formal suits and other sophisticated looks. In the meantime, Arnaz's personal life garnered more significant publicity when he and Lucille Ball were married. After they completed their promotional tour for *Too Many Girls*, they wed on November 30, 1940. Ball's greater fame

A young Desi Arnaz, in a publicity still for the film version of *Too Many Girls* (1940).

at the time is evident in the press coverage; headlines such as "Lucille Ball weds Cuban actor" were common.[21] Notable in this coverage is the fact that Arnaz's foreign status is emphasized—in other words, that he was promoted as a white foreigner rather than a racialized American, and that the Arnaz-Ball marriage was not viewed as violating taboos of miscegenation. Thus, the Arnazes were interpreted as a bicultural but not biracial couple, and as fitting role models for other American newlyweds. For example, belief in the public's interest in the newlywed couple was illustrated when they graced (with their dog, Tommy) one of the first covers of *Movie Life* in June 1942. After their wedding, Arnaz and Ball returned to Los Angeles to resume work; they soon moved to a ranch they purchased in Chatsworth, which they named Desilu.

In Arnaz's first film for RKO, *Father Takes a Wife* (1941), he had a small role that was overshadowed by stars Adolph Menjou and Gloria Swanson. The contrived story is about an operatic tenor, Carlos Bardez (Arnaz), whose appeal draws the attention of a married woman who wants to support his career and sparks her husband's jealousy. Arnaz was able to demonstrate his youthful romantic appeal and sang some numbers in the film, but he received little attention from reviewers for the role. He fared somewhat better with his next film, the comedy *Four Jacks and a Jill* (1941), in which he had a dual role as a taxi cab driver and a king who exchange identities. While both *Variety* and *Hollywood Reporter* praised the film and Arnaz's performance, he would later comment that he hoped it would be forgotten.

His final film in fulfillment of his contract, the patriotic war film *The Navy Comes Through* (1942), similarly offered Arnaz a flimsy role. He was seventh-billed, after such stars as Pat O'Brien and Jane Wyatt. In one of his few Cuban roles, Arnaz played an earnest man who had chosen to fight for the United States because it had earlier "freed Cuba." The film didn't garner a lot of attention, although *Variety* commented that he "sparks much of the interest" in the film.[22] Before his contract ran out, RKO also sent Arnaz with other studio actors to Mexico City on a goodwill tour, taking advantage of his ability to speak Spanish. But as he notes in his autobiography, the studio didn't take it very seriously when he told them he had learned that Mexicans were suspicious of the studio's sudden interest.[23]

These marginal roles and the lackluster promotion that Arnaz received from RKO seem directly reflective of the white American centrality of Hollywood storylines and casting in this time period. Even while Carmen Miranda was the top moneymaker for Twentieth Century-Fox in the mid-1940s, it was generally unthinkable at the time to create protagonist roles for Latina/o actors, even "white Latins," outside of the Latin musicals. Arnaz's lack of easy fit in the industry's usual categories of Latino "types" arguably also hampered his casting possibilities.

The obstacles that Arnaz faced at this stage in his career also can be seen as related to the studios' continued lack of concern for appealing to Latina/o moviegoers in the United States, even while Latin American audiences were sought. In truth, in this period the standing of Mexican Americans and other U.S. Latina/os was far more complex and less optimistic than the Good Neighbor films would seem to imply. While Cuban immigrants in this era were of varying class status, Mexican American communities were struggling in the aftermath of the Great Depression. Some Mexican Americans hoped that assimilation would bring about greater equality, and advocacy groups such as LULAC (the League of United Latin American Citizens) had succeeded in having their racial designation changed from nonwhite to white on the census.[24] But with respect to employment discrimination, segregation in public school systems, and other social problems Mexican Americans experienced, their racialized status was unchanged.[25] And while the G.I. Bill offered some Mexican American and Puerto Rican veterans opportunities to achieve a higher education that had not previously existed, it was not always honored. In Los Angeles, home of the media industries, the construction of multiple freeways in the city from 1940 to 1960 also carved up thriving Mexican American neighborhoods, fragmenting the community and destroying some of its most important districts, as Rudolfo Acuña and other scholars have documented.[26] The new freeways also effectively sheltered most film industry executives from their Mexican American neighbors.

The studios apparently had little fear with respect to challenge from Mexican American and other Latina/o advocacy groups, moreover. In this period, such groups typically were focused on securing equal rights for Latina/o citizens in areas such as employment, voting rights, and education; media images were seldom challenged in any significant way in these years. As Chon Noriega found in surveys of Production Code Administration files on films featuring Mexican American characters in the 1950s, the Hays Office appeared concerned only with whether they might offend Latin American viewers, for instance.[27]

This is not to imply that all of the studios were blind to the potential appeal of a handsome young Latino actor such as Desi Arnaz, however. He was eventually signed by Louis B. Mayer to a new contract with MGM, soon after the RKO contract expired. This led to what was perhaps Arnaz's most compelling film role in his career, in MGM's *Bataan* (1943), a war drama about a U.S. Army regiment defending a bridge for the Americans to use in their escape from Bata'an in the Philippines.

Although to a degree it could be said to memorialize the important contributions made by Mexican Americans in World War II through the inclusion of Arnaz's character, *Bataan* still is adamantly white-centric.[28] In it, Arnaz played soldier Felix Ramirez, a Mexican American who is proudly from

California. He is part of a thirteen-member, multiethnic regiment which, Hollywood-style, is completely color-blind, as racial or ethnic differences are never mentioned. It really isn't necessary, however, as the soldiers of color are characterized by common stereotypes (the African American soldier can't stop singing, while Felix Ramirez is mechanically inclined and loves the new American music of Tommy Dorsey) and utilized in the narrative only as color in the background. Ultimately, they willingly sacrifice their lives for their country and for the white lead characters. Ramirez, for example, serves valiantly, even while critically ill, until he dies of malaria early in the narrative. Arnaz was praised for his performance (the *Hollywood Reporter* posited, "Desi Arnaz is his usual self-assured self as a Latin-American private"),[29] and he was later recognized by *Photoplay* for best performance of the month. He did not receive a great deal of promotion from the studio, however. MGM's promotional thrust can be discerned from the publicity posters, none of which feature the Latino or African American soldiers. Rather one, in full color, features four of the Anglo-American soldiers, next to the subtitle, "The Story of a Patrol of 13 Heroes." Of interest also is that there was no discussion in reviews or other media commentary as might be the case today that Arnaz, a Cuban, was portraying a Mexican American character. It appears that the film industry's creation of homogenous Latina/o images that lumped various groups together in an undifferentiated manner went unquestioned in the 1940s, to the advantage of Desi Arnaz in this instance.

Soon after the film wrapped, Arnaz began his own two-year enlistment in the army, where he both became an American citizen and, in a move reminiscent of his character in *The Navy Comes Through,* had his name legally shortened to Desi Arnaz. Upon his release from the service, Arnaz found that he was not getting film roles from his MGM contract. In one case, a musical with a role for a Latin love interest, Mexican newcomer Ricardo Montalban was offered the part before Arnaz could vie for it.[30] Arnaz ultimately managed to get out of his contract and formed a band again. He was one of the best paid bandleaders in the country during those years, as Pérez-Firmat notes, though his work required a great deal of travel.[31]

There were troubles in his marriage, moreover, particularly because Arnaz and Ball's work often kept them in different cities and reportedly because he was involved in infidelities. News items in late 1944 reported that Lucille Ball Arnaz had filed for divorce, and then reconsidered. The couple's difficulties were heavily dramatized in the press, which only seemed to feed the public's interest in both stars. The *Los Angeles Times,* describing their marriage in verbiage that relied heavily on ethnic associations, romanticized their problems as due to "An explosive romantic formula—a redheaded woman and a fiery Latin."[32] At least some of the difficulty for the couple resulted from Arnaz's inability to secure steady work in Los Angeles, however. He found acting roles occasionally, and also led the band for Bob Hope's television series for a season. But despite working with a dialect coach to lessen his accent, he generally was not considered for lead film roles. It was this obstacle that motivated him and Lucille Ball to find a creative project on which they could collaborate.

Arnaz's last film before embarking on *I Love Lucy*, *Holiday in Havana*, in fact bears striking similarities to his later role as Ricky Ricardo. A 1949 musical set in Cuba, it was one of the few films that correctly situated him with respect to his heritage. In its predictable romantic storyline about a misunderstanding between two Cuban musical performers—played by Arnaz and a miscast but jovial Mary Hatcher as Lolita Valdez—who ultimately are meant to be together, *Holiday in Havana* offered an ideal though lightweight showcase for Arnaz and his music (his "Holiday in Havana" and "The Arnaz Jam" are included among the songs). The character of Carlos in fact called for him to be both a heartthrob and a tame, family-friendly romantic lead. He marries Lolita so as not to besmirch her reputation when she uses this cover story while on the lam, for instance, even though they have not so much as kissed yet. In his portrayal of Carlos Estrada, Arnaz established a successful negotiation of tensions inherent in playing a Latin romantic lead in this period, a negotiation that set the stage for what would make Ricky Ricardo so popular with American viewers.

The Good Neighbor on Prime Time: *I Love Lucy*

The success of *I Love Lucy* and promotion of Desi Arnaz as a television star is best understood in relation to what was happening in the country at the time. For white Americans it was a time of prosperity; marriages and home ownership were on the rise, along with a "boom" of births. The Arnazes were in sync with other U.S. couples in this regard. In 1949 and 1950, Desi Arnaz and Lucille Ball were featured as a couple in the news again. News items reported that they were planning a second wedding and were going to celebrate their tenth wedding anniversary, as well as that Ball was pregnant; her miscarriage later sparked further sympathetic news coverage. And around the time that they began production on their upcoming television series, *I Love Lucy*, it was announced that Lucille Ball was pregnant again.

It was in these years that television began to be a viable commercial medium in the United States. As a medium that could be accessed in viewers' homes, it supported other consumer trends of the time, particularly the increase in home buying and other consumer purchases. Family-based comedies set in the homes of the characters fit well within this rubric, with the success of domestic comedies such as *I Love Lucy* leading this trend.[33] In the first years of commercial television, sponsors also were extremely influential, as series were financed by just one sponsor which then had a voice in, if not complete control over, creative decisions. Given the resulting dominance of advertisers over the direction of television programming for several years, it is illuminating to note again that Mexican Americans and other Latina/os were not courted by advertisers in this era, apparently because they were viewed as a negligible market with respect to both numbers and buying power.

There is an interesting twist in this history of television programming, however. While 1950s television has often been critiqued as a bastion of whiteness, in its earliest commercial years the networks broadcast a number of situation comedies about ethnic American couples and families.[34] As television scholars note, this was due in part to an FCC freeze from 1948 to 1952 on the growth of commercial television after the first network stations had been established primarily in large cities. Shows like *Life with Luigi* (1952), about Italian Americans; *I Remember Mama* (1948), which focused on a Norwegian immigrant family; and *The Goldbergs* (1949–56), about a Jewish American family, thus were broadcast in part because of the presumed ethnic—though strictly white ethnic—diversity of the mainly urban television audience.

This was the industrial scene in which Desi Arnaz and Lucille Ball conceived and pitched their new series to CBS and NBC. At the time, Lucille Ball's successful radio show, *My Favorite Husband,* was in negotiations to be remade into a television series, and Ball and Arnaz decided that they would push to have Arnaz cast as her television husband. Despite the more urban audience in 1951, they found they still had to convince network executives that the American public would watch a series about a bicultural couple that included a Cuban husband. While Lucille Ball's success in film and radio was enough to spark interest in the deal, the network brass apparently balked at casting Arnaz, as Arnaz and biographers have noted. Arnaz and Ball took to the road, doing a nightclub act together to change their minds, and ultimately convinced CBS in December 1950 to finance the series pilot.[35] They still needed a sponsor to get the series on the air, however, and reportedly it was difficult to attract one in the cultural climate of the period. Finally, their agent, Don Sharpe, was able to garner the interest of Biow advertising agency, which secured Phillip Morris, the cigarette manufacturer, as their sponsor; with a sponsor in place, they were set to begin production. In the drawn-out process of negotiations that then took place in establishing the series contract, Arnaz quickly demonstrated business acumen and shrewd instincts as a producer. He pushed to film rather than merely broadcast the show, and to base production in Los Angeles. When the network balked at the cost, Arnaz and Ball offered to take cuts in their salaries so that their newly established Desilu company could purchase the episodes outright, a move that was instrumental to their eventual financial windfall and that pioneered the system of syndicated reruns that would be critical to the future of the television industry.

As Pérez-Firmat notes, the next challenge for the show's producer, Jesse Oppenheimer, and writers Madelyn Pugh and Bob Carroll Jr., was to convert *My Favorite Husband* into a vehicle for Ball and Arnaz. This narrative cast Ball as a housewife opposite a banker husband; but everyone involved, including Ball and Arnaz, were sure Arnaz would not be seen as a credible banker (which is ironic, considering the stature that Arnaz's family had enjoyed in Cuba). The team ultimately figured they should capitalize on Arnaz's real life; his character became a Cuban bandleader, while Lucy Ricardo became a daffy housewife constantly trying to break out of the confines of domesticity and especially to enter to world of entertainment in which Ricky worked daily. They envisioned Lucy Ricardo as a whirlwind of comic activity, in light of which her husband was often exasperated. But at the end of the day, he always still loved his wife. The series title, a way to offer both stars top billing while capitalizing on Lucille Ball's greater (and likely to CBS and Phillip Morris, more palatable) fame, also aptly described the series premise.

Interestingly, the title also dovetailed well with the promotion of the series. As mentioned above, *I Love Lucy* was conceived as a project that would allow Arnaz and Ball to stay in the same city, preserve their marriage, and raise a family, information that was shared in news items that publicized the fledgling series.[36] In addition, reports of *I Love Lucy's* first season production often highlight Ball's pregnancy, sharing such information as the fact that baggy clothes were used to hide her growing size before the birth of the Arnazes' daughter, Lucie, on July 17, 1951. Such glimpses into Arnaz and Ball's personal life likely fed the interest of viewers, resulting in what Mary Desjardins describes as an intense fascination that audiences have had with the couple since the series first aired (and which, I would argue, began prior to *I Love Lucy*).[37] Fitting Martha Nochimson's definition of a "synergistic" star couple, Desi Arnaz and Lucille Ball soon became a favored celebrity couple in large part because of broad public interest in their on- and off-screen marriage and perceived on-screen chemistry, in addition to Ball's considerable comedic talents as showcased on their series.³⁸ This appeal was no doubt aided by star discourses that established Arnaz as a white Cuban star.

The Arnazes Become America's "First Family"

In the first episode of *I Love Lucy* viewed by the public, "The Girls Want to Go to a Nightclub," the audience was introduced to Lucy and Ricky Ricardo and their best friends, neighbors Fred and Ethel (played by William Frawley and Vivian Vance).³⁹ They're meant to be seen as typical American couples, aside from the fact that Ricky is a Cuban bandleader, which is gradually revealed in the storyline. It is a convoluted narrative, especially for an introductory episode. Lucy and Ethel try to get their husbands to take them to a nightclub that night to celebrate Fred and Ethel's anniversary, but are turned down, as Fred and Ricky want to go to a boxing match. Unhappy, the women claim they're going to the nightclub anyway—with dates (though they have none and have to conspire to find some). Ricky and Fred then want to check up on their wives, and strategize to go to the nightclub with dates also.

To turn to some of the underlying character construction in this episode, it is clear that Ricky Ricardo is meant to be introduced as more a loving husband than a Latin lover. In order for this to be possible, narrative moments are included that clearly dispel any doubt in this regard. For instance, as Ricky and Fred try to think of ways to invite some women to join them, we learn that Ricky used to have an address book with former girlfriends' phone numbers ("'A' alone was worth over a hundred dollars!" he deadpans), but that Lucy had convinced him when they got married, not long after he came to the United States, that it was an American wedding tradition for the groom to burn his phone book. Throughout the episode, moreover, Ricky demonstrates his patience with and clear love for his wife, even after Lucy has contrived to get back at him by posing as his hillbilly date. The construction was to endure and in fact arguably become one of the central appeals of the character of Ricky Ricardo on *I Love Lucy*.

The episode, like most, also included both Desi Arnaz's music—Ricky, with Fred's help, sings the song "Guadalajara," accompanying himself on the guitar—and a Phillip Morris plug, when Fred suggests that they all have a cigarette and Lucy gives away her identity by knowing exactly where they are kept in the Ricardos's living room. Also like most *I Love Lucy* episodes, it ends on a warm note, with a final, humorous glimpse of the two couples out on the town to celebrate Fred and Ethel's anniversary (at the fights Lucy and Ethel were trying to avoid). It goes without saying that Guadalajara is a city in Jalisco,

Mexico, rather than in Cuba. Its popularity in Arnaz's musical repertoire is an example of how he liberally blended influences from various Latin American countries in his music, as well as of their typical conflation in U.S. popular culture in this era. Arnaz incorporated similar "American Latin" numbers and shtick in his performance of Ricky Ricardo throughout the many-season run of *I Love Lucy*. Ricky Ricardo, and Desi Arnaz by extension, thus expressed Latinidad within a white American framework that continually reaffirmed the fantasy construction of a safe and entertaining Latinidad.

Similarly, in the next episode, "Be a Pal," Lucy Ricardo attempts to recreate Cuba in the Ricardos's home in order to get the attention of a distracted Ricky. To do so, she brings in such props as a donkey, a supposed sleeping man in a sombrero, and serapes, and also cooks tacos and other Mexican food items. Lucy also does a Carmen Miranda imitation, lip-synching to a recording of Miranda's "Mama Yo Quiero." Again, the conflation of Mexican, Brazilian, and Cuban cultures goes unquestioned. Ultimately it doesn't matter, as the series was never about Ricky's Cuban heritage as much as Americanization and American identity, which we learn from Ricky Ricardo that anyone can achieve—with love. As he tells Lucy after learning why she has gone to such extremes to try to recreate Cuba in their home, "If I wanted to stay in Cuba, I'd have stayed in Havana. That's the reason why I married you, because you're so different from everyone I knew in Cuba."

The first episode of *I Love Lucy* was popular with most critics, although some were lukewarm in their comments. *Variety* called it "refreshing" and praised Lucille Ball's comedic abilities, but also noted that "the story line wasn't exactly inspiring."[40] The *Hollywood Reporter*, meanwhile, commented that Ball was "America's number one comedienne in her own right" and that "Half a step behind her comes husband, Desi Arnaz, the perfect foil for her screwball antics and possessing comic abilities of his own more than sufficient to make this a genuine comedy team rather than the one-woman tour-de-force this almost becomes."[41] Critics' reviews only got warmer as more episodes were broadcast. Within a few months, the series was in the top three in the ratings, and by the end of April 1952, it was in the number one spot. Critics raved about the show's ascension and further fed public interest in its stars' private lives with such headlines as "Everybody Loves Lucy! Especially orchestra leader Arnaz, who knows what a dangerous gamble movie star Lucille Ball took for the sake of their marriage."[42] While Desi Arnaz did not receive as much attention as Ball with media critics, he was generally well received, as when the *Hollywood Reporter* called him the "most underrated performer on network television" in January 1952.[43] The series was the top-rated show for four of the next six seasons, and among the top-three rated series during its other seasons. The series and its stars also were feted with multiple Emmy awards; in fact, Desi Arnaz was the only actor of the four series leads to not be given an Emmy for his acting.

As a part of their Phillip Morris sponsorship, Desi Arnaz, Lucille Ball, and other series regulars had to maintain a public image that the company felt would reflect well on them. This was interesting, considering the product sold by Phillip Morris; this meant they had to maintain what was viewed as a family-friendly and American image. It appears that Arnaz's Cuban heritage was not seen as precluding this American image, when he was paired with Lucille Ball. There were concerns on the other hand about the risk of hiring actor William Frawley, who played Fred, because he had a reputation as an alcoholic before his time on the series.[44] Series episodes typically opened with Arnaz and Ball in a Phillip Morris commercial (for the first five episodes, this was an animated segment in which a cute, miniature Lucy and Ricky scaled a giant Phillip Morris cigarette box, cavorted, and then announced their series), as well as including occasions for the characters to smoke a cigarette or mention smoking. Arnaz and Ball also appeared in print ads for Phillip Morris in major magazines of the time such as *Life* and *Look*. (The dialogue ascribed to their elegantly attired images in one 1956 print ad: "Smoke for pleasure *today,* No cigarette hangover *tomorrow!*") Phillip Morris was to continue as sponsor of the series through 1956, despite the fact that its sales did not go up substantially during the years that it underwrote the show.

The selling of Lucy and Desi as a celebrated star couple was further cemented when Lucille Ball became pregnant again. The couple decided that rather than hiding the pregnancy, this time they would have Lucy Ricardo become pregnant as well, a television first. Sharing in Ball's pregnancy in this way arguably further encouraged viewers to identify with Lucy/Lucille and Ricky/Desi. The seven-episode pregnancy story arc also further reinforced the major theme of Ricky's great love for his wife. This story arc was kicked off with the episode "Lucy Is Enceinte" ("Lucy Is Expecting" in French), in which Lucy tries to find the right moment to tell Ricky that she is pregnant and Ricky is visibly touched and overjoyed to hear the news. This narrative moment was and is extremely popular with audiences, to the extent that a publicity still that captures it is one of the most iconic images of the television couple; it is easily accessible for purchase today from star memorabilia vendors. The episode in which the Ricardos's baby is born, "Lucy Goes to the Hospital," later made television history on January 5, 1953, when it garnered forty million viewers, approximately 72 percent of all homes with television

Lucille Ball and Desi Arnaz sharing a tender moment as Lucy and Ricky Ricardo in the "Lucy Is Enceinte" episode of *I Love Lucy* in 1952.

sets.[45] What followed were years in which *I Love Lucy* continued to dominate the ratings and Desi Arnaz and his family were in high demand in a variety of media outlets as role models for the American family, with audiences clearly intrigued with the parallels between the couple's "real life" and "reel-life" lives, as Mary Desjardins notes.[46] For instance, a doting Desi Arnaz and

Lucille Ball, along with their two young children, graced the cover of *Life* magazine on April 6, 1953, alongside the headline, "TV's First Family." The Arnazes were asked by journalists for their marriage and parenting secrets, among other things.

The couple's image was so positive that it wasn't noticeably marred by stories in September 1953 that Lucille Ball had come under question during the McCarthy era Communist witch-hunt due to her grandfather's past political leanings. At Arnaz's urging, they held a press conference at which they reassured the public that it was all a misunderstanding. Gossip columnist Hedda Hopper was invited and reported on the conference on the front page of the *Los Angeles Times*, while Walter Winchell also weighed in. Desi Arnaz also made an impassioned statement decrying Communism and defending his wife, who he said was "100 percent American." He ended with the line, "I want you to meet my favorite wife—my favorite redhead—in fact, that's the only thing red about her, and even that's not legitimate—Lucille Ball!"[47] With this, the matter was put to rest. With respect to Arnaz's Cuban nationality, he was not questioned regarding his own political alliances, although this might have been the case in the 1960s as Cuba became associated with Communism in the American imagination. Arnaz in fact commonly criticized Cuba and expressed public appreciation for the many opportunities his life in the United States had brought to him. While he was well known in the media industries as Cuban or "Latin" and as a bandleader he hired many Latina/os of various nationalities, it appears that, like most Latina/os of the era, he did not embrace a pan-ethnic U.S. Latino identity.

Notably, with respect to this overall survey of evolving opportunity for Latinos in the media industries, Desi Arnaz had a great deal of creative control over the development of his character and *I Love Lucy*. He was named executive producer of the show by 1952, and according to numerous sources, always, along with Lucille Ball, had ultimate control over its development. Arguably Arnaz's agency in this regard was instrumental in allowing him to create and portray a character that, while incorporating Anglo-centric notions of Latina/o cultures, didn't necessitate that he become a permanent butt of jokes or not be seen as a talented musician, loving husband, and solid provider for his family. Arnaz didn't mind poking fun at and exaggerating his accent for laughs, and Ricky's broken English was often central to the comedy, but as series producer Oppenheimer pointed out, audiences only found this gag funny when Lucille Ball, as his loving wife, was the one to poke fun at Ricky, so the creative team deliberately limited its use in this regard.

Perhaps unsurprisingly, Ricky Ricardo's position as "straight man" to Lucy and the rest of the series cast meant that Arnaz's acting was typically overlooked in comparison to that of his costars. Over time, his work as president of Desilu Productions also began to overshadow his star image as an actor or musician. Arnaz was well respected for his business decisions and accomplishments; news stories in 1957 and 1958 focus on Arnaz as a series producer and television executive.[48] Desilu's sale of the *I Love Lucy* episodes to CBS had made Arnaz and Lucille Ball the first television millionaires, while Desilu Productions also had grown by leaps and bounds, reportedly expanding to eight hundred employees by the late 1950s. It presided over such shows as *December Bride* (1954) and *The Untouchables* (1959), while Arnaz was described in news coverage with such headlines as "The Biggest Man in Hollywood," as the *Chicago Tribune* called him.[49] By this time, the studio was producing twenty-two television series. In 1957, Desilu Productions had even purchased the RKO studio lot—ironically, the studio that had done little for Arnaz's career—making it the largest television studio in the nation. In other words, he was seen in these years as an American success story.

Arnaz's life as a *vivo* and *vividor* was to spin out of control, however. There were many allegations that Arnaz struggled with drugs and alcohol and workaholic tendencies, in addition to engaging in multiple infidelities, and the star ultimately fell prey to such self-destructive behavior by 1959. In September 1959, Arnaz was stopped for drunk driving; news briefs noted that he failed to appear in court when scheduled. He and Ball had separated again and Ball began to be more publicly critical of Arnaz, as was the case in a 1960 magazine interview that appeared in *Cosmopolitan*.[50] They announced their impending divorce, which was finalized in 1961. Arnaz noted in a public statement issued by Desilu Studios that he and Lucille Ball "deeply regret that, after long and serious consideration, we have not been able to work out our problems and have decided to separate."[51] He announced their planned divorce and that it would be worked out amicably. Viewers expressed intense sadness at the news; eight thousand letters were reportedly sent to Lucille Ball from fans asking her to reconsider.[52]

Ball wed comedian Gary Morton later that year. In November 1962, Arnaz resigned his Desilu posts; it was announced that Ball had been appointed the new head. In 1963, Arnaz also remarried, to Edith Mack Hirsch. For the most part, Arnaz retired from acting and producing; a notable exception took place on February 21, 1976, when he was guest host, along with his son, Desi Arnaz Jr., on *Saturday Night Live*, then in its first season. On the show a visibly aged Arnaz and the *SNL* cast took part in skits that poked fun at *I Love Lucy*, with Desi Jr. playing his father and Gilda Radner standing in for Lucille Ball. Arnaz also performed "Cuban Pete" and "Babalú," and the show culminated with Arnaz leading the *SNL* cast, which at the time included such actors as Radner, John Belushi, and Dan Aykroyd, in a last, historic conga.[53] In his later years, Desi Arnaz focused mainly on his racehorses, his wife, children, and grandchildren, his continued friendship with ex-wife Lucille Ball, and the writing of his autobiography, before his death in 1986.

* * *

There are many reasons why Desi Arnaz is important to the history of U.S. Latina/o stardom as an actor, performer, producer, and executive. In his 1940s films, he challenged producers through resisting the traditional stereotyping of Latino actors, while he possessed a boyish but clean-cut charm that female viewers in particular noticed even when he was cast in negligible roles. Arnaz also clearly broke ground by making his way into the living rooms of 1950s households, although with a portrayal that aimed to be appealing more than authentic to the experiences of Cuban Americans or other U.S. Latina/os. At the same time, he also played characters and performed in a manner that emphasized dignity and good will. In so doing, he adeptly surmounted the obstacles that Latina/os typically faced in Hollywood and delivered Latinidad in a package that the American public apparently enjoyed in this era, with a heavy dollop of sweetness and deliberately artificial spice.

Arnaz's success in television went unmatched for almost two decades; it would not be until 1974 that a Latino actor would again have a lead role in a U.S. series, as I discuss in chapter 5 on *Chico and the Man* and its star, Freddie Prinze. How and why was Desi Arnaz so successful as a television star at a time when Latina/os were typically excluded from starring roles? Likely because of how he and Lucille Ball portrayed a loving husband and wife and the struggles and foibles of marriage in a manner that audiences identified with, in performances that typically transcended race and ethnicity even while they involved outrageous events and poked fun at Arnaz's accent. In addition, Arnaz's real-life financial and business success, as a veritable illustration of the American Dream, may have contributed to viewers identifying with and looking up to the star.

On the other hand, Desi Arnaz, like his television alter ego, was a role model of Latino assimilation. Although he played a Mexican American character in one of his films (*Bataan*), Arnaz was distanced in his star promotion from the racialization that many Mexican Americans and other U.S. Latina/

os experienced; I argue that he was promoted as a white Latino star and experienced greater opportunity as a result. Despite not denying his Cuban roots, Arnaz often publicly expressed that his spiritual home was the United States; it is not unrelated that his image was one of an exceptional foreigner rather than that of an ethnic, American Other. As he noted in his autobiography, "I cannot think of another country in the world in which a young man of sixteen, broke and unable to speak the language, could have been given the chances to accomplish what I did, or the welcome, *cariño* (affection), praise and honor which were given me."[54]

Much of Desi Arnaz's assimilation to American culture and the Hollywood star system, moreover, rested on the vehicle of marriage; his "love of Lucy" both on television and in his own life was likely central to Arnaz's appeal and success as an American star. Even today, Arnaz is typically characterized in this manner, as in the U.S. postage stamp created in 1999 that features the well-known image of Lucille Ball being kissed on the cheek by Arnaz. Notably, the public and news media demonstrated an interest in the Arnazes long before *I Love Lucy* debuted, considering that stories on their marriage, pregnancies, and relationship difficulties were also well publicized throughout the 1940s. This fascination probably existed in part because of the tension of U.S. racial borders that was invoked but not crossed in their on- and off-screen marriage, while Desi Arnaz and Lucille Ball's talent and comedic performances further intrigued the public.

3

A Fight for "Dignity and Integrity"

Rita Moreno in Hollywood's Postwar Era

> I played the role [of the Latin spitfire] to the hilt, but at least
> it got me attention. It amused and charmed people. "Isn't
> she something! What a firecracker!" If that's all I could get
> then that's what I settled for. There was never a possibility
> of being anything else in my head, in my perception. The
> people around didn't help; the society didn't help.
>
> —Rita Moreno, as quoted in Susan Suntree, *Rita Moreno*
> (New York: Chelsea House, 1993), 49

The Latin spitfire. Readers likely already have an image of this stereotypical Latina figure in their heads. She is curvaceous, hypersexual, and emotionally irrepressible, and a historically entrenched trope of Hollywood star publicity. We saw hints of her in the publicity that surrounded Jennifer Lopez in 1998, when her voluptuous body and outspoken refusal to adapt to Hollywood beauty ideals were the focus of obsessive media attention. The spitfire, described as the Latina "harlot" by Charles Ramírez Berg, can be traced to the early years of silent film, and earlier, to frontier literature.[1] An image that possessed both admirable and denigrated traits, the spitfire/harlot was an image that actress Rita Moreno found she was often saddled with in 1950s film and star promotion.

Moreno, who acted in her first film as an eighteen-year-old in 1950, began her career often typecast as a spitfire and promoted in a manner that capitalized on such imagery as well. For instance, the young actress posed inside a life-size firecracker for a 1954 publicity photo, a physical embodiment of the energetic, explosive nature associated with this Latina stereotype. While Moreno eventually sidelined her film career in order to be able to play more diverse and challenging roles, she had no such options as a young actress.

As she notes in the quote above, she at times played up her exuberance and flamboyance at premieres and other public events because it was what garnered her publicity, which she needed to maintain and advance her career. Her comments call to mind how Desi Arnaz as a young bandleader learned to perform Latinidad in a manner that was comfortable for his mostly non-Latina/o American audiences. Given that neither chose to downplay their Latin heritage, both had to adjust to U.S. ambivalence regarding the status of Latina/os in these decades. In Moreno's case, this was distinctly influenced by the confusion that existed over whether Puerto Ricans were American citizens (as they have been since 1917) or eternal immigrants, as film and other media representations often seemed to reinforce.

As an actress, dancer, singer, and all-round performer, Rita Moreno is notable in many ways. Most often, she is remembered as the media industries' most critically lauded Latina. Moreno's talent was officially recognized by the Hollywood community when she won an Academy Award for Best Supporting Actress in 1962 for *West Side Story* (1961), one of few Latina/os to this day to win an Oscar.[2] She topped this feat in 1977 with the distinction of being one of only a handful of performers ever to have won all four of the major U.S. entertainment awards, including awards in theater (the Tony), film (the Oscar), sound recording (the Grammy), and television (the Emmy, which she has won twice).[3] Rita Moreno's early career and public image are notable as well, on the other hand, for illustrating the obstacles that Latina/os typically faced in attempting to establish and maintain an acting career in post–World War II Hollywood. As she has told interviewers, she was often blocked from being cast in roles that would challenge her acting abilities, or in being promoted as a potential star. "When you were Latina and at that time . . . it was perceived that there was no possibility of someone like myself becoming a person of note," Moreno said in a 1995 interview. "[I]t's not as though they resisted the possibility, the possibility didn't exist in the minds of most people."[4] Rita Moreno thus serves as an example both of the most a Latina could achieve and how Latina actresses were viewed as not quite American in these decades, revealing the narrow parameters of Hollywood Latinidad in the 1950s and '60s.

The challenges that Rita Moreno faced introduce a number of new questions useful to a study of how Latina/o stardom has evolved. How did gender norms, narrative constructions of romance as imagined in 1950s and '60s films, and the racialization of Latinas as nonwhite play into the opportunities and promotional efforts that were experienced by a young Latina actress hoping to become a star? What was (and is) the allure of the spitfire image for

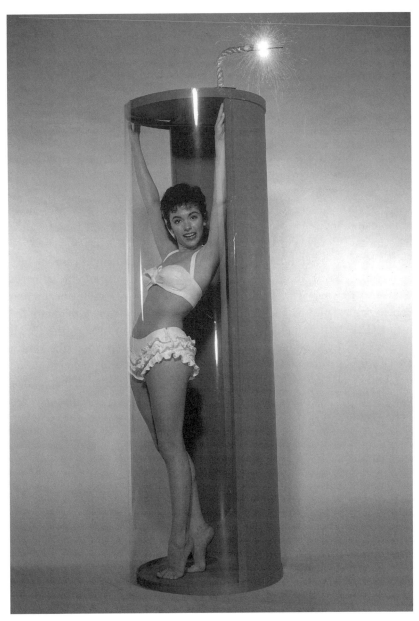

Film starlet Rita Moreno in a 1954 publicity photo. 20th Century Fox / The Kobal Collection.

the American public, and how can we better understand it in relation to the history and evolving status of Latina/os as a racialized ethnic group in this time period in the United States? And to consider Moreno's specific heritage and family history, what was the impact of her Puerto Rican heritage and blue-collar family background on her image as a Latina star? To explore these questions, I return to the 1950s, this time focusing on Latina opportunity and star promotion in the film industry, and exploring 1960s shifts as well.

Rita Moreno has maintained an active and distinguished career; it continues today in the areas of film, television (recently in appearances on *The George Lopez Show* and *Ugly Betty*, after a long stint on the HBO drama *Oz* [1997–2003]), and theater. It is because of this chapter's focus on the climate Latina/os faced in the 1950s and '60s film industry that I focus here almost exclusively on the first two decades of her career. The one exception is an exploration of Moreno's turn as Puerto Rican singer Googie Gomez in *The Ritz* (1976), a reprise of the role she portrayed in the successful Broadway play of the same name. This role and the positive acclaim Moreno received for her performance—a highly exaggerated, comic parody of the former spitfire roles that she used to portray—highlight shifting paradigms of Latina/o representation by the 1970s. Googie Gomez and Rita Moreno's creative agency in the character's development is instructional also regarding the importance and impact of Latina/o creative control in the construction of Hollywood portrayals of Latinidad and promotion of Latina and Latino stars.

Rosita/Rita and the "Debbie Reynolds World" of Postwar Hollywood

As noted in chapter 2, conservative trends had a substantial impact on the film and television industries in the 1950s, as were felt in the era's representational norms manifest in the Hollywood star system. As Rita Moreno described in an interview, "I was limited to certain roles by reason of being a Latin. It was a Debbie Reynolds world and there was no way I could flex my acting muscles in it."[5] In this climate, unambiguously white stars such as Reynolds were given clear preference in the casting of lead roles, while she as a Latina was not considered qualified for such roles. The era's conservatism also extended to scrutiny of the political leanings of actors and other film professionals. The Cold War was well under way early in the decade, as Senator Joe McCarthy and other politicians attempted to ferret out perceived Communists and other threats to U.S. ideology and politics, often described vaguely as the "American way." The fallout included a witch hunt for and the subsequent blacklisting of politically left-leaning film and television professionals, suspicion of films and television programs that contained overt social or political critique, and a return to conservative ideologies in many films. This led once again to increased emphasis on "all-American" (unambiguously white) actors and characters, such that Latina/os often worked in vain to be cast in lead roles.

In addition, the major studios were scrambling to respond to other challenges within the industry. After the Paramount Decision forced them to sell their theaters and dismantle other studio system practices, their domination would never be as certain. In addition, filmgoing had declined dramatically since the mid-1940s. The rise of commercial television and migration of many white Americans from large cities to the growing suburbs were among the reasons why fewer people were frequenting movie theaters, especially in city centers. Often these shifts resulted in extreme caution and a desire to stick to proven formulas and stars. Aspiring actors of all ethnic backgrounds thus faced a more tenuous situation. They also were less likely to benefit from the job security of a studio contract and instead had to campaign for roles on a project-by-project basis.

Latina actresses faced the additional obstacle of Eurocentric casting standards against which they continued to be marginalized. An illustration of such standards was the Miss America pageant.[6] While established in 1920, it became an important site for the display and celebration of feminine ideals after World War II, when it became more "patriotic and respectable" for middle-class young women to take part.[7] Identifiably ethnic Latinas, with olive or darker complexions or with Spanish surnames, were nowhere to be found at the pageant. Moreover, after the United States became involved in World War II, the privileging of fair coloring was clearly emphasized in Hollywood. As Shari Roberts argues, military foes were portrayed in World War II films through casting and makeup "that stressed dark hair and dark skin," while blonde hair and fair skin was more likely to be constructed as American.[8] Latina/os who might have been able to play lead characters in the 1920s thus were confined to the background (or B-pictures such as Lupe Velez's *Mexican Spitfire* series) if they chose not to anglicize their appearance or names. Mexican Americans and Puerto Ricans also had to contend with negative attitudes from non-Latinos in this era, fed in large part by mass media representations. As Rubin and Milnick note, in this period "Puerto Rican 'spics' of the East Coast" joined "the Chicano 'greasers' of the zoot suit era" in the public imagination.[9] Puerto Ricans were increasingly represented as "problem" people, particularly as more people moved from the island of

Puerto Rico to the mainland of the United States[10] and after activists who sought the island's independence from its status as a U.S. commonwealth were portrayed as criminals in news coverage.[11] It was in this less-than-welcoming climate that Rita Moreno began her career as a film actress.

Rita Moreno was born Rosa Dolores Alverio in Humacao, Puerto Rico in 1931, the daughter of Maria Rosa Marcáno and Paco Alverio. She moved to New York City as a child to live with her mother and stepfather, Edward Moreno, in the Spanish Harlem neighborhood of Manhattan, at the time a fairly ethnically diverse neighborhood. Her family was part of a wave of Puerto Ricans that moved to the States during the Great Depression because of the potential for better work opportunities on the mainland; her mother reportedly went to work in a garment factory. However, as Moreno's family and many others discovered, conditions were also harsh in the States. Puerto Ricans in the New York City area, like Mexican Americans throughout the Southwest, typically had to contend with such obstacles as substandard education, housing discrimination, and a lack of lucrative job opportunities in their pursuit of the American Dream.[12]

This underscores the financial sacrifice Moreno's family made to ensure that she could attend dance classes from a very young age. The young Rita Moreno, then called Rosita and who later took her stepfather's last name, reportedly showed great talent as a performer. At the age of five, Moreno had her professional debut, dancing in a nightclub, and she soon began to perform in children's theater and at parties. Moreno has shared in interviews that she dreamed of dance as her ticket to success, as Puertorriqueña/os in her neighborhood had few options for achieving an education that would enable any other way of rising to middle-class status. "It was accepted at the time that as Puerto Rican boys could pull themselves out of poverty by excelling in boxing or baseball; girls could achieve success by becoming exceptional dancers," she has been quoted as saying.[13] As a child performer, she beat the odds and found work in nightclubs as well as in radio, theater, the new medium of television, and dubbing Hollywood films into Spanish.

Even at this young age, Moreno realized that playing to stereotypes could at times be helpful, and she cultivated a boisterous, exaggerated performance persona (notably, these were also the years of Carmen Miranda's heyday in Hollywood musicals) because it helped her obtain work as well as attention. One of the New Jersey clubs that she performed in, which was decorated like a jungle, even billed her as "Rosita the Cheetah." Moreno didn't need a publicist to tell her to tone it down when she had a chance to break into film, however. The five-feet-two-inch, slight teen dropped the exaggerated act and reportedly tried to look as much like a young Elizabeth Taylor as possible when she had a chance to meet Louis B. Mayer, then head of MGM, an approach that worked. On December 26, 1949, Moreno, then eighteen and an unknown, was signed to an MGM contract. The studio management suggested that she change her stage name to Tina Moreno. "[Mayer] thought the name [Rosita] too corny, even for a Spanish spitfire."[14] She compromised and became Rita Moreno.

Although the studios were losing their stranglehold on the national film industry at the time, MGM, the largest, was still producing expensive, often Technicolor features, with musicals comprising 25 percent of their output.[15] It also was still signing some actors to multiyear contracts. The studio philosophy meanwhile reflected the nation's turn toward more conservative politics. Dore Schary, head of film production at the time, though previously known for left-wing leanings, had promised when he began his tenure that the studio would focus on making "good films about a good world."[16] As Rita Moreno and Desi Arnaz would both learn at the studio, this "good world" was a tenuous place for a Latina/o actor, however, particularly as the vogue for the Latin musical was on the wane.

It was at the end of 1949 that Moreno arrived in Los Angeles to begin work for MGM. She had already acted in one film soon to be released, *So Young So Bad* (1950), billed as Rosita Moreno. In this United Artists film Moreno portrayed Dolores, a depressed, presumably Mexican American teenager picked up for vagrancy,[17] and now a ward at a corrupt girls' reform school. She is mistreated and eventually commits suicide. Moreover, Dolores is characterized as damaged goods, with her ethnicity blamed for this in subtle ways. While there are hints at the deleterious effects of racism (Dolores had begun running away after being shamed when her mother visited her Anglo-dominant school), ultimately the narrative implies that as a Mexican American, Dolores is naturally prone to mentally unbalanced thinking and actions. Clichés about Mexican American culture abound in the film as well. The few moments when Dolores appears happy are when she moons over her Virgin of Guadalupe figurine and when she sings a song in Spanish, accompanying herself with a guitar. The only publicity still found for *So Young So Bad* that features Moreno captures the moment in which her character engages in this odd musical interlude. The photo of the then-unknown Rosita emphasizes her youth and innocence, what might even be called a "girl-next-door" purity. Thus, Moreno was promoted by United Artists in a manner that echoed the star construction of her predecessor, Dolores Del Rio, and that of her contemporary, Desi Arnaz, as an appropriate (and unthreatening) ethnic.

Upon her arrival, MGM gave Moreno a lackluster publicity launch, including brief news items in the Los Angeles newspapers on December 26, 1949. The *Examiner* referred to Moreno as a "vivacious" Puerto Rican performer whose "dancing, singing, and acting talents led to her discovery by Metro-Goldwyn-Mayer scouts."[18] The *Times* added that Moreno had "trained for the stage all her life" and proved herself through screen tests.[19] It is telling to compare this publicity to that which launched Dolores Del Rio in film and Desi Arnaz as a television star. In the absence of a famous patron or spouse or an economically privileged background, credibility in Moreno's case was achieved through publicizing that she had proven her exceptional talent with respect to her theatrical, musical, and dance abilities. Rita Moreno's Puerto Rican background, moreover, was not a neutral element in her star publicity. The fact that many Puerto Ricans and other Latina/os in New York (and some Mexican Americans in the Southwest) referred to themselves by the whitewashed label of "Spanish" in this time period attests to the ambivalence expressed toward Puerto Ricans and Mexican Americans in these years.

That Moreno never disavowed her Puerto Rican heritage and chose not to straighten her hair or change her last name thus posed stumbling blocks to opportunity in Hollywood. MGM did offer Moreno some benefits from the former studio system, as the young actress took dance and acting classes at the studio five days a week and received the salary for contract players. She was never promoted as a potential star, however, and the roles she was offered were not substantial. Moreno appeared in two MGM films in the next two years, first as a young Cajun woman in the Mario Lanza–Kathryn Grayson romantic musical, *The Toast of New Orleans* (1950), and later, in brownface makeup, as a Tahitian girl in *Pagan Love Song* (1951), an Esther Williams bathing beauty musical.

In *Toast of New Orleans*, a musical that combined opera and Cajun-inspired musical numbers, Moreno's dance background and high energy were put to good use. In the film she plays Tina, a fiery Cajun woman in love with a local fisherman, Pepe (Lanza). He, however, only has eyes for Suzette (Grayson), a white opera singer. When Moreno and Lanza performed in several numbers together, the precedent began that would haunt Moreno throughout her early film career: Her character, Tina, is the woman in "his" arms, but he ultimately has eyes only for the white female with whom he falls in love. Given how Tina is characterized primarily as energetic and passionate, this could be considered Moreno's first role as a spitfire, an ethnically marked woman who is excessive on multiple counts, particularly as "a slave to her passions."[20]

She also is an expendable love interest that the audience is not meant to take seriously. Such qualities came to define many of Moreno's subsequent roles.

Unsurprisingly, the actress received little promotion from the studio in connection with the film, even in Spanish-language versions of the studio's press books (books sent to film exhibitors that included possible film posters and stills, as well as advertising suggestions). Despite this, Moreno received positive mention in reviews. *Variety* described her as "vivacious," while the *Los Angeles Times* predicted that "the girl may go places."[21]

Moreno received less promotion and critical attention for her small role in *Pagan Love Song*, again with no mention in the English-language exhibitors' press book and scant mention in the Spanish-language version. Moreno and Charles Mauu play a Tahitian brother and sister in the film, a colonialist fantasy in which the Tahitian natives are portrayed as working for free, having no sense of money, and only living for the moment and bodily pleasure. Moreno, as a house servant, is a constantly cheerful, colorful foil for the American leads, played by Howard Keel and Esther Williams. This was only the first of many films in which she was to play a non-Latina, "ethnic" character in this era in which Latina/o actors were often liberally cross-cast in this manner.

Moreno was soon dropped by the studio, after less than two years. The actress said later that MGM musical producer Joe Pasternak "fought like a tiger" for her, but that "unfortunately there was nothing in any of the pictures coming up for a little Latin type, so he had nothing to back him up."[22] The racialized politics of casting of the era, which viewed Latina/os as all-purpose ethnic types but made it taboo to cast a Latina in an unambiguously white role, likely played into the executives' lack of interest in finding better vehicles for the young actress.

The Mid-1950s: Barefoot Roles and "Firecracker" Publicity

Working in the industry without a studio contract of course was increasingly the reality for film actors in these years, as an agent-based system was coming to take the place of the former studio contracts. While no longer having to abide by a studio's stringent choices about films in which they would appear or about their star image offered a new flexibility to actors, it also meant that they had to rely on their agents and their own wits to secure jobs on a film-by-film basis. Similarly, with the end of her MGM studio contract, Moreno and her agent had to seek out each of her film roles over the next few years. The most successful film in which she appeared was MGM's *Singin' in the Rain* (1952), in which she played the part of (non-

Latina) tattletale Zelda Zanders. It was a minor role, however, and a survey of promotional materials for the film indicates that Moreno was not featured in them. More typical of Moreno's opportunities in this period, this was followed by a string of what she has termed "Señorita roles" in Latin musicals (some of the few still being produced) and Westerns. These included roles in Republic's *The Fabulous Señorita* (1952), Warner Bros.' *Cattle Town* (1952), and MGM's *Latin Lovers* (1953) (unique in that Moreno's bit part was that of an upper-class Brazilian).

The rise of independent production companies such as Republic also did not typically offer improvement in the quality of Moreno's roles. Republic was typical of the independent companies making their mark in these years. While they provided acting jobs, these companies, in need of risk-free projects, "were tied to formulas to an even greater extent than ever before," as Robert Sklar notes.[23] Most produced genre films such as Westerns, adventure dramas, and war dramas; themes of white and U.S. superiority are reinforced in many of these films, and the unwritten casting guidelines still applied. Thus, at the time that Desi Arnaz was the star and executive producer of the top-rated television series, few Latina/os were considered film stars. The most successful alongside Rita Moreno included Ricardo Montalban, Cesar Romero, Katy Jurado, and Anthony Quinn. These actors similarly found themselves often typecast in Latin lover and fiery ethnic roles, with the exception of perhaps Anthony Quinn, who, because of his mixed (Mexican and Irish), not identifiably Latino ancestry and international film career, was likely considered to be a more versatile actor.

An exception to such traditional casting for Rita Moreno was her role as a clean-cut Mexican American girl and girlfriend of the protagonist in *The Ring* (1952). This social problem film about a Mexican American young man who becomes a boxer in an attempt to help his family rise from poverty was unique in its realistic approach to the discrimination Mexican Americans often still experienced. In fact, it was one of a handful of films produced in the postwar era that aimed to sympathetically address segregation and other inequities that Mexican Americans had and often still did experience. Importantly, such films as *Salt of the Earth* (1954), *A Medal for Benny* (1945), and *The Ring* (1952) offered both realistic and educational critiques of U.S. Latina/o experience, as Ramírez Berg and Noriega note, and some opportunities for Latina/o actors to be cast in lead roles.[24] In addition, *The Ring* offered Moreno her first lead role; her character, Lucy, was pivotal to the storyline. When Tommy, the protagonist (played by Lalo Rios), finds himself exploited as a prizefighter, it is Lucy's unwavering integrity and steadfast love that helps him to persevere and

Publicity still of Rita Moreno and Lalo Rios in *The Ring* (1952). Courtesy of the Academy of Motion Picture Arts and Sciences.

do the right thing. Moreno has noted in an interview that the film was unique with regard to its positive portrayal of Mexican American characters.

Promotion for *The Ring* illustrates how a publicity campaign can capitalize on negative and hegemonic attitudes even when these are not evident in a film narrative, however. Exhibitors were offered a choice of promotional posters by United Artists that, through differing wording and art, ran the gamut in tone from sensitive (focused on the issues of discrimination addressed in the film), to clearly sensationalized and implying nonexistent sexual and violent content. For example, some of the posters for *The Ring* depict the romantic leads in lurid pulp-novel style drawings. In others, actual photos of Moreno and Rios are used, but in a sexually provocative pose that misrepresents their characters. The poster most ambiguous in tone included the tagline "They call me 'Dirty Mex' but still they chase my women!" displayed in such a way that the words "Dirty Mex" are particularly prominent. Such sensational- ism seems to thinly mask anti-Mexican sentiment in this example. Likely this was how United Artists attempted to appeal to theaters in regions with mixed attitudes toward Mexican Americans.

One of United Artists' promotional posters for *The Ring* (1952). Courtesy of the Academy of Motion Picture Arts and Sciences.

Although having again received positive reviews for her role in *The Ring,* Rita Moreno was still a relatively unknown actress. If she did receive publicity in these years, it tended to be of the double-edged variety. Reporters might register their surprise that Moreno could speak English or highlight aspects of her daily life, true or untrue, that they deemed particularly exotic. Howard McClay, for example, described his reaction to meeting Moreno in a 1952 column in the *Los Angeles Daily News:* "[I]t's rather surprising to hear this pretty, black-haired Latin beauty rattle off the dialog [*sic*] like some doll who had been raised in Manhattan all her life."[25] Another news feature focused on Moreno's purported dream to become a bullfighter.[26] Moreover, the actress was still only offered roles of poor and passionate nonwhite women, self-sacrificing Indian maidens, or the cantina girl the romantic lead might kiss, but never marry. Some of the films in which Moreno next played the ethnic, barefoot woman included the Warner Bros.' Western *Cattle Town* (1952), Columbia's war drama *El Alamein* (1953), Paramount's jungle adventure film *Jivaro* (1954), and Allied Artists' *Fort Vengeance* (1953).

But the actress continued to work steadily, both in film and early television, and received an unexpected career boost when she was cast as Ray Bolger's dancing partner on the new ABC variety show *The Ray Bolger Show* (1953–55).[27] When a photographer for *Life* magazine took pictures of Moreno for a story on the new television series on the networks, she unexpectedly ended up gracing the cover that month, on March 1, 1954. Notably, the headline of the inside story was "Rita Moreno, An Actress's Catalog of Sex and Innocence." The accompanying photos and captions related the "story" of how Moreno could easily express the desired range of an actress (or of a Latina actress?) in any audition; this reported repertoire ran the gamut from "All Innocence" to "Sexy-Wild." Meant as satire, nonetheless it is difficult to know if readers interpreted it as such in 1954. Also considering that Moreno's reported "range" seemingly ran the gamut from sexy to sexier, it could be said that *Life* playfully posed that perhaps it was her innocence that was just an act.

Moreno was not alone in experiencing such sexuality-focused star promotion, however. As Diane Negra elucidates in her analysis of white ethnic female stardom since the film era, "off-white" stars have often been promoted in a manner that foregrounds notions of "excessive physicality," whether in the form of exaggerated bodies, appetite, sexuality, or dress.[28] In the case of Latin spitfire imagery, this promotional pattern, as noted in the introduction, has also been described as an emphasis on "tropicalism," which characterizes Latinas as particularly passionate ("hot"), sensual, and sexual.[29]

As noted earlier in the chapter, the image of the emotionally and sexually irrepressible and possibly untrustworthy Latina has a long history in U.S. film and literature that is related to the country's colonial history with respect to Mexican Americans and U.S.–Latin American relations.[30] For example, as Antonia Castañeda discusses, stereotypical notions of *Mexicana* attractiveness after 1848 were strongly linked to assumptions in Anglo society about their ambivalent "race," and by extension, presumed virtue and marriageability; taboos regarding miscegenation therefore colored how newly American Mexicanas were described alternately as earthy, primitive, colorful, and sexually inviting in both fictional and nonfiction narratives.[31] The ambivalently white/nonwhite status of Latinas similarly raised tensions that necessitated negotiation in Hollywood film roles and star promotion texts. Physical and personality characteristics thus have marked Latinas as distinct from white females—often constructed in classical Hollywood in relation to norms of idealized femininity as controlled and chaste—and in the process serve an important racializing function. The spitfire/harlot imagery that Moreno found hard to escape can be traced to this history—the better to differentiate Rita Moreno from a "Debbie Reynolds," perhaps.

This long history likely played a major role in the resonance this image appeared to have for Moreno's potential audience and for industry executives on the lookout for potential stars. At the time that the *Life* issue came out, Moreno was in Mexico for the filming of Twentieth Century-Fox's *Garden of Evil* (1954). She was playing a Mexican cantina singer, a role that was more of the same for Moreno but marked her singing debut in film. Pleased with her performance and aware of her recent publicity, Daryl Zanuck, then head of the studio, asked who Moreno was and wanted to put her under contract—as long as she could speak English. Apparently, in the minds of Hollywood executives of the era, a "Latina" actress was often construed as foreign and non-English-speaking. Moreno assured the studio brass that she could indeed speak English and was signed to her second studio contract. At the time she was twenty-three.

Interestingly, the *Life* cover story also resulted in a twist in the publicity for Moreno's next film, *The Yellow Tomahawk* (1954), which was produced independently and distributed by United Artists. In the Western, Moreno plays another Indian maiden. Her character, Honey Bear, is in love with a scout played by Rory Calhoun, who in the end, no surprise, falls in love with Peggy Castle's character. Naturally, the promotional posters are dominated by a photo of Calhoun and Castle. A small box was inserted in the corner of almost every poster, however. In it was a photo of Moreno (from the "sexy" photograph of Moreno and Lalo Rios used in some posters for *The Ring*), accompanied by the words, "See Rita Moreno: *Life*'s 'Sex and Innocence' cover girl!" Sexiness clearly was becoming a predominant theme in Moreno's star publicity. In a social era when "nice girls" were expected to be chaste and only mildly interested in sex, promoting Moreno as an outgoing, sexy, and sexually aware young woman played to fantasies, based on historical tropes, of the seductive Latina. One illustration of how such notions played out in film merchandising can be found in the product tie-ins for *Yellow Tomahawk*. While Peggy Castle's image was associated with the Gotham Blouse, a staid, proper design in the film's marketing campaign, the product tie-in for Rita Moreno was Luc-Ray lingerie.

At the onset of Moreno's new contract, Twentieth Century-Fox orchestrated the actress's first studio-generated promotional campaign; dueling images of sex and innocence, with sex typically winning, can be found in the publicity materials. In photos and biography materials commissioned in 1954, Moreno is alternately portrayed as a proper "Latina next door" and as a 1950s-style Latin vamp. And while her new studio biography included a quiet critique, presumably by Moreno herself, that she had unfortunately been typecast in many "bare-foot parts" in the past, Fox publicists assured journalists and thus Moreno's potential fans on that potentially controversial topic that "she doesn't mind that too much."[32] Moreover, many of the publicity images did not strive for subtlety; the photos, for example, include the firecracker shot mentioned early in this chapter. Perhaps it comes as no surprise then that a majority of Moreno's fan mail at this time came from servicemen. Possible "pinup titles" later suggested by the studio's publicity department included "Puerto Rican Pepper Pot, Queen of the Home Show, Air Force ROTC Queen, Queen of Little Baseball, The Cheetah, and Chile Pepper."[33] Twentieth Century-Fox also stressed in her publicity that she was interested in dating "Americans." Her 1954 bio ends with mention of how Moreno "doesn't go along with the way Latins treat, or mistreat, as she sees it, their women. . . . So she plans to marry an American."[34]

Moreno also received some unwanted, sensational publicity around this time because of events in her personal life that became known to the public. She was involved in an on-again, off-again relationship with actor Marlon Brando that often drew unwanted attention in the press. During a period of disillusionment with Brando, she also dated heir George Hormel. There was a well-publicized scandal when Hormel was arrested for possible marijuana possession while he was with Moreno, though he was later cleared of the charges, and Moreno also was cited for a physical altercation with a police officer when the arrest took place. This coverage further positioned Moreno as a fiery and sensation-seeking ethnic.

Ultimately, Moreno was not able to escape being offered more "barefoot roles" by Twentieth Century-Fox. These included roles in the films *Untamed* (1955), *Seven Cities of Gold* (1955), and—an exception—*The Lieutenant Wore Skirts* (1955). *Untamed,* a Technicolor adventure film set in South Africa, was perhaps the most spectacular of the three. Moreno plays a biracial African girl in the film; Richard Egan plays her love interest, at least until Susan Hayward comes along. ("But she doesn't want him. I stick with him until he dies," Moreno reported later.)[35] *Seven Cities of Gold,* notably, offered Moreno perhaps the most notoriously stereotypical role of her film career. In the film she once again plays an American Indian woman, Ula, who loses her love to a white woman. Moreno has described the scene in which she later commits suicide (including the infamous line, as parodied by Moreno, "Why joo no luv Ula no more?") as a classic in the "Yonkee peeg" school of screenwriting and acting that she often had to endure.[36] In a change of pace, in *The Lieutenant Wore Skirts* (1955), a play-on-gender-roles military comedy, Moreno got to act a little and show her ability to do comedy. The actress also was cast as Princess Tuptim in Twentieth Century-Fox's musical spectacle *The King and I* (1956), but her work in the film wasn't heavily promoted.

Unsurprisingly, stereotypical imagery was central to the next major promotion campaign she experienced, this time by Paramount. The studio commissioned a series of photographs of the actress in 1955 to promote the musical adventure film *The Vagabond King* (1956). In *The Vagabond King,* an operetta set in France during King Louis XI's reign, Moreno played Huguette, an irrepressible tavern wench. Huguette, who is in love with the rogue bandit hero of the film, leads the ensemble in several oddly Latin-inspired musical numbers. The Paramount publicity photos meanwhile incorporated stereotypes of fiery, erotic Latinas. For example, Moreno is photographed kicking up her heels in a flouncy Spanish dress, lounging in baby-doll pajamas, and wearing strapless dresses and a come-hither look. Most interesting, racialized body concepts are evident in the touch-up marks that I located on a set of original photos.[37] The pen marks and instructions stamped on the back of the photos, communication between Paramount employees, indicate how the photos were to be airbrushed to give the dancer-lean Moreno a more prominent bosom, while other marks indicate the need to cover up Moreno's upper thighs. Her studio-enhanced *décolleté* points to the perceived necessity of such enhancements in the packaging of Moreno as a star. While actresses of all ethnicities were likely enhanced in a similar manner, it arguably was especially important to the marketing of a star being promoted as a Latin spitfire.

Meanwhile, the entertainment news media in 1955 and 1956 further emphasized this image when reporting on Moreno. The studios set up interviews with entertainment writers; the resulting articles reported such things as "[her] alleged 24-hour use of perfume (even in bed), her temper, her love of earrings and high-heeled shoes with straps."[38] The publicity that surrounded Moreno at this juncture is particularly striking when compared to Dolores Del Rio's promotion in the late 1920s, which points to the more blatant racialization of a home-grown Latina from a working-class background during this period, versus that experienced by a wealthy, foreign-born actress in the mid-1920s. Aside from the emphasis on Moreno's body, another marked contrast can be seen with respect to a rhetoric of labor and ambition. For instance, the *Los Angeles Times* called attention to the fact that Moreno, the "Puerto Rican firecracker," was taking it upon herself to send out "pinup shots personally to columnists and editors," not wanting to wait for Twentieth Century-Fox publicity personnel.[39] As noted in chapter 1, Del Rio, in contrast, had been promoted as a privileged young woman who never had to work to further her career.

An Oscar, but Still No "Integrity and Dignity"

Moreno has reported in interviews that she struggled with her self-esteem in the late 1950s with respect to obstacles she continued to encounter when being cast in film roles. In an interview with Ally Acker, she reported: "It took six years of therapy trying to get my 'ethnic' problems untangled. . . . I'd get to the point where I'd feel great, really sure of myself, and then audition for an important part only to have the producer say, 'Terrific. But really, honey, for this part we need a Mitzi Gaynor—we need an American.'"[40] While Moreno was able to play and overplay spitfire characters with aplomb, she never stopped wanting more challenging roles and developed a keen awareness of the limitations she faced in Hollywood. By the end of the decade, she had made a decision only to play Latinas "with integrity and dignity. No more wild, Chiquita Banana mamas who would get what was coming to them. No more fooling around with the leading lady's hunk only to get dumped."[41] Given the difficulty of achieving this in Hollywood at the time, Moreno turned her attention to theater in the late 1950s. She began a stage career in New York and London, playing, among other starring roles, teacher Annie Sullivan in *The Miracle Worker;* Lola, a temptress literally from Hell, in *Damn Yankees*; gutsy cabaret singer Sally Bowles in *I Am a Camera;* and long-suffering girlfriend Adelaide in *Guys and Dolls*. This wide range of roles highlights the greater openness that she experienced in theater. These achievements in turn encouraged her casting in film roles, the best remembered being her role as Anita in *West Side Story* (1961).

A retelling of Shakespeare's *Romeo and Juliet*, *West Side Story* is set in Manhattan amidst a turf war between the Sharks, a Puerto Rican gang, and the Jets, consisting primarily of second-generation Polish immigrants. While the lead role of Puerto Rican heroine Maria was played by white actress Natalie Wood, Moreno beat out five other actresses for the role of second female lead, Anita, for which she subsequently won the Oscar for Best Supporting Actress.[42] The film in fact garnered ten Oscars, including Best Picture, as well as proving to be one of the most financially successful film musicals ever. Critics also were pleased with Moreno's performance in the role of the newcomer to New York who aimed to make the most of her life in the States. *Variety*, for example, asserted that she "score[d] hugely in the role."[43]

Moreno in fact led perhaps the best-known song from the film in "America." A high-energy musical number in which Anita leads her friends in a song that is simultaneously patriotic and anti–Puerto Rican, an expression of the dream of what Puerto Ricans could accomplish stateside in "America," and (from the men in the group) a testament of the racism Puerto Ricans often experienced in the States, it posed Anita as a brassy model of American assimilation who is happy to forget Puerto Rico. As she begins, "Puerto Rico, my heart's devotion . . . let it sink back in the ocean! Always the hurricanes blowing. Always the population growing. And money owing. And the sunlight streaming. And the natives steaming. . . . I like the island Manhattan. Smoke on your pipe and put that in!" Moreno's talent, charisma, and humor shine through in the competitive song and dance that ensues between the Puerto Rican men and women (including a number of white performers in brownface) about whether "America" is the true land of promise that Anita claims. It is a tour-de-force for Moreno, despite the problematic way in which it characterized Puerto Rico and Puerto Ricans.

As that scene illustrates, the film itself is ambiguous with respect to its representation of Latinidad. As Rachel Rubin and Jeffrey Melnick note, the film and the play on which it was based make allusions to Puerto Ricans as immigrants "no different from the Jews, Italians, Poles and so on," when in fact Puerto Ricans moving from the Island to the States were American citizens.[44] As Laura Briggs has argued in relation to media representations of Puerto Ricans more generally,[45] the film performs ideological work that reinforces the construction and marginalization of Puerto Ricans (and thus, of Latina/os more generally in the public imagination) as eternal foreigners who pose a threat to American ideals and progress.[46]

Moreover, given the casting of Natalie Wood and George Chakiris in the lead Latina/o roles, the production reiterated the frustrating tradition by which Latina/o actors were not even considered good enough to act in their "own" starring roles. *West Side Story* was unique and important, however, with respect to also portraying Puerto Ricans as active subjects, with the character of Anita a major illustration, and for including information about discrimination that they commonly experienced (though in a manner that is typically overshadowed by the white-centric patriotism of the narrative).

Rita Moreno has related to interviewers that she had been optimistic that winning the Oscar would lead to offers for the more compelling, complex roles that she wanted to portray. But in retrospect it didn't increase her opportunities in Hollywood. Given societal stereotypes, it appears many in the Hollywood community did not grasp that Moreno was in fact acting in this Puerto Rican immigrant role. Moreno found she was more typecast than ever. Rita Moreno's other role that year likely didn't help in this regard. As Rosa Zacarias in *Summer and Smoke,* she was the wild daughter of a Southern town's presumably Mexican American casino owner. Rosa wears black, drinks, gambles, speaks her mind, and flirts, managing to catch the eye of the confused romantic lead, Johnny. She is the always-available ethnic Other who ultimately is rejected by Johnny, because of her background, behavior, and presumably her ethnicity, which arguably is presented as the root of her unseemly behavior.

Moreno was not afraid to voice her disappointment in having to embody and thus perpetuate Latin stereotypes in her film roles; articles on the star at this juncture often took up this topic. She also began to get involved in the anti-war and civil rights movements, including participation in advocacy efforts in Hollywood aimed at increasing diversity in front of and behind the camera. For example, in 1962, Moreno spoke out in a letter to the editor in *Daily Variety* against actress Bette Davis, who had criticized activist efforts for increased minority representation in film. She argued that Davis didn't speak for everyone, adding, "[S]o long as any American citizen or group of citizens is deprived of dignity and freedom, then my own freedom and sense of personal dignity are also inevitably threatened."[47] Referring to the industry's racial barriers in traditional casting practices, she also called in these years for ending "Hollywood Jim Crowism . . . in all its aspects."[48] Moreno in many respects was fighting against the tide in her efforts, however, as the film industry tread lightly with respect to addressing these issues, particularly in these years before studios and networks likely felt they had much to fear from ethnic advocacy groups.

Because of the lack of challenging or dignified roles she was offered, Moreno acted only sporadically in film in the 1960s, appearing as a Filipina guerrilla fighter and love interest in *Cry of Battle* in 1963, as a criminal involved in the kidnapping of an heiress (with former boyfriend Marlon Brando) in

Night of the Following Day (1969), in the detective film *Marlowe* (1969), as the girlfriend of a single father in *Popi* (1969), and as a prostitute in *Carnal Knowledge* (1971). While these parts offered variation from Moreno's former roles and more well-developed characters than in the past, they still tended to be fairly peripheral to the narratives and thus did not greatly propel her film career. Of these films, *Popi* was unique in that it offered Moreno her first role in a Puerto Rican–themed film, a development that reflected the rise of consciousness and pride of the Puerto Rican community, as well as incipient interest in ethnic-inflected films in Hollywood. Moreno's character is one of the most positive in the film, a bittersweet comedy about a Puerto Rican father (sensitively portrayed by Jewish actor Alan Arkin) who tries to pass his sons off as Cuban refugees so that they will be adopted by a wealthy family. Even so, the role offered little for Moreno to do aside from make coffee for Arkin's character and look attractive.

Throughout this time Moreno was highly lauded for her work in theater. She had moved to London, then New York, where she threw herself into a successful acting career. In 1965, she wed Lenny Gordon, a physician specializing in cardiology, who eventually became Moreno's manager. They later had a daughter, Fernanda. Her desire to spend more time with her daughter played a part in Moreno taking a job with the children's television program *The Electric Company* in 1970, when she was asked to join by original ensemble members Bill Cosby and Morgan Freeman. Produced by The Children's Television Workshop, the goals of the show and its multicultural cast included increasing children's reading skills and self-esteem, which dovetailed well with Moreno's values. As she told Neil Hickey of *TV Guide*: "I am Latin and I know what it is to feel alone and ignored because you are different. When you are ignored, you have lost your sense of identity. So I can be the Latin on this show and my presence there can tell a lot of children and some adults, 'yes, we do exist, we have value.'"[49]

She ended up staying for five of *The Electric Company*'s six seasons. Meanwhile, she also performed in musical and theater endeavors. She was awarded a Grammy in 1972 for an ensemble-effort soundtrack recording of *Electric Company* songs, and won a Tony in 1975 for the role of Googie Gomez, a part written especially for her in the play *The Ritz*, later remade as a film, discussed in the following section. This was followed by two Emmy wins, in 1977 and 1978, for performances on episodes of *The Muppet Show* (1976–81) and *The Rockford Files* (1974–80), respectively. With her first Emmy win, Moreno joined the elite ranks of a small handful of performers to have won all of the top awards in the fields of theater, film, music, and television.

Rita Moreno as Googie Gomez, with Jack Weston in *The Ritz* (1976). Warner Bros. / The Kobal Collection.

Given this survey of Rita Moreno's first decades as a film actress, the role of Googie Gomez, which Moreno played in *The Ritz* both on Broadway and in the film version, offers a telling counterpoint. The tale, a mistaken-identity sex farce set in a gay bathhouse in Manhattan, offered Moreno what she has described as the role of a lifetime. A flamboyant, aspiring Puerto Rican singer hoping to gain fame via the bathhouse route that had given Bette Midler her start, Googie Gomez is a caricature who constantly calls attention to her own outrageousness and thus to the absurdity of the societal assumptions on which such characters are based. The role was written with Moreno in mind by playwright Terrence McNally after seeing her do an impromptu performance at a party. From these beginnings, the role of Googie Gomez was a perfect showpiece for Moreno's talents and one which she was able to help craft. Critics in turn praised her performance variously as "'pure beauty,' 'wonderfully atrocious,' and 'a comic earthquake,'" as one *New York Times* reviewer summarized.[50] She later reprised her role in the film, again receiving almost universally exuberant praise for her performance.

Moreno told Shaun Considine of the *New York Times* that playing the role was cathartic to her, in offering a chance to "thumb her nose" at Hollywood writers who had, in seriousness rather than humor, written the demeaning roles she had played over the years: "By playing Googie, I am thumbing my nose at all those Hollywood writers responsible for lines like 'You Yankee peeg, you rape my seester, I keel you!' Those writers were *serious* and Terrence is not. All the characters in 'The Ritz' are outrageous caricatures and that's how I play Googie, outrageously!"[51] Moreno indeed portrays Googie Gomez as an überspitfire, who takes everything to the extreme, from her dress to her confidence. For instance, she never gives in to self-doubt, even when others think she's a drag queen (just one of the mistaken identities in the narrative). As Googie had to say for herself in the film version: "(Singing) Everyting's coming up roses, por me and por ju . . . (Speaking) One of dees days, ju is going to see de name of Googie Gomez in lights and you gonna ask juself (gasps) 'Gwas dat her?' An den ju gonna answer juself, (gasps) 'jes, dat gwas her!' Well, let me tell you something, Mister: I gwas ALWAYS her, just dat nobody knows it!" Moreno's appeal in and apparent enjoyment playing the role of Googie Gomez serves as a vivid illustration of the power of satire, when accompanied by creative agency, to begin to lessen the power of Latina/o stereotypes. When Moreno finally had a voice with respect to the writing, directing, and acting of a so-called spitfire role, she was able to skewer it with style and verve, helping to create a character that commented on former spitfire roles in Hollywood film with humor and a knowing wink.

Given that Googie Gomez roles were not common in Hollywood, however, Moreno continued to focus on acting in theater and other projects. For Rita Moreno, these choices offered freedom and relief in a number of respects. In interviews, Moreno enthusiastically reported her interest in producing and otherwise working to promote positive images of Latina/os in the media, exemplified by her involvement in a documentary about the making of the 1954 docudrama *Salt of the Earth*. Dignity in fact has become an overriding signifier of her career in the last decades, as Moreno's position as a grand dame of film, television, and theater has only solidified. She has starred in such films as *Slums of Beverly Hills* (1998), *Piñero* (2001), *Casa de los Babys* (2003), on countless television series, and in her own one-woman cabaret shows. Moreno also played Sister Peter Marie on HBO's critically acclaimed series *Oz* (1997–2003), a hard-hitting drama about the inmates and employees of a maximum-security prison, and a Cuban American family matriarch on the television series *Cane* (2007). That year, Moreno also celebrated her seventy-sixth birthday. She continues to pursue an active career and lives in Berkeley, California with her husband, daughter, and grandchildren.

* * *

As Rita Moreno's career and early star image illustrate, the 1950s and '60s were marked by the continuation of a number of film industry traditions that limited the possibilities for Latina/o stardom. For one, Latina/os continued to find one of their most likely points of entry as dancers or singers. The challenge, then, as Moreno discovered, was to be seen by producers, casting directors, and publicists as more than entertaining and titillating bodies and voices. This was almost impossible to accomplish during this period, however, as the film industry's unwritten rules of casting in the 1950s designated a Puerto Rican actress and Latina/os as nonwhite and non-American and enforced a racialized line that they typically were not allowed to cross. The roles they might subsequently be offered overwhelmingly were underdeveloped and of a variety of nonwhite ethnic types. Notably, much of the opportunity to be found in 1950s films was in independently and studio-produced Westerns and adventure dramas, postcolonial fantasies that supported notions of white and U.S. superiority and typically posed nonwhite characters as inferior, tropicalized ethnic others. Aside from the obvious denigration such roles intimated toward ethnic performers deemed nonwhite, they also offered little opportunity for demonstrating potential star appeal. If Moreno's filmography can be taken as an example, her image lacked the upper-class elegance that had tempered Dolores Del Rio's in the 1930s, an illustration both of the differing sexual mores of the two eras and of how Del Rio's wealthy background, her foreign-born status in a period more accepting of foreigners, and perhaps her more European look softened her star publicity. Evolving ideals of American identity and particularly of relative notions of idealized femininity that continued to characterize and marginalize Latinas and Latinos as residing on the fringes of white American society (even while Latina/os were now able to claim whiteness as a racial designation on the U.S. census) undergirded the obstacles that Moreno faced as she attempted simply to stay employed as an actor.

Moreno's career also illustrates how publicity was often a double-edged sword for Latina film actresses in the post–World War II period. Promotion naturally was necessary to become known to audiences, but there was a cost if star images took on an overtly sexualized tone. Moreno's spitfire star image, manufactured in particular by the studios and production companies that produced her films, capitalized on historical tropes of Latinas as seductive but ultimately trifling sex objects. While white actresses at times experienced similar "cheesecake" marketing, with Betty Grable, Jane Russell, and Marilyn Monroe's pinup posters as vivid illustrations, Latinas, particularly U.S.-born Latinas such as Rita Moreno, typically had no opportunity to be marketed in any other manner than as excessive and inviting bodies. In Rita Moreno's career trajectory, she was hampered in her desire to be cast in more challenging roles by this type of promotion.

Rita Moreno acknowledges that she milked the spitfire myth for as much publicity as possible in her early career, which may have encouraged the typecasting that she experienced. However, this situation did not improve for Moreno after winning the Oscar for Best Supporting Actress for *West Side Story*. If anything, it proved how entrenched stereotypical notions of Latinidad were in Hollywood at the time. Rita Moreno's role as Googie Gomez offers an interesting coda to this summary of Moreno's early career, however, as it highlights how Latina/o creative agency promised to upset the racial paradigms that typically confined Latin actors with respect to the characters they could portray and the promotion they might receive. As Latina/os began to have some input into and creative control over the roles they played, opportunities for stardom could shift in far-reaching ways, as the following chapters will illustrate.

4

The Burden of Playing Chico

Freddie Prinze and Latino Stardom in Television's Era of "Relevance"

The 2005–6 series *Freddie* quietly marked a milestone of sorts in Latina/o television representation. Its star and co-executive producer, Freddie Prinze Jr., dedicated the pilot episode to his famous father, Freddie Prinze, who died before he was old enough to know him. Notably, *Freddie*'s protagonist was half Puerto Rican and half Italian, and the storyline included a Puerto Rican grandmother (Jenny Gago) who spoke only Spanish. Freddie Prinze Jr.'s ability to get this series on the air, reportedly with the support and assistance of actor and producer George Lopez, whose series, *The George Lopez Show* (2002–7) performed well for five years, speaks to shifts in Latina/o television representation—and in Latina/o media advocacy and clout in relation to television programming—since Prinze's father experienced his rise to national fame in *Chico and the Man* in the mid-1970s.

Freddie hearkens from a contested legacy in the form of *Chico and the Man* and Chicana/o activist lobbying of the Big Three networks for improved and increased representation of Mexican Americans and other Latina/os in the 1960s and 1970s. The NBC situation comedy, which aired from 1974 to 1978, was an anomaly at the time for featuring the only Mexican American lead character to be found among the "socially relevant" television programming of that decade. It continued to be exceptional as the only network series with a Latina/o protagonist for the next two decades to survive beyond a season.[1] Starring Jack Albertson as Ed Brown and Puerto Rican and German-Hungarian Freddie Prinze as Francisco "Chico" Rodriguez, *Chico and the Man* focuses on an *Odd Couple*–pairing of a crotchety white auto shop owner and the young, happy-go-lucky Mexican American man who works and lives with him in a barrio of East Los Angeles.[2] They eventually become fond of each other, learn from one another, and come to see each other almost as father and son. As far-fetched as this premise may seem, and despite protests from Chicana/o and other viewers that the series portrayed Chico and other Mexican Americans in a demeaning light, it became a hit upon its debut, finishing as one of the top five–rated shows of the season. In the process, it made young comedian Freddie Prinze a star.

Prinze was just nineteen but already a seasoned stand-up comedian performing on the *Tonight Show Starring Johnny Carson* when he was noticed by television writer-producer James Komack, the creator of the series, and invited to audition for the role. As a result of his sudden visibility on the series, Prinze became a virtual overnight sensation. He held a unique status as a young Latino television star until 1977, when tragically, he committed suicide. A testament to his intense popularity, *Chico and the Man* was so popular that NBC renewed it for another year after Prinze's death, albeit to increasingly lower ratings throughout the 1977–78 season, when it was eventually cancelled.

Prinze's stardom and the intense negotiations that took place over the development of his character thus provide important inroads into understanding a television network's portrayal of a popular Mexican American character and of Hollywood Latinidad more generally in this time period. On even a cursory examination, it is clear that a number of ideological limitations marked the representation of Chico and other Latina/o characters on the series, while Prinze as a stand-up comedian naturally experienced more freedom of expression with respect to his public appearances and star promotion outside the series than the typical actor. It is unsurprising that audience reception was mixed about the character of Chico as it was originally constructed; as one of very few images of a Mexican American in the mass media, it carried a unique burden of representation and was the focus of intense scrutiny, debate, and negotiation. Chicana/o and Latina/o advocacy groups by the mid-1970s were offering their opinions (which were often not heeded) to the networks regarding portrayals deemed unflattering, and threatened boycotts and well-publicized protests were a threat that the networks had to contend with for the first time. Freddie Prinze meanwhile was both criticized for taking on the role and embraced as a youthful and radical new Puerto Rican (or rather, "Hungarican," as he termed himself) star, and one of the top comedians in the country, all before he reached the age of twenty-two. He was heavily promoted, and in his few years in the public spotlight he had a substantial presence on the comedy circuit and as a guest star on television talk shows, in addition to his weekly role on *Chico and the Man*. Outside the series, his irreverent and socially incisive comedy in particular gave him a distinct voice that was unusual for a Latina/o in mainstream culture at the time. He was still often equated with Chico in the public imagination, however, a limitation that Prinze was beginning to protest in interviews around the time of his death.

Given this history, the production and promotion of *Chico and the Man* and its star, Freddie Prinze, are important illustrations of common attitudes toward Latina/os within Hollywood media industries and the construction of Latina/os in television story worlds of the 1970s. How did series producers envision Mexican Americans in this time period, and what assumptions did they make about the attitudes and interests of their viewers? How did the producers respond to potential viewer and advocacy group critiques of the show? And given Prinze's mixed racial background, history, and personal performance style, how did he negotiate his star image, particularly with regard to the diverging expectations of the network, the series producers, Latina/o critics, and his fans, of a Latino television star?

Despite his importance with respect to Latina/o representation, there has been relatively little scholarship on Freddie Prinze or *Chico and the Man*, with the work of Chon Noriega and Greg Oguss serving as notable exceptions.[3] To begin to remedy that, in this chapter I analyze the marketing of Freddie Prinze as a young star in the context of the production and reception of *Chico and the Man*. To do so, I explore behind-the-scenes negotiations and public relations related to Prinze's work on the series from 1974 to 1975, with a particular focus on its first season. I do so as this was when Chico and the other characters were developed, often in response to viewer criticism, and when Prinze was launched as a national star. In addition, I focus on the various promotional texts that constructed Prinze as a star, explore the show's construction of Chico Rodriguez and of Mexican American and other Latina/o cultures and identity more generally, and also consider how Prinze's comedy performances expressed his unique "Hungarican" and Puerto Rican perspective on U.S. social life and popular culture.

Chico: At the Crossroads of TV "Relevance" and Chicana/o Activism

The 1960s brought about a number of social and industrial shifts that were to have an impact on the racial politics of casting in film and television. As noted in the previous chapter on Rita Moreno's experiences in 1950s–'60s

Hollywood, social shifts in the 1960s included rising social awareness on the part of many young Americans of various ethnic backgrounds. This shift only intensified by the end of the decade. During this period, in which young people were often questioning U.S. social institutions, there was a sharp spike in interest and involvement in the civil rights, antiwar, and women's and gay rights movements, among other social causes. As these children of the Baby Boom aged, they also had a greater impact on the direction of popular culture. By the late 1960s, a major portion of the audience for film and television was under thirty, and they began to more directly influence casting and the related star system. Many of the most popular films of the decade reflected the preoccupations of the new, young adult audience—including a greater social consciousness, cynicism, and desire for sensation. Popular genres were often reformulated, as more mature subject matter and graphic sexual and violent content became the norm, trends that were aided by the scrapping of the Production Code by 1968.[4]

Such trends were soon felt in television production as well as the networks aimed to reach the same audience. CBS in particular set its sights on targeting younger and more educated viewers. In 1971, their success with *All in the Family* (1971–79), which frankly incorporated such issues as racism, sexism, and antiwar sentiment into its storylines as fodder for laughs and featured nonwhite actors in guest and recurring roles, marked the network's transition to a new cycle of more socially conscious programming, what has been described by scholars such as Todd Gitlin and Erik Barnouw as a turn to "relevance."[5] Other series that followed often focused on African American experience, such as *Sanford and Son* (1972–77), and later *Good Times* (1974–79) and *What's Happening!!* (1976–79). Within this cycle of programming, Latina/os were not typically represented, however. While Latina/os comprised almost 5 percent of the population in 1970, and Mexican Americans were a sizeable community in Los Angeles, Latina/o characters only appeared in walk-on roles in series such as *All in the Family* and *Sanford and Son*. Mexican American characters in particular were conspicuously absent. This was a gap that James Komack, the creator and producer of *Chico and the Man,* aimed to fill when he wrote the initial pilot script for the series in 1973.

The series as it developed over its first season also was influenced by the rise of Chicana/o civil rights activism and particularly activism with a focus on Latina/o mainstream media representation and employment both in front of and behind the camera. In the late 1960s and early 1970s, in response to continuing social problems related to poverty, blocks to decent employment and wages, and educational inequities, many Mexican Americans and

Puerto Ricans became involved with civil rights activism, fighting in a more visible and militant manner than ever before for equal rights and respect for Latina/os in U.S. social institutions.[6] It was during this period that the term Chicano (and with reference to women and girls, Chicana) began to be embraced as a label of pride by many Mexican Americans. As Neil Foley notes, in this process Chicana/o activists were "renounc[ing] their status as white" and choosing instead to identify racially as "'brown,' partly as a legal strategy but mostly as a consequence of the Chicano movement's emphasis on the Indian and mestizo heritage of Mexican people."[7] Given that many of these Chicana/o and Puerto Rican activists were the first generation to have been raised on television, their activism also often included awareness of the power of the media images and of creative control in their production.

As Chon Noriega documents, around 1968 Chicana/o activists began staging visible, wide-scale demonstrations to protest what was seen as negative Latina/o imagery in film, television, advertising, and radio. Most notable were protests against the Frito Bandito, an animated bandit figure in Frito-Lay commercials who couldn't help but "steal those cronchy corn chips," and the Chiquita Banana, a dancing Carmen Miranda-esque mascot for Chiquita Brand fruit who wore fruit of her own on her head, images that were criticized as reinforcing stereotypical notions of Latinas and Latinos as criminals and frivolous tropical dancers. Activists also demanded increased access to and employment of Latina/os within the media industries themselves.[8] With respect to television, Chicana/o and Latina/o activists had a strong case to make regarding Latina/o invisibility and negative characterization, as Latina and Latino characters were seldom seen on television, and often appeared in marginal or criminal roles.[9]

Established Latino advocacy groups such as LULAC and the Mexican American Political Association (MAPA) engaged in such protests targeting the media industries, joining newer organizations such as the Mexican American Legal Defense and Education Fund (MALDEF) and the National Council of La Raza (NCLR). A number of groups also were organized in this time period with a primary focus on Chicana/o and Latina/o media representation and employment; a few were Los Angeles–based and included individuals who were working in Hollywood or wished to be. Among these groups were CARISSMA, the Council to Advance and Restore the Image of the Spanish-Speaking and Mexican Americans, the Puerto Rican Action and Media Council, and Justicia (Justice), also known as Justice for Chicanos in the Motion Picture Industry. Justicia in particular lobbied the commercial television networks, advocating for the hiring of Mexican American actors and creative professionals and for the right to proffer feedback on scripts that included Latino characters; it was the most successful of the advocacy groups in gaining the ear of the networks in the early 1970s.[10] Notably, however, the networks managed within a few years to contain the fervor of these groups through a number of measures, including offering a few traineeships and low-level jobs to group members, providing small grants to fund group activities, cultivating a relationship with just one advocacy group, or making promises for future improvements that later were not kept, as research on Latina/o and other ethnic media advocacy and my own interviews with media professionals who were involved in these activities has documented.[11] On the other hand, the networks were now aware of the public relations hassles that could result if Latina/o viewers and one of these groups in particular became unhappy with a series, and would go to great lengths to avoid such problems, as the history of *Chico and the Man* bears out.

Latina/os working in film and television as actors and creative professionals also began to organize and agitate within the industries, both for improved representation and to foster a more supportive climate for fellow Latina/os. For instance, the actors' advocacy group Nosotros (Us) was founded by actor Ricardo Montalban in Los Angeles in 1970. Among other activities, Nosotros began to sponsor an annual awards show, the Golden Eagle Awards, which continues to honor achievements by Latina/os in the entertainment industries each year.[12] Even so, Latina/o creative professionals found opportunities hard to come by in these years, when the realms of writers, directors, and producers in particular were still overwhelmingly white and Latina/os had intense difficulty gaining the necessary experience to join the professional guilds and otherwise gain entry to the creative realms of film and television. On a related note, as Donald Bogle attests and as this exploration of Freddie Prinze's career highlights, nonwhite audiences, in addition to pushing for more responsiveness from studios and networks, also began to demand more political correctness from nonwhite actors and particularly from high-profile stars in the 1970s.[13]

High Hopes and Damage Control: The Series before Its Debut

Chico and the Man, as noted above, was envisioned as an *Odd Couple*–like pairing, with the added twist of a culture clash between an older white American and a younger Mexican American man. It was conceived and written without input from Mexican American or other Latina/o writers or media producers, however, making Freddie Prinze's impact on the series all the more significant. Series creator James Komack (1930–97), of Jewish American descent, had grown up in New York City and was a successful stand-up comedian before moving into the television industry. He then worked as a writer for *My Favorite Martian* (1963–66) and *Get Smart* (1965–70) and as executive producer of *The Courtship of Eddie's Father* (1969–72), among other projects, before serving as executive producer for *Chico and the Man*. Freddie Prinze apparently considered him a friend; Prinze, for instance, gave his newborn son (Freddie Prinze Jr.) the middle name of James in honor of Komack.

James Komack always maintained that his interest was to showcase a Chicano character who could be seen as a positive role model. However, Komack's original script for the series pilot, titled "Now, Chico!" and retitled "The Man Meets Chico" in its final version, is rife with problematic elements in the construction of Chico. Many of these elements were improved upon by the final version, co-written by Komack, Don Nicholl, Michael Ross, and Bernie West. For instance, Chico is described in the first version of the script as knowing how to fix cars because "he's been stripping-them-down and ripping-them-off [*sic*] for years."[14] While he is written as a twenty-five-year-old Vietnam veteran, he also has no job before he meets Ed Brown and merely wanders around "whistling modern day Rock tunes."[15] Perhaps most problematic, and this story premise was *not* changed in the final pilot script, Chico is constructed as having no family ties or friends in the neighborhood he calls home; he apparently lives in such isolation that he needs to live in Ed Brown's garage.

The series was considered promising, however, to the extent that NBC authorized the making of the pilot and first season episodes. In this preproduction stage, the auditions would appear to illustrate the good intentions of the producers. Reportedly as many as forty-one Latino actors were considered. As James Komack told journalists, "We contacted all the activist groups and we auditioned every Chicano available. We narrowed it down to five people, two Chicanos, two Puerto Ricans and a Cuban."[16] Freddie Prinze ultimately beat out the other actors, including Mexican American actor Isaac Ruiz, who was to play his best friend Mando on the series. Much of the decision was apparently based on performance dynamics; Prinze and Jack Albertson reportedly had the best chemistry together. According to many, once Prinze was cast in the role of Chico, the role began to be developed with his brand of brash ethnic humor in mind. His comedy routines were mined for material. (Prinze, however, is not included in the writer's credits on most of the episodes.) Bits borrowed from his comedy act included "Eez not my job," a thickly accented line from Prinze's act that he used to lampoon his Puerto Rican apartment building superintendent and other Puerto Rican characters. When some viewers expressed their belief that this supported notions of lazy Latina/os, this was often replaced with Prinze's drawn out "Looking good!" another of his comedic trademarks.

So how did a Jewish American television producer from New York strive for credibility in his series about a young Chicano in primarily Mexican American East Los Angeles? Komack often claimed in interviews that he based the character of Chico on the lives of Mexican Americans that he knew. In such discussions he occasionally mentioned Cheech Marin, who at the time was a successful stand-up comedian performing with Tommy Chong as the duo Cheech and Chong, in the years before his work as an actor, writer, and director in films such as *Up in Smoke* (1978) and *Born in East L.A.* (1987). More often, Komack claimed he had based the role on a lesser-known actor by the name of Ray Andrade.[17]

Ray Andrade, an actor and occasional military-technical advisor on film shoots, not coincidentally had been the president of the media advocacy group Justicia. (The group had been technically defunct since 1972, but reportedly was still remembered and feared by the networks, according to Kathryn Montgomery.)[18] Early on, Andrade was signed on as a consultant on the series, under the title associate to the producer and later under the higher-status title of associate producer. The incorporation of Andrade into the show's production, while possibly well meaning, was arguably also a defensive maneuver; his presence was often mentioned in defense of the show's representation of Chico and other Mexican American characters. This containment strategy soon backfired, however, as Andrade later spoke out against the series, as detailed further below.

Despite these maneuvers, the series quickly came under fire. The hiring of Freddie Prinze, a Latino of Puerto Rican and Anglo descent, marked the beginning of clashes over the character of Chico that would continue throughout his three years on the show. Not hiring a Mexican American actor so soon after the networks had made promises to Chicana/o advocacy groups to increase Mexican American employment in the industry was seen as a major affront.

NBC screenings of the pilot had network executives excited, however. Yet the network did want reassurance that the series would not arouse fatal protest; one way that this was accomplished was through pre-screening episodes in various markets. Notably, a screening strictly with Latina/o viewers was not arranged (although documentation in the production files indicates that Komack did this informally with Justicia members and perhaps other Chicana/o viewers); instead, the pilot was tested in March 1974 with audiences in San Francisco; Akron, Ohio; Kingsport, Tennessee; Grand Junction, Colorado; and at the NBC studios in Burbank. This preview indicated that audiences generally liked and took no umbrage with this episode. Interestingly, however, it is noted in the internal NBC memo on the pre-screening that the audience in Burbank "seemed a bit sensitive about racial remarks," and that this may have been related to the Mexican American population in the Los Angeles area.[19] Overall, the results were interpreted as confirming that the series had good potential to succeed on the air. A second preview screening, this one of the second episode, "Second Thoughts," that was pre-screened in September 1974 in San Francisco did not return such favorable reactions, however. Audiences viewing this episode, who had not seen the pilot, felt that Ed treated Chico in a manner that was "belligerent and hostile," and that it made no sense that Chico allowed this to happen and chose to stay with Ed.[20] The network clearly wished to avoid this type of reaction and thus put a great deal of emphasis on publicity before the show's premiere.

As a part of this pre-publicity, Komack did a number of interviews before the debut of the series, taking pains to explain his various ties to the Mexican American community and the inclusion of Ray Andrade as consultant on the show. As a UPI newswire story on the production on June 30, 1974 noted, Komack was "deeply involved with the Hispanic culture and lifestyle" and had "talked to hundreds of Chicanos" before working on the series.[21] Komack was also quoted as saying he hoped to use *Chico and the Man* as a means to rectify the invisibility of Mexican Americans on television. He added, "They are a proud and beautiful part of the American scene, and I think viewers will take them to heart."[22] In addition, publicity stills of Freddie Prinze and Jack Albertson as Chico Rodriguez and Ed Brown were shared liberally with the press and used to illustrate a number of the eventual reviews after it premiered.

Chico and the Man debuted on September 13, 1974, with a theme song scored and sung by José Feliciano (like Prinze, also of Puerto Rican descent). From its first episode, the series storylines attempted to capitalize in a humorous way on the theme of ethnic conflict. Ed drove business away with his cantankerous demeanor, while Chico cleaned up the garage and brought business in with his positive attitude. Throughout the series episodes he encouraged Ed to clean up and enjoy his life as well. Ethnic humor often drove these early episodes; the jokes are especially barbed in the pilot and second episode. For example, this is the dialogue that ensued when Chico and Ed met for the first time in the pilot, after Chico rides into Ed's garage on a bicycle:

Jack Albertson and Freddie Prinze in a promotional photo for *Chico and the Man* in 1974.

Ed: What are you doing in here?

Chico: Who me?

Ed: Yeah, you. Do you see anybody else in the garage?

Chico: Garage? It looks to me like *un basurero.*

Ed: What's that supposed to mean?

Chico: *Basurero.* It means junk yard.

Ed: Get out of here! And take your flies with you.

Chico: What flies?

Ed: Your flies. You people got flies all around you. And while you're standing here your flies are getting together with my flies and making more flies!

Chico: (somewhat sarcastically) You're a nice man.

Ed: Would you get out of here and get back to your neighborhood?

Chico: This is my neighborhood. I grew up watching this garage run down! . . . You need me.

Ed: For what?
Chico: I'm Super Mex!
Ed: Who's Super Mex?
Chico: Super Mexicanic! Ask anybody about Chico Rodriguez.

As evident from this exchange, even though Ed adds that Chico's flies are now mating with his flies, the sting of the ethnic slur is not completely absorbed by this reframing. Perhaps because of the comic charm of Freddie Prinze and chemistry between Prinze and Albertson, the series was a quick hit, however, earning a number three spot in the ratings. Television critics were generally positive. Lee Winfrey of the *Philadelphia Inquirer*, for instance, called it a "remarkably good show . . . consistent and always refreshing," while saying Freddie Prinze "may be the best new comic who has developed anywhere in this country during this decade so far."[23] *Time* called Prinze the "hottest new property on prime time TV." And television critic Cecil Smith similarly called Prinze "one of the most gifted young comedians to come along in years."[24]

Freddie Prinze: "Hungarican" Comedian

Such reviews marked an influential transition in the career of the young Freddie Prinze, who became a national star overnight. According to various biographies on Prinze, Freddie Prinze was born Frederick Karl Pruetzel on June 22, 1954, in New York City. His mother, Maria, was Puerto Rican, and his father, Karl, was Hungarian of German descent, which led to Prinze later declaring himself in his comedy act to be "Hungarican." Freddie Prinze grew up in Washington Heights, a multiethnic neighborhood in upper Manhattan. While it had a fair number of middle-class residents, Prinze interestingly characterized it as a working-class ghetto. He often used it as fodder for his comedy, emphasizing its dangers and hopelessness for many of its residents, perhaps in tune with American notions of the period of urban Latinidad. For instance, he cracked that it was such a slum that "even the birds were junkies."[25] He also noted in more serious moments with journalists that many of his childhood friends had died from overdosing or were still struggling to make something of their lives.[26]

As he noted in interviews, Prinze was an overweight child who struggled with bullies, but learned that he could avoid being picked on if he made other kids laugh. Soon he was known for telling jokes and doing impersonations. He also was interested in music and singing, and reportedly his mother enrolled him in ballet classes to help him lose weight. He took it upon himself to audition for the Fiorello H. LaGuardia High School of Performing Arts.

There he focused on acting and dance. He shared with interviewers that he had especially loved entertaining his friends with improvised comedy in the school bathroom, and he soon tried his hand at stand-up in city nightclubs. He dropped out of high school before graduating because it interfered with his nightclub comedy performances, which he began at comedy clubs such as Catch a Rising Star and The Improv by the age of sixteen. It was at one of his performances that he caught the attention of David Jonas, who became his first manager and secured comedy gigs for Prinze at the Playboy Clubs and other East Coast nightclub venues. Later Prinze was to switch to West Coast managers Marvin "Dusty" Snyder and Ron DeBlasio to manage his then Los Angeles–based career when Jonas refused to move from New York.

It was through Snyder and DeBlasio that Prinze secured his first television appearance in 1973, performing comedy on the late-night talk show *The Jack Paar Show*. This led to other television appearances, the most important being his first on *The Tonight Show Starring Johnny Carson*. On December 6, 1973, Prinze came out on *The Tonight Show* stage smiling and proceeded to smartly skewer his urban neighborhood and irreverently poke fun at authority figures and neighborhood thugs alike. He also offered social critique from a Puerto Rican point of view, asking for instance why there couldn't be a Puerto Rican astronaut, or a Puerto Rican president? Such critique was softened by Prinze's good humor and spot-on timing, and he scored a huge round of applause at the end of his set. Johnny Carson was visibly excited about Prinze's performance, gushing that there was "no greater thing than seeing a comic start their careers on the show!" and spontaneously invited the momentarily speechless Prinze to sit on the couch and talk with him afterward—making him one of only a small handful of comics ever given this opportunity. Prinze appeared on the show many times after that, and also served as guest host a few times in 1976.

As a stand-up comedian, Freddie Prinze was able to be a social critic and proffer his opinion on a wide variety of subjects, putting him in a drastically different position with respect to the construction of his public image than was or is the case for Latina/o performers who work only as actors. His humor presented an irreverent, urban underdog point of view that had seldom been witnessed in the national arena. A smattering of one-liners from his act:

My parents met on the subway—picking each other's pockets.

My mother's always talking about the wedding. "You shoulda been there," she says. She doesn't remember. I was there, and so were my two brothers.

To survive in the ghetto, you gotta look tough. The best way to look tough is to have a broken arm.[27]

He quickly became known as a brash comedian skilled in ethnic humor (as noted by Daniel Bernardi, Prinze was an "observation comic," and his comedy typically included broad ethnic humor and impersonations that made fun of all ethnic groups), as well as for sharply observed satire about U.S. race and class relations.[28] As he was quoted in one set at Catch a Rising Star in 1974: "Hey! Rockefeller! . . . he's Spanish for a day, dig, he comes uptown going 'HO-LA, MI HER-MA-NOS PORTOREE-KANYOS Y LATEEENOS. . .' We say, 'Hey, man, give us some money. . . .' Hey! Nixon! . . . says he won't go to jail . . . up' im . . . put bars on San Clemente."[29] And another line from one of his stand-up performances underscored: "We live in a society that cripples people, and then punishes them for limping. . . ."[30]

With the debut of *Chico and the Man,* Freddie Prinze and his humor, albeit sharply tempered for television audiences, made their way to prime time. The actor, then twenty, was promoted to mainstream audiences in a manner in tune with the social consciousness and edgy aesthetic of the times. In stark contrast to Desi Arnaz in the era of 1950s television, as discussed in chapter 2, Prinze could be a television star without a family-oriented image outside the series, and in fact was likely considered appealing to younger viewers in part because of his youth-oriented and edgy image. Magazines and newspapers such as *Newsweek, Time, Rolling Stone,* and the *New York Times* ran feature stories in the fall of 1974 and early 1975 on the young star, as did teen-oriented media outlets such as *Seventeen* and *Sixteen* and counterculture tabloids such as *Playboy.*[31] Most constructed Prinze as an urban man of the times; for example, *Rolling Stone*'s cover story on Prinze was titled "The Undiluted South Bronx Truth."

In these feature stories and appearances, Prinze's "Hungarican" background is often mentioned, alongside his hardscrabble childhood in Washington Heights. Bits of his comedy act also made their way into interviews, as Prinze was known for incorporating them as he embellished liberally on his childhood for interviewers. Prinze as a Latino and Puerto Rican star thus was marketed to the public in a unique manner. For one thing, it seems that he was called to respond to an intense curiosity on the part of the public regarding his ethnic background and where he came from. His responses underscore his complex ethnic identity as both Latino and "Hungarican"; this was to become even more complex as he was called to stand in for *Chicanismo* in the role of Chico Rodriguez. This would be increasingly contentious as Freddie Prinze was criticized for taking on the role and imbuing it with his own comedy style, as I note further below. Notably, it appears that Prinze did no interviews with the Latino press at the time (or during the rest of the series run), despite the signs in the *Chico* pre-screenings that Latina/o

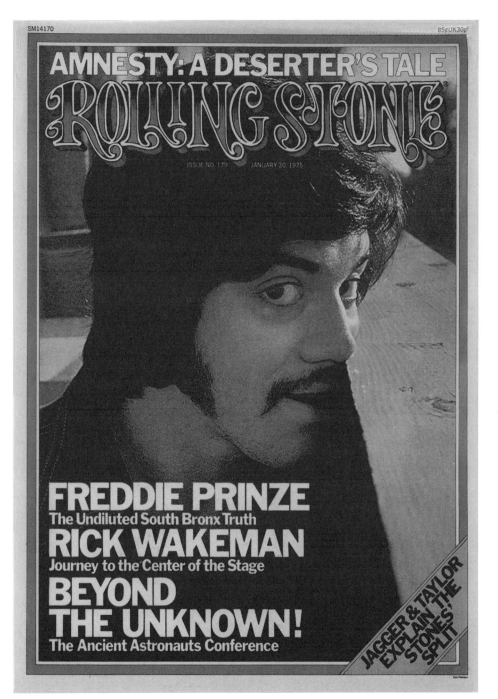

Freddie Prinze gracing the cover of *Rolling Stone* on January 30, 1975. Cover by Don Peterson from *Rolling Stone,* January 30, 1975. © Rolling Stone LLC 1975. All Rights Reserved. Reprinted by Permission.

audiences might take issue with the series and with his casting in the title role. Chicana/o and other viewers soon made it clear that they would not be ignored, however.

"Now, Chico!" Critics and Producers at Odds

As noted above, the series debut of *Chico and the Man* inaugurated a unique and often rancorous relationship that the production had with Chicana/o and other viewers and media advocates. At the time of the series debut, protesters picketed NBC's Burbank studios and wrote letters protesting the casting of Prinze, Chico's inaccurate accent, and what they termed his demeaning and non-macho demeanor. Perhaps not surprisingly, many viewers also found the premise of the series, that of a Mexican American young man who wishes to work for a bigoted older white man in East Los Angeles, problematic. Letter writers, both Latina/o and non-Latina/o, also complained to the producers and NBC about how Mexican Americans were being represented. For instance, to provide a sampling of the complaints shared with series producers and the general public, a repeat letter writer, Vincent P. Tobias, asserted to the show's producers that the series "portray[ed] Mexican Americans as non-contributors to our society by its innuendos, slurs and cheap petty statements,"[32] while educators who taught at the Los Angeles Hispanic Urban Center wrote in the *Los Angeles Times* that the series presented Chicana/o youth in a manner that "reinforces or elicits racist Anglo-American feelings of superiority over Chicanos by ridiculing the character of Chico."[33] And many critics, such as Caesar C. Cantu, president and chair of the Mexican Heritage Cultural Board in Columbus, Ohio, complained that there were no Mexican American writers working on the show.[34] Ray Andrade, then an associate producer on the series, also spoke out publicly against the series producers in early October 1974. Siding with the critics, he relented that "the show does indeed lack authenticity. . . . And it's the result of non-Chicano writers. . . . There are good Chicano writers, but they won't hire them, now. They'll wait until the show is a solid hit before taking a chance on them."[35]

Members of the Chicana/o and Latina/o theater consortium TENAZ (Teatro Nacionales de Aztlán) and other Chicana/o and Puerto Rican groups also picketed the NBC studios, while the Chicano Coalition and Felix Gutierrez, then an assistant professor at California State University of Northridge, filed a petition to the FCC to deny the renewal of the license of the NBC affiliate in Burbank, KNBC, stating in their affidavit that *Chico and the Man* was a series of the type "detrimental to the self-image of Chicano children who watch it."[36] Boycotts of the series and its advertisers also were threatened by a number of Chicana/o organizations. Much of the focus of the protest, notably, was whether Chico was an appropriate or positive Chicano role model. Some critics, on the other hand, felt if changes were made and Chicana/os were employed behind the scenes that it could improve problematic elements on the series and salvage the opportunity the series presented. As Alicia Sandoval and Paul Macias noted in an op-ed piece in the *Los Angeles Times,* "Some viewers believe that if Freddie Prinze can improve his imitation of an East Los Angeles Chicano, and if Chicano script writers are eventually hired, the format can be salvaged."[37]

In response to the controversy, the show's producers attempted to appease the most vocal of critics and to widely publicize their hard work in doing so. As journalist David Winder wrote in the *Christian Science Monitor,* the production team's response included "a series of meetings, a willingness to compromise, and an expenditure of a good deal of money to alter the show."[38] Ed Brown's racist tendencies were softened, while Chico's Mexican American identity became more fluid, as was noted in a new round of news articles.[39] In the next episodes the East LA neighborhood where the garage was set was referred to with less specificity, while Chico was revealed to be half Puerto Rican and raised in New York, and even to have a grandmother who could "speak a little Hungarian."[40] Freddie Prinze told journalists that it had been decided that he should aim to be a "general Latin" in his approach to the character.

As noted earlier, employment was also used as a public relations strategy. In this period when virtually no Latina/os had managed to break through the color barriers to get training and the experience to be considered among the ranks of working television writers, *Chico* had an all-white creative team.[41] James Komack's hiring of Ray Andrade in fact was unusual. Moves such as these could backfire, however, considering that Andrade eventually spoke out publicly against the series. Aside from his complaints about the lack of Mexican American writers, he also noted to *Daily Variety* that his input was typically not solicited or utilized by producers and that he found some elements of the show offensive, including Chico's subservience and "lack of machismo."[42] He was not asked back to work on the series after the first season. And as Andrade alleged, the production team did not rush to hire Latina/o writers. This was despite the facts that dozens of unsolicited scripts were being sent in by Chicana/o and Latina/o writers and that Chicana/o organizations were agitating for this sort of inclusion. In response, a $10,000 fund was created by NBC to assist in the development of scripts by promising

Chicana/o writers and other writers of color.[43] Documentation in the series production files indicates that there were disagreements over who would actually choose the scripts and mentor the writers, however; it does not appear that any writers actually benefited from the fund.[44]

For their part, journalists' coverage of the controversy also often minimized its importance, through referring to the small size and supposed negligible buying power of the Mexican American audience, or through implying that the only critics of the series were Mexican Americans in the Los Angeles area. As Cecil Smith wrote, "I doubt the controversy means a thing outside Southern California, or even much beyond the city limits of Los Angeles."[45] Even the *Los Angeles Times* op-ed piece by Sandoval and Macias that was largely supportive of the critics of the series made the concession that the Chicana/o audience was being ignored because it was a "relatively small, low-income segment of the TV audience"—although they inserted the important critique that this perception existed in part because Latina/os were not being properly polled in the Nielsen ratings of television viewing.

Prinze, for his part, defended with his usual irreverent humor his right to portray the character of Chico. For instance, he was quoted as saying, "If I can't play a Chicano because I'm Puerto Rican, then God's really gonna be mad when he finds out Charlton Heston played Moses."[46] He also would raise questions about how to create a culturally accurate portrayal of a Mexican American. As he told a journalist for the *Los Angeles Times,* "I wish I knew what they wanted. . . . They say Chicanos talk a certain way, walk a certain way. I know lots of Chicanos. All different. They don't want an actor. They want a stereotype: a wind-up Chicano."[47] While Freddie Prinze continued in the next seasons to insert his own brand of Latinidad into the character and the ratings would indicate that he was popular with many viewers, he could never fully transcend the limitations inherent in the role of Chico Rodriguez. It also seems apparent that by the third season of *Chico and the Man,* and Prinze's last, he no longer was as engaged in the narrative, perhaps in part due to the fact that he did not have ultimate creative control over his character.

The Cipher of "SuperMex": Multivalent Latinidad (and Lost *Chicanismo*) on *Chico*

The issue of creative agency is of extreme importance with respect to *Chico and the Man* and the controversy that came to be associated with Freddie Prinze's stardom. As previously mentioned, it appears that there were no Latina/o writers among the more than sixty who worked on *Chico and the*

Man, aside from Freddie Prinze, who received a co-writer credit on at least one episode. Missteps in the characterization of Chico Rodriguez can thus be understood within a framework of well-meaning cultural ignorance. From its outset, the narrative premise demonstrates the limitations of an all-white production team; Chico's need for Ed to give him a job and a home in East Los Angeles is a foundational tale that never fully rings true. Despite Ed's racist sentiments, he also is supposed to be understood as merely a cranky benefactor who will help Chico find his way. The rapid-fire comedic exchanges, in Vaudeville tradition, between Prinze and Albertson that were central to the series also often were typically constructed at the expense of Chico's character, with the young man's response one of cheerful good will. Such exchanges arguably illustrate the producers' creation of a "safe" Chicano (and later, Latino) and Anglo Odd Couple for their imagined television viewers of this period.

This is not to say that *Chico and the Man* didn't offer counter-hegemonic humor and potential, however, which kept the series from conforming to a complete marginalization of its Mexican American and Puerto Rican characters. Most consistently, such potential was alluded to in the opening and closing credits included with most of the series episodes, as Greg Oguss has also noted.[48] A montage of East Los Angeles street scenes that change slightly for each episode, the footage shows local scenery and Mexican American families enjoying a day in a park, including such sights as young men playing soccer, Chicana/o murals, a small boy toddling among the pigeons, a young woman in a wedding dress, and a couple enjoying a ride in a lowrider car painted with flowers. Almost no Anglos are seen; they are peripheral. The sequence thus hints at the many stories that could be told about Mexican Americans. As such it could be considered a promise, one the series never delivered, of something that hadn't been experienced in television before: a portrayal of daily life from a Mexican American perspective. Notable as well is that Chico Rodriguez and Ed Brown are not shown interacting in this world.

The character of Chico as portrayed by Freddie Prinze did challenge former tropes of Hollywood Latinidad that designated Latina/o and particularly Mexican American characters as ineffective and inferior, moreover. For one, the presence of a character written as Chicano and the hiring of a Latino actor to portray Chico offered transgressive potential in and of itself—although arguably, not to the same degree as if a Mexican American actor had been hired.[49] It was also a first to have a major character that was proudly Chicano on prime-time television. And Chico's *Chicanismo* is made central as early as the pilot. In the episode storyline, Chico decides to sneak back into

Ed's garage and to clean it up and move in, despite Ed's refusal to give him a job the day before. Some police officers come by and want to arrest him on suspicion of some thefts in the area, even though they have no proof that he was actually involved. They ask if he even has papers to prove he's legal, and this is his response: "Why; you got papers to prove where you were born? I'm a Chicano, man; I was born in this country. And what's more, we had it first! *Una pregunta chota* [Chicano slang for "a typical cop question"] . . . And you people are the outsiders. I *hablo* your English; why can't you *habla* a little Español?"

The reaction from the studio audience was one of raucous applause after this monologue, very likely a prime-time first with respect to its blatant expression of Chicana/o identity. (It goes without saying that Chicana/o political activism was co-opted later in the episode, however. When Ed subsequently provides an alibi for Chico, his glib response is "Viva la Raza!") While the series never followed through on further constructing a Chicano identity for Chico, aside from such props as a "Chicano power" badge sewn to his jacket and Pancho Villa poster hung in the van that he made into his bedroom, moments such as these were powerful ruptures in the typical televisual representation of Latinidad.

In addition, analysis of episodes throughout the three seasons that Freddie Prinze was on the show reveals other moments of ideological rupture. Even while the character of Chico often can be viewed as subservient to Ed, as portrayed by Freddie Prinze he also was a cocky "SuperMex," an effective motivator, businessman, and light-hearted rebel poking fun at mainstream notions of propriety. (As Chico notes in "Lifestyle" in the first season, "Life is chicks, kicks, and champagne!" To which Ed retorted it would soon be "pills, bills, and prune juice.") And given Prinze's considerable talent and energy, his performances typically spilled beyond the bounds of his character, for example in his constant mix of accents and ethnic impersonations, which made clear that Chico himself was an impersonation. Prinze also often inserted moments from his comedy performances into his characterization of Chico. For example, in "Veterans," Prinze as Chico launches into a humorous commentary on the importance of having credit to get credit in the United States, into which he manages to insert a satirical critique of class privilege. A less politically incisive example was a warmly funny monologue in the third episode, "Old Dog," in which Prinze used various accents to demonstrate the personalities of an Italian car, a Japanese car, and a British car.

The series in fact consistently offered up moments, as Oguss notes, "to engage with and interrogate cultural signs of Otherness in comparison with whiteness."[50] In other words, occasionally it was whiteness rather than Latino identity that was made strange and de-centered in the dialogue and, less often, narratives of the series. The surprise reversal of Latina/o stereotypes and Spanish was used at times at the expense of Ed and other white characters. For example, Spanish was occasionally used in a manner that privileged bilingual viewers, as when Chico made comments to himself in Spanish that demonstrated his true frustration with Ed's behavior, or in scenes in which English-speaking characters misunderstand the Spanish being spoken around them. Oguss cites an example that occurred in "Natural Causes," in which a doctor talks to Chico about his dying car—and Ed thinks it must be him that is dying.[51]

Through moments such as these, a Latino and Prinze's own sensibility is at times prominent in the series. Such moments of rupture, while perhaps contributing to the popularity of *Chico and the Man* for many fans, were nonetheless targeted by producers by the end of the second season as disruptive to its success. A memo recapping a development meeting of the creative producers indicated that their plans to improve the show included: "Reestablish Chico's original wide-eyed enthusiasm and play down the cynical, smart aleck attitude which has crept into his performances."[52] While in part the producers may have been commenting on the acting of a more downbeat Freddie Prinze by the end of the second season, it also seems possible that his "smart aleck" demeanor was just too confident for (their vision of) a Latino character; it was too challenging to the hegemonic ideals that continued to undergird the series. It seems unsurprising that Freddie Prinze often told reporters before his death that one of his dreams was to produce and star in a series of his own making.

* * *

Despite the production team's attempt to portray Latina/os in a politically correct manner in *Chico and the Man,* the series suffered from its lack of Latina/o creative input and the difficult negotiation between ethnic humor and a "can't we all get along" fantasy on which the storylines were based. Ultimately, negotiations between the series producers and Chicana/o critics of the show broke down because "each wanted something quite different for Chicanos within episodic television," as Noriega points out.[53] Freddie Prinze, in a related note, had to deal with fame that was constantly under fire because of his role as a contested Mexican American (and later, more generally Latino) character within the series, even while he also lived with the burden of being the only actor in a Latino lead role on U.S. television.

Given his youth and inexperience with the industry, it isn't surprising if he found his fame and the myriad expectations that came with it to be stressful, exacerbating his battles with depression and drug addiction that led to his eventual death by drug overdose.

The multivalent and contradictory representation of Chico Rodriguez and of Freddie Prinze as an American star, and particularly the negotiations that took place behind the scenes of *Chico and the Man,* provide a telling illustration of the evolving negotiations and shifts that were taking place in network television with respect to Latina/o representation in this time period. While the Big Three networks were experiencing pressure from advocacy groups to increase and improve Latina/o and particularly Mexican American representation, there were virtually no Latina/o writers or producers with enough experience within the industry to be included on the production team—or at least that is what the producers appear to have believed. Notably, a few other Chicana/os and other Latina/os were employed in nominal, but not creative positions (two Latina/o production assistants were added to the series production staff in the first season, for instance). The visibility and success of Freddie Prinze as a result of the series, meanwhile, offered a reminder of the Latina/o voices that were still not included in narrative programming. In this regard, the series and Prinze's stardom reflected and also challenged network and national notions of Mexican American, Latina/o, and American ethnic identities and remained a contested forum of Latina/o representation during its time on the air.

As mentioned earlier, the series continued to be a ratings success while Freddie Prinze was on it, despite complaints by some viewers. The stars also were critically recognized for their work; Jack Albertson was awarded an Emmy in 1976, while Prinze was nominated for a Golden Globe the following year. Reportedly in the fall of 1976, he had signed a new contract with NBC, which was to provide over $6 million for five seasons of work. Prinze also had begun to work in other arenas, as well as continuing to perform stand-up comedy. For instance, he starred in a made-for-television movie, *The Million Dollar Rip Off,* as an electronics genius who pulls off a heist with the assistance of four "lady friends," in 1976.[54] Not long before his death, he also had performed at President Jimmy Carter's inauguration celebration.

Recent years have brought about a resurgence of appreciation for Freddie Prinze's genius and particularly for the importance of his presence in mid-1970s popular culture, particularly after *Chico and the Man* episodes were re-run on the TVLand network in 2001. In November 2004, Prinze was honored posthumously with a star on the Hollywood Walk of Fame, at a ceremony where his son emotionally accepted this recognition for his father. The name of Freddie Prinze Jr.'s production company, Hunga Rican, Excitable Boy! and the company's verbal signature, Prinze Sr.'s "Looking good!" also serves as a constant reminder of Freddie Prinze's legacy.

As a series like Freddie Prinze Jr.'s *Freddie* illustrates, Latina/o opportunity in the television industry has in some respects improved dramatically since the days of *Chico and the Man*. The new ABC series *Ugly Betty*, which is performing strongly in the ratings and garnered Golden Globes and Emmys both for the series and its star, America Ferrera, in 2007, in particular points to increasing potential for Latina/os in the realm of television. The under-representation of Latina/o characters and culture on U.S. television outside a few series like *Ugly Betty* is a cause for continued concern, however; while the proportion of Latina/os in the United States has continued to grow, television story worlds have not kept pace.[55] There also continue to be challenges to representing Latina/o characters and culture, considering that Latina/os still make up typically less than 2 percent of creative professionals in the industry.[56] So have we really come that far since *Chico and the Man* and Freddie Prinze's struggles as the only Hungarican Chicano on TV?

5

The Face of the "Decade"

*Edward James Olmos and
Latino Films of the 1980s*

Latina/o creative agency was to bring about the next influential shift in Hollywood Latinidad, with the 1980s the backdrop for this turning point. While not the full-blown "Decade of the Hispanic" trumpeted by the mainstream news media, it was a period when the first Latino-helmed feature films,[1] most produced independently but distributed by both independent and Hollywood-backed companies, reached national audiences.[2] A handful were financially successful, and many received critical and popular acclaim. These films, built upon the legacy of Chicano independent cinema, included *Zoot Suit* (1981), *El Norte* (1983), *La Bamba* (1987), *Born in East L.A.* (1987), and *Stand and Deliver* (1988). With respect to films that received at least limited distribution, this period also witnessed the first feature films by Cuban American filmmakers, including *El Súper* (1979) and *Crossover Dreams* (1985).[3] Collectively these films presented a Latino perspective on U.S. history and contemporary life, in stark contrast to films of classical Hollywood that had typically posed Latina/os as outsiders or at best sidekicks or temporary love interests. They also offered more interesting and compelling roles to Latina and Latino actors than had existed in feature films to date—key with respect to opportunities for audience identification and, ultimately, stardom.

In the mainstream press coverage that ensued about the new Latino films and the growth of Latina/os as a population and consumer market, Mexican American actor Edward James Olmos was the individual who received the most attention; he was promoted particularly in the late 1980s as a rising star and a symbol of the reportedly "new" Latina/o visibility in U.S. film and popular culture. For instance, Olmos's visage in an urban mural graced the cover of a *Time* magazine special issue on Latina/os in U.S. popular culture on July 11, 1988. He also was the only actor to be profiled at length in the issue. A decade later, Olmos's centrality and fame in relation to the Latino films of this period were immortalized in an illustration by Mexican American cartoonist Lalo Alcaraz when he put Olmos at the center of his "Pochtecha Calendar of Raza Popular Culture."[4] This humorous take on a Mexican calendar appeared in a special section of the *San Francisco Bay Guardian* in March 1998. The caption notes that Olmos, dubbed "Olmotzin," is deified in the calendar because of his ubiquitous presence in Latina/o popular culture, "from *Miami Vice* to every major film featuring Latino subject matter."[5]

As Alcaraz and others since have noted, Olmos was a central feature in this first wave of Latino feature films and particularly in their mainstream media coverage. Among other performances, he appeared as El Pachuco in Luis Valdez's musical play and film *Zoot Suit,* as Gregorio Cortez in Moctesuma Esparza and Robert Y. Young's *The Ballad of Gregorio Cortez,* and as teacher Jaime Escalante in Ramón Menéndez's *Stand and Deliver.* He also worked actively to promote and at times helped produce these films. Partly as a result of his subsequent visibility, he was anointed a star by the mainstream media, which made him the public face of what was variously called "Hispanic Hollywood" or the "Decade of the Hispanic," labels that were problematic for reasons that I detail in this chapter. Many other actors busy in this Latino film wave received little notice, however. The rise of Olmos to become the most recognized star of these Latino-directed films thus raises questions regarding Hollywood's treatment of Latina/o and particularly of Mexican American actors and filmmakers in this time period.

As a star, Edward James Olmos has been promoted in a manner that has emphasized his Mexican American heritage and humble roots. As related in biographies of the actor-producer, Olmos was born in Los Angeles on February 24, 1947, to Eleanor Huizar and Pedro Olmos, who were, respectively, of Mexican American and Mexican descent; he grew up in the multicultural neighborhood of Boyle Heights in Los Angeles and in Montebello, California. Similarly, his star image has never rested on playing glamorous or romantic lead roles, but rather has been associated with character roles and multiple accolades for his talent. In fact, Edward James Olmos has been consistently recognized for his acting abilities; over the years, he has been awarded an Emmy, two Golden Globes, an Academy Award nomination, and a Tony nomination, in addition to multiple ALMA awards (American Latino Media Awards) and other accolades.[6] While he continues to make a vital contribution to the evolution of Hollywood's representation of Latini-

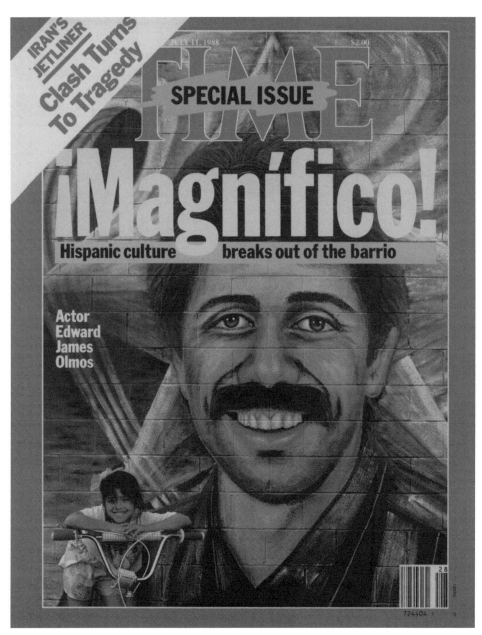

Edward James Olmos, featured on the cover of *Time*'s special issue on Latinos entering the mainstream of U.S. popular culture, on July 11, 1988. Reprinted through the courtesy of the Editors of TIME magazine © 2008 Time Inc.

dad in his current career and instrumental association with projects such as the Los Angeles International Latino Film Festival, in this chapter I focus on Olmos's early career and promotion, given the importance of his stardom in the 1980s to the evolution of Latina/o representation and creative agency.

A number of questions guide this exploration. As Latino filmmakers and Latino-themed films became visible in the Hollywood landscape during this decade, why was Olmos singled out for star promotion by the typically non-Latino news journalists? What was it about Olmos's performances, public persona, and/or critical response that led to the intense publicity that he received? And given the dearth of well-known Mexican American actors continuing to the present day, what can be learned from the promotion that surrounded Olmos in the 1980s regarding the treatment of Mexican American actors and actresses in Hollywood and how this relates to U.S. racial histories, borders, and identities?

1980s Hollywood and the Rise of Latino Films

The opportunities and stardom that Olmos experienced in the 1980s were made possible in part because of the growing visibility of films by Latino and (now at times) Latina film producers and other developments within the film industry. More specifically, alongside blockbuster production trends in this New Hollywood industry era, ethnic-oriented television programming and independent filmmaking began to be viewed as potentially profitable, encouraging the regional and national distribution of Latino-oriented films. As it became clear by 1980 that Latina/os were projected to surpass African Americans as the largest nonwhite group in the United States, that many Latina/os watched English-language and bilingual films and television, and as economic incentives such as tax breaks for film financiers encouraged financial investment in independent film projects, targeting the Latina/o audience was increasingly viable and of interest to investors and film studios.[7] A cadre of Latina/o and other nonwhite actors found acting opportunities and in fact compelling starring roles in the films that were subsequently produced during this period.

Shifts in the dominant racial paradigms that guided casting and star promotion began to be evident in the Hollywood star system in these years, seen most prominently in the success of African American actors Whoopi Goldberg and Eddie Murphy. Both starred in hit films, while Murphy was one of the top ten box office draws of the decade.[8] The earlier success of such television comedies as *All in the Family* (1971–77) and *Chico and the Man* (1974–78), and in the 1980s of *The Cosby Show* (1984–92), also encouraged Hollywood producers to develop projects that featured nonwhite actors in starring roles. Latina/os still experienced obstacles with respect to casting, however, particularly considering that *Chico and the Man* didn't achieve the long-term ratings peaks and consumer marketing potential that the *Cosby Show* franchise later experienced. But while opportunities in studio-backed films and on prime-time television had not substantially improved, Latina/os were beginning to take matters into their own hands with respect to filmmaking.

Latina/o feature filmmaking, much like Latina/o media activism targeting the mainstream media industries as discussed in the previous chapter, has its roots in the Chicana/o and Puerto Rican civil rights movements. As Chon Noriega, Charles Ramírez Berg, and Lillian Jiménez document, the first Latina- and Latino-directed films were produced by activist filmmakers utilizing their media production skills in support of their communities.[9] The first wave of films produced by these filmmakers in the late 1960s and 1970s was inspired by, at times recorded the activities of, and meant to support the goals of Chicana/o and Puerto Rican activism, and typically was motivated by such objectives as educating their communities about their history and encouraging ethnic self-pride. Documentary production was at first emphasized, in part because documentaries were affordable to produce, but also because they lent themselves well to these goals. Contemporary filmmakers whose early work was a part of this first wave of Chicana/o and Puerto Rican independent cinema include Luis Valdez, Moctesuma Esparza, Lourdes Portillo, Susan Racho, Jesus Treviño, Carlos De Jesús, and Beni Matías.

To focus on Chicana/o filmmakers, the first wave of media producers of this tradition initially aimed to create films by, for, and about Chicanos rather than for a national audience.[10] Another goal was to make films that would counter those of Hollywood, which were viewed by many activists as reiterating negative stereotypes and turning its few Latina/o employees into sellouts. A number of these early Chicana/o films, such as Jesus Treviño's *Yo Soy Chicano* (1972) and Susan Racho's *Garment Workers* (1975), were produced in conjunction with and appeared for the first time on the Chicano or Puerto Rican public affairs programs that aired on public television stations in the early 1970s.[11] Meanwhile, other Latina/o producers of the 1980s had gained experience working on the public affairs shows or in bilingual children's programming of the 1970s, such as the children's series *Carrascolendas,* which aired on PBS affiliate stations from 1970 to 1978.[12]

These individuals thus were among the wave of filmmakers of color that came into the public consciousness in this decade. As films such as Wayne

Wang's *Chan Is Missing* (1982), Spike Lee's *She's Gotta Have It* (1986), and Gregory Nava's *El Norte* made a splash at film festivals and with critics, they called attention to the potential profits to be earned from low-budget films for ethnic niche markets and art house audiences. *El Norte* and Luis Valdez's *Zoot Suit* were among the first Latino-oriented films that garnered critical attention, though neither made a great deal of money. They were joined by such films as *The Ballad of Gregorio Cortez* (1983), Cheech Marin's *Born in East L.A.* (1987), Valdez's *La Bamba* (1987), and Ramón Menéndez's *Stand and Deliver* (1988), in what was described in the mainstream press as a flourishing of Latino-written and -directed films.

With respect to Hollywood's construction of Latinidad, this amounted to a sea change of representation. Clearly, these films offered Latina/o actors some of their most interesting and well-developed roles to date. Actors and actresses who were showcased in Latino-helmed films included Mexican Americans Edward James Olmos, Lupe Ontiveros, and Elpidia Carrillo. A number of Latina/o actors of a variety of nationalities also broke into the mainstream in this decade in both Latino and mainstream films; they included Cuban actor Andy Garcia, Puerto Rican Raul Julia, Irish-Cuban Mercedes Ruehl, and Maria Conchita Alonso, a Venezuelan of Cuban descent. Some of the so-called rising Latina/o stars of the 1980s were not even of Latino descent, however; in particular, Lou Diamond Phillips, the heavily promoted star of *La Bamba* and *Stand and Deliver,* was of mixed Philippine descent and not Mexican American as was initially believed.

As Henry Puente notes, these films did not make a huge amount of money, but all had been produced and marketed on very small budgets.[13] The small-scale successes of these projects thus helped spark an awareness in the industry of the Latina/o audience. The success of *La Bamba,* about the life of Mexican American rock star Richie Valens, made a particular impact because of Columbia's successful, simultaneous release of the film in a first-ever Spanish-dubbed version, resulting in record profits for a Latino-focused film. As it became known that the Latina/o population was growing at a rate of 65 percent and had rapidly expanding buying power, the media industries, along with advertisers, increasingly began to recognize them as a potential consumer force and to track their media habits, as Arlene Dávila and Puente note.[14]

As a result of such shifts, a handful of film projects and television series with Latina/o themes began to be developed by studios and production companies in the 1980s. Gary Keller notes that the growing "population power and consequently political, economic, and cultural importance [of Latina/os] spurred all sorts of film, television, and video initiatives for and by U.S. Hispanics."[15] While only a minute number would actually make the leap to production through the early 1990s, this attention in the realm of development acknowledged that it would be wise to address Latina/os as a potential audience.

Olmos's First Years as an Actor: Scrambling for Opportunity

Throughout his career, Edward James Olmos's acting abilities and critical popularity have been acknowledged through multiple awards and award nominations for his performances. He also has chosen roles wisely. In addition to the seminal roles that he has played in Chicano and Latino films, he has appeared in highly successful mainstream projects such as the film *Bladerunner* (1982) and the television series *Miami Vice* (1984–89), and more recently *Battlestar Galactica* (2003, 2004–).

His star promotion, even more notably, has emphasized how Olmos has built his career through determination, hard work, and sacrifice. This begins with his biography, which Olmos has shared with numerous journalists. According to the details of his childhood that he has shared, when he was a child his parents divorced; he turned to baseball to distract himself and found he enjoyed the challenge of perfecting his skills on the ball field. He later shifted his attention to rock music. Before graduating from high school, Olmos formed his first rock band. He wasn't a great singer, he has stressed, but he applied himself to improving. He was known in particular for his energetic performances on stage.[16] Some years later his band, Eddie James and the Pacific Ocean, was popular enough to play at nightclubs on the Sunset Strip in Los Angeles. Despite having little time to study while a musician, he pursued a college education. It was at California State University–Los Angeles that he took his first acting classes, initially just to improve his stage presence as a musician. Soon acting became equally important to Olmos, and he began to pursue a career as an actor. While still a musician, Olmos had met a young woman named Kaija Keel, the daughter of actor Howard Keel, former MGM musical star (who coincidentally had been the star of *Pagan Love Song,* one of Rita Moreno's first films). They married in 1971 and later had two sons, Bodie and Mico. Olmos continued to study acting and pursued roles in plays, films, and television. To support his acting, Olmos founded a business moving antique furniture.

Edward James Olmos reportedly had to scramble to find roles, and his first were minor parts that offered little acting challenge. He got occasional television roles, as small-time criminals and bartenders, on such series as *Hawaii Five-O* (1968–80) and *Kojak* (1973–78). (He once noted to an interviewer: "I was the only person Jack Lord [the star of *Hawaii Five-O*] shot in the back, ever. That's how bad I was.")[17] His first, small roles in films also included a part as a Mexican American hoodlum in *Aloha, Bobby and Rose* (1971) and as a drunk in the more socially conscious *Alambrista!* (1978), an independently produced film about the struggles of a Mexican undocumented immigrant. This film, which earned the Palm d'Or at the Cannes Film Festival, began his friendship with its director, Robert M. Young, who has since directed Olmos in multiple projects.

In 1978, Olmos had a major breakthrough in a musical play directed by Luis Valdez, *Zoot Suit*, after an audition that he reportedly stumbled upon. His role was that of El Pachuco, a larger-than-life pachuco figure who struts and speaks the frank truth of Mexican American experience.[18] Based on historical events, the play related the story of the Sleepy Lagoon trial in the mid-1940s, when a group of young Mexican American men were wrongly accused of a murder and did not receive a fair trial. This miscarriage of justice is now considered an illustration of the discrimination Mexican Americans commonly experienced in this time period.[19] In Valdez's retelling of the event, the trial of the fictionalized Henry Reyna (played by Luis Valdez's brother, Daniel Valdez, in the original play and film versions) was brought to life with swing music numbers and sweeping drama, held together in large part by the El Pachuco figure, who serves as narrator.[20] Perhaps unsurprisingly, the promotional poster centrally featured Olmos as El Pachuco, standing proudly in his drapes (slang for the suit favored by the pachucos), an iconic illustration of the proud Chicano ethos of the narrative.

The play, which opened in 1978 at the Mark Taper Forum in Los Angeles, was a smash hit, selling out both this theater and later the Aquarius Theater in Hollywood over many months. When it subsequently traveled to the Broadway stage in 1979 it did not do well, however; it closed after five weeks with a loss of $825,000.[21] Yolanda Broyles-Gonzalez, in exploring the reasons for the play's failure on Broadway, found that some critics of the East Coast theater establishment, in particular those reviewing the play for the *New York Times* and *New Yorker,* harshly panned it in a manner that implied a defensiveness over *Zoot Suit'*s focus on racism, in addition to a predisposition against its *rasquache* aesthetic and upstart status as a play that had arrived as a West Coast hit.[22] Although critics from other news outlets praised the play, theatergoers may have been swayed by the negative reviews and did not flock to see it.[23] Despite the attempt to target Latina/o communities in the New York region in *Zoot Suit*'s marketing campaign, it appears the campaign did not reach its target audience, and Latina/os did not see the play in great numbers. Broyles-Gonzalez speculates that this was likely because of associations of white-centric exclusivity attached to Broadway theatergoing, while the lack of a large Mexican American population among New York-area Latina/os likely also played a role.[24]

Olmos's performance on Broadway still garnered positive attention, however (even, notably, from the *New York Times*), and he was later nominated for a Tony and awarded the Los Angeles Drama Critics Circle Award and Theater World Award for his performance. When the play was later adapted into a film with backing from Universal Pictures, Olmos recreated his performance. In *Zoot Suit* (1981), Edward James Olmos as El Pachuco is simultaneously narrator, conscience, and trickster who bears historical witness to the injustice experienced by Henry Reyna and his friends. As he warns Henry after his arrest, "Look out, ese. You don't deserve it, but you're going to get it anyway!" As El Pachuco, Olmos skillfully conveyed cool, pride, and outrage in a mesmerizing performance. Again, most of the promotional posters and publicity stills for the film centered on the figure of El Pachuco, standing defiantly.

While critics' reactions to the film were varied (on the negative end, *Variety* noted that it was unclear whether audiences would be interested in "the specialized material," and the *New York Times* was again unimpressed), many praised Olmos's acting and the unique character he portrayed.[25] For example, Kevin Thomas of the *Los Angeles Times* called El Pachuco "the ultimate mythical zoot-suiter, the epitome of cool."[26] Edward James Olmos was to learn later in his career that Mexican Americans who saw the film considered him not just a star but a legend because he had played El Pachuco. Latina/os who were not Mexican American did not always consider his character a positive role model, however. As Puente notes, diverging reactions to the film by Latina/os around the country pointed to the complexity of attempting to garner a universal Latina/o film audience, an impossibility given the distinctly different histories, cultures, and relationships to U.S. social institutions experienced by Mexican Americans, Puerto Ricans, Cuban Americans and other Latina/os in various regions.[27]

Despite the fact that the film wasn't seen widely, it garnered Olmos's first promotion as a national star. In a development that was to become a trend in his budding career, a feature story on *Zoot Suit* that was published in the *New York Times* ended up focusing largely on Olmos himself, addressing among other things his childhood in multicultural Los Angeles and efforts since to establish himself as an actor. Olmos explained that one of his early

Edward James Olmos as El Pachuco in the film version of *Zoot Suit* (1981). Universal / The Kobal Collection.

inspirations was witnessing work on film sets with a friend when a guard at one of the studios would let them in, providing a hint of how Mexican Americans might see themselves as outsiders looking in on a film industry literally situated in their backyard. Olmos also spoke eloquently about the importance of Mexican American representation in the mainstream media. "If I never again play anything but a Mexican American, I will feel fortunate," he was quoted as saying. "There are so many stories that have to be done, and somebody has to do them. Who am I going to leave them for? Marlon Brando?"[28] With this statement the actor posed a provocative comparison with the mention of Brando, who had played the Mexican revolutionary hero Emiliano Zapata in *Viva Zapata!* in 1952, in just one of many instances of "brownface" performance of a Latino character in a Hollywood film. Edward James Olmos's own rise to fame in fact was a sign of the shift within the film industry as Latina/os began to be able to produce films based on their own perspective and stories and as Latina/o actors were much more likely to be cast in compelling Latina/o roles. His growing career also signaled the new possibilities for Latina/o stardom in the shifting media landscape.

Discourses of Determination and Talent: Olmos's 1980s Films and Promotion

On the wings of *Zoot Suit,* Olmos soon had roles of a variety of ethnicities offered to him. He appeared as a Mohawk Indian and shape-shifting wolf man in *Wolfen* (1981) and was offered the title role in *The Ballad of Gregorio Cortez* (1982). With respect to the first role, Olmos told journalists that he insisted that the film producers first make a concerted effort to find an American Indian actor before he would consent to taking the role, to the extent that his casting later received official tribal sanction.[29] Olmos's performance reportedly also convinced director Ridley Scott to cast him in the role of Gaff, a mysterious police informant in the now-classic *Bladerunner* (1982), set in the futuristic twenty-first century. As a citizen of the future, Gaff is appropriately multicultural; Olmos as Gaff has blue eyes and what seem to be Asian features, and speaks multiple languages. Although Olmos was not promoted heavily with the release of the series, the film's critical success and cult status with audiences ensured that he was taken more seriously as an actor. Olmos next reportedly turned down a role in *Scarface* (1983), saying, "I just couldn't find myself in that movie."[30] His promotional texts in this period thus already painted Olmos as an actor who took the craft seriously and would go to great lengths to successfully embody a role, which served to construct his public image as accomplished and talented, a serious actor that Christine Geraghty in her taxonomy of stardom would describe as a "star-as-performer."[31] This characterization would serve Olmos well throughout this decade.

Olmos next starred in a film financed through the PBS American Playhouse series and broadcast on public television, *The Ballad of Gregorio Cortez* (1982). The film, based on historical events that have been made legend through a well-known Mexican American corrido, told the story of a Mexican American man in South Texas at the turn of the twentieth century who becomes the target of a posse of Texas Rangers after killing a sheriff in self-defense.[32] The shooting had taken place because of a misunderstanding based on language barriers. Producer Moctesuma Esparza, who wanted to bring this tale of cultural misunderstanding and Mexican American bravery to the screen, cast Olmos as Gregorio Cortez and reportedly allowed him to pick his own director; Olmos picked Robert M. Young. Olmos also had a creative voice as they considered the approach the film would take. For instance, he spearheaded the idea of having the characters speak whatever language was historically accurate, without subtitles, to make audiences experience a sense of the language barriers that contributed to the incident.[33] Olmos also portrayed Cortez using very little dialogue. Rosa Linda Fregoso has commented that the character is reminiscent of the stereotypical American Indian "noble savage" because of Cortez's almost mute status throughout much of the film narrative.[34] Interestingly, for many non-Latino reviewers this dynamic often only added to the poignancy of the character and his story. As Tina Daniell of the *Hollywood Reporter* noted, "It is a part with few spoken lines, which makes Olmos' extraordinarily moving performance all the more remarkable. Cortez' fear, sadness, pride and anger are expressed unmistakably in Olmos' weatherbeaten face."[35] While the film was not seen widely, it added to Olmos's cultural capital and reputation as a committed actor.

Given that the film debuted on television, distributors were reluctant to take it on for a national theatrical release, however. This thus marked Olmos's first foray into film exhibition and promotion; he made it his mission to have the film seen by many audiences as possible. What followed was several years of Olmos and Moctesuma Esparza "fourwalling" the film—literally renting out a screen at theaters in cities such as San Antonio and Los Angeles, and personally offering screenings, advertised largely through Latina/o organizations and word of mouth.[36] These actions ultimately led to the film's distribution deal. An extension of these efforts was the indirect promotion of Olmos as an actor, promoter of Latino-themed film representation, and increasingly as a star.

In 1984, a very different opportunity came Edward James Olmos's way when he was offered a recurring role as Lieutenant Castillo of the Miami police department on the television series *Miami Vice* (1984–89). Initially reluctant to take on the role, Olmos was able to negotiate a contract that allowed him not only to work on other projects but also to have a great deal of creative control over the development of his character, both stipulations that were instrumental in his success at that time. While the lead characters of Miami police detectives Sonny Crockett and Ricardo Tubbs (Don Johnson and Phillip Michael Thomas) were clearly the stars of the show, Lieutenant Castillo became known as its heart, the moral center of the series. Olmos provided a serious and compelling presence in the role and was recognized many times for his solid acting. His contractual flexibility also allowed him to work on occasional films, such as *Saving Grace* (1986). Olmos plays an Italian bully in this drama about a pope who decides to pose as an ordinary person in order to experience life among the populace.

Throughout this period, Olmos spent much of his free time as a community activist. Feature articles on the actor after the *Ballad of Gregorio Cortez* release often detailed the many community organizations to which he would lend his time and lectures that he would give in the community, particularly at schools, youth organizations, and prisons. As Pat Aufderheide noted in *Mother Jones* in 1983, Olmos began to receive invitations to speak for organizations in part because of the symbolic importance of his character of El Pachuco to the Latina/o communities.[37] He estimated that he spoke to as many as three thousand people a week at various functions. Again, a rhetoric of hard work and determination was emphasized and often appeared to bring Olmos further media coverage.

Olmos's personal commitment to social service and acting career dovetailed with his next project. He reportedly became interested in the story on which *Stand and Deliver* was based after reading a newspaper article about teacher Jaime Escalante. Escalante, a calculus teacher at Garfield High School, a primarily Latina/o neighborhood of Los Angeles, was being recognized for his excellence as a teacher. Record numbers of his students had passed the national Advanced Placement Test for calculus, only to be accused of cheating; they were finally vindicated after passing the test a second time. When Tom Musca and Ramón Menéndez wrote a script about Escalante's story, Olmos signed on to play the teacher and also became a co-producer of the film.

Olmos reportedly threw himself into the role in true Method actor fashion. He was noted to have undergone extensive work to fill Jaime Escalante's shoes on screen, including spending hundreds of hours poring over videotapes

Edward James Olmos as calculus teacher Jaime Escalante in *Stand and Deliver* (1988).

of Escalante in the classroom, gaining forty pounds, and otherwise pains-takingly embodying Escalante. After the film wrapped, he also engaged in countless screenings for educator associations, advocacy organizations, and even then-President Ronald Reagan that played a key role in the visibility and later success of the film. Olmos is quoting as saying to an enthusiastic audience of United Farm Workers, "This film about our people will touch the nation. It shows we can achieve anything we want."[38]

The film ultimately grossed about $14 million domestically. Reactions by critics also were overwhelmingly positive. Donna Britt at *USA Today,* for instance, called *Stand and Deliver* "a small-scale marvel—proud without preaching, sympathetic without condescending, and funny," while *Newsweek* declared it "tremendously compelling."[39] Olmos was constantly singled out for praise as well. Janet Maslin noted in the *New York Times,* "Mr. Olmos seems to be living and breathing this role rather than merely playing it, and his enthusiasm really catches on."[40] The discussion soon buzzed about a potential Best Actor Academy Award nomination, which was later made official.

Unsurprisingly, feature coverage of the film focused on parallels between Olmos and the teacher he portrays in *Stand and Deliver,* in particular through discussion of Olmos's dedication to social activism and to communities in Los Angeles. As the *Los Angeles Weekly* noted: "In real life terms, Olmos never really left. He's a fixture in the LA arts community, as well as a community activist."[41] Olmos himself was quick to praise Jaime Escalante in interviews. As he said in one, "[Escalante] has an ability to motivate people, to do things of value like self-education, self-discipline, perseverance, determination."[42] To which journalist Pat Hilton added, "He [Olmos] might be describing himself."[43]

Representing the "Decade of the Hispanic"

As noted earlier, *Stand and Deliver* and other of Olmos's films were part of a cycle of feature films by Latino filmmakers in the 1980s; these were some of the first films with national distribution that told stories from a distinctly Latino point of view and related such scenarios of U.S. Latina/o life as coping with immigration-related conflicts and generational differences, blending Latina/o and Euro-American perspectives in raising a family, and coping with racial misunderstanding and prejudice. As Jason C. Johansen noted in a *Los Angeles Times* op-ed piece in 1981, film executives were divided on whether there was enough of a market for such films.[44] Susan Merzbach, then-vice president of creative affairs for Twentieth Century-Fox, noted that after the success of *Zoot Suit* on stage, "Maybe only now . . . do some of us feel a little more confident about the film market potential."[45] News coverage of films such as *La Bamba* and *El Norte* also fed this trend. Many in the industry were not convinced, however. An unnamed Warner Bros. executive called the film version of *Zoot Suit* a "luxury," implying that it would not be of interest to a mass audience.[46]

Interestingly, the handful of Latino-oriented film successes was treated dramatically in the mainstream press, which declared these films part of a new "Hispanic Hollywood" or "Decade of the Hispanic," in much the same manner as the so-called Latin Explosion was more recently declared in the late 1990s. The emphasis on the term "Hispanic" was timely, and also meaningful. The term had come into federal government parlance in 1980, when it began to be used as a pan-ethnic term on the U.S. Census. It was (and is) increasingly seen as a problematic label by many Latina/os because of how it privileged Spanish, and thus European, over indigenous ancestry and elided the specific histories of Mexican Americans and other Latino groups, however.[47] This clash of opinions provides insight into the problematic aspects of the media coverage that accompanied and to a large degree constructed Hollywood's "Decade of the Hispanic."

First, the news coverage of Latino-themed films had an odd tone that marked them as distinctly new and different from other U.S. films. (The phrase also happened to have its genesis in the realm of advertising; it was used by Coors to advertise beer to Latina/os in a short-lived commercial campaign. In response, the Chicano comedy troupe Culture Clash was known to quip in their 1992 act, "The Decade of the Hispanic turned out to be a weekend sponsored by Coors.") For example, on August 18, 1987, *Newsweek* trumpeted a "new Latin beat on celluloid."[48] Bruce Corwin, the owner of the largest Spanish-language theater chain in the nation, was quoted describing *La Bamba* as a breakthrough with respect to reaching out to the Hispanic market. It did not, however, note that Hispanic viewers were already a part of the larger American audience. The article also posited what chroniclers of Latina/o popular culture already knew, the understanding that "Hispanic actors can be stars."[49]

As can be discerned in *Newsweek*'s comment, an ambiguous strain ran through the mainstream media's description of these films and their stars. In addition, the term "crossover" began to be used to describe financially successful Latino films, as well as to label the Latina and Latino actors that appeared in these films, regardless of whether they were American or Latin American–born and whether they spoke English, Spanish, or both. Ultimately, Latina/o actors were made to appear more exotic through many of their descriptions in this coverage. For instance, *Time*, in its special issue with Olmos on its cover, reported much the same "news" on rising Latina/o visibility in popular culture that *Newsweek* had a year earlier, stating: "More and more, American film, theater, music, design, dance and art are taking on a Hispanic color and spirit. Look around. You can see the special lighting, the distinctive gravity, the portable wit, the personal spin. The new marquee names have a Spanish ring: Edward James Olmos, Andy Garcia, Maria Conchita Alonso."[50] While on its surface such commentary appeared celebratory, ultimately it only reinforced figurative boundaries of U.S. popular culture. Even U.S.-born Latina/os thus were marked as foreigners and racialized as nonwhite—not coincidentally, at exactly the juncture when Latina/os were finally able to speak for themselves in film. Kathleen Newman aptly describes the problematic and ultimately limiting aspects of this spin on Latina/o culture and Latina/o stars, asserting that "*Time* magazine believed it permissible to state that (a) Latino culture is not U.S. culture, (b) it is new, and (c) it principally involves entertainment and aesthetics but not the political-economic structures of the nation."[51] Ultimately, the desire to reassure (presumably white) readers that Latina/os and Latina/o culture still resided at the margins of U.S. society appears central to the media discourse in the late 1980s.

It was within this social context and industrial "buzz," coupled with ambivalence expressed in the news media around Latino-themed projects and stars, that Edward James Olmos became the most heavily promoted Mexican American and in fact Latino star in Hollywood promotional texts. In exploring Olmos's roles and publicity in these years, a number of themes emerge that begin to explain why he became the face of the Decade of the Hispanic. For Olmos to become "Olmotzin," he had to represent what was most palatable for mainstream producers, reviewers, and audiences about what was now being construed as "Hispanic Hollywood." This was accomplished in part through the establishment of Olmos's image as a hard-working and talented actor of the Method variety, as noted earlier; in this sense it could be implied that he had "earned" his membership in the Hollywood star system through hard work and the sheer intensity and verisimilitude of his performances, rather than through simply being an American actor of considerable appeal. This was made possible through his star image being painted in broad strokes in the mainstream media, often by Olmos himself in interviews, as the star's promotion in this period stressed his storied acting career in socially conscious roles, discipline, and community service work.

Promoting Olmos as central to "Hispanic Hollywood" thus could reassure that not only were Latina/os still in marginal positions in U.S. popular culture, but they were also uplifting their race through the minor visibility that they had achieved. Given the foregrounding of his acting abilities and of a "discourse of citizenship," as Newman terms it, in his star promotion, it makes sense that Edward James Olmos was chosen to represent the Latino film wave of the 1980s.[52] Such associations arguably were necessary for a Latino and particularly for a Mexican American actor to be comfortably embraced in mainstream, popular culture texts at the time.

In addition, Olmos's status as a character actor and a physical appearance that likely precluded producers from viewing him as a romantic lead, arguably ensured that his stardom did not disturb the film and television industry's racial paradigms even while he was held up as a representative of the new "Hispanics" in Hollywood. Given Hollywood's preferred "Latin look" and the comfort of producers with casting Latina/os as a range of nonwhite ethnicities, Olmos's tan skin tone, indigenous features, and rough-hewn skin mark him as always, comfortably ethnic. As Victor Valle notes, despite the variety of roles that Olmos played and the ethnic fusion that he felt was central to his personal identity, in 1980s media coverage the actor almost unfailingly was portrayed as an "ethnic artist . . . *Stand and Deliver* underdog and son of immigrants preaching the bootstrap gospel of hard work and self-responsibility."[53]

The roles Olmos portrayed in this decade further established his non-threatening status in this regard. He played a number of secondary characters in mainstream film and television projects, such as his roles in *Bladerunner* and *Miami Vice*. Admittedly in this New Hollywood era such roles were at times more compelling and dimensional than in the past; Olmos also has always been skillful at fleshing out and subverting roles that might appear one-dimensional on paper through his performances. Ultimately these characters serve to support the more idealized lead characters, however. His Latino roles of the 1980s fit within the character actor mold in a number of ways as well. While he portrayed several Latino heroes, these typically were humble characters that achieve their accomplishments through intelligence and perseverance rather than through force or bravado. Examples include Gregorio Cortez and Jaime Escalante.[54] Association with such characters likely offered comfortable difference but not challenge to Hollywood paradigms and the U.S. star system.

Edward James Olmos's star image as a tireless worker for the community also supported the comfortable construction of the 1980s Latino films by the mainstream news media as colorful and well meaning, but not overly aggressive. Clearly, the wave of Latino films raised questions regarding the history of Hollywood "Jimcrowism [*sic*]" as experienced by Latina/os (to borrow Rita Moreno's term as mentioned in chapter 3) and continuing misperceptions of the Latina/o audience. But these films and filmmakers for the most part represented a sea change since the days of radical Chicana/o and

Latina/o cinema, as they sought entrance to the mainstream film industry rather than working completely outside or against it. Perhaps it is unsurprising, given the tensions that existed around such a shift, that performers who were perceived as nonthreatening would receive particular acclaim. As Newman has argued in relation to Hollywood narratives and Olmos's role on *Miami Vice,* a "trope of sacrifice" was foregrounded in Olmos's image; this was particularly the case in his role as Jaime Escalante.[55] The dominance of *Stand and Deliver*—a film that stresses self-sacrifice and hard work rather than interrogating the racism of the U.S. school system—in both Olmos's star publicity and that of "Hispanic Hollywood" of the late 1980s thus should be viewed as no coincidence.[56]

A smart self-promoter, Edward James Olmos skillfully engaged in this era in the construction of his "hardworking underdog" image, often while personally promoting his films. His keen sense of public appeal and effective way with words further supported his image construction in this regard. In particular, his quotes to the press often aimed to educate and inspire regarding the need to increase and improve media images of Latina/os and other people of color. For example, he told Charlotte Wolter of the *Hollywood Reporter* in 1989, "Would Martin Sheen have made it as Ramon Estevez? I think so . . . I think our industry is governed by a common base that supersedes color, race, or creed; that's the dollar. If you know how to make it, inevitably the industry turns its face away from what color you are."[57] He did not stop there, however, adding, "Our society does not value the human element enough to use the art form to explore different colors. Americans are of almost every race and culture in the world, but we look at only a very minute portion of it in our art forms."[58] The mainstream media's wish to provide a recognizable face for the string of Latino-produced films and film producers' desire for a bankable star through which to market their films also arguably played into these developments. As Reba L. Chaisson documents, the favoring of "name" actors continues to dominate the financing and distribution even of independent films, given the intense need for guaranteed audiences when producing even low-budget feature films and the boost that a star's name recognition and popularity can offer in this regard.[59] While Olmos was in fact the most ubiquitous actor in the string of Latino-directed films that were released in the 1980s, the media coverage that ensued about these films made him seem even more so. A telling illustration of this dynamic that Newman noted in her analysis of this period is the origin of the mural of Edward James Olmos that appeared on the cover of *Time* in 1988. As it turns out, the mural was not captured by a photographer but actually had been commissioned by the magazine (as the editors note, in the spirit of the "uplifting" tradition of mural art in Latina/o neighborhoods).[60] The *Time* editors, in glibly imitating this populist art form that Chicana/o (and similarly, Puerto Rican) artists and community members began to take up in the late 1960s as a means to creatively express their values and struggles with oppression, arguably elide Mexican American experience, activism, and art with an art work that instead reflects a distinctly nonpolitical "Hispanic" identity.[61] Edward James Olmos in the process is uplifted to hero standing in relation to this newly constructed pan-Latina/o group, his image replacing the more controversial figures that have graced actual community-produced murals, such as Pancho Villa, Emiliano Zapata, and Che Guevara. In the process, popular culture usurped politics, while *Time* created a national star. Such an artistic construction also could reassure readers that "Hispanics" were not threatening because they no longer needed or wished to fight political battles. Major economic and social disparities still existed between Mexican Americans and unambiguously white Americans, however; the mural and its symbolism merely posed a fantasy resolution.

In the 1990s, Edward James Olmos continued to make choices and get involved in projects that aimed to educate and inspire audiences. In 1992, he co-produced, directed, and starred in *American Me,* about gang life and the toll it was taking on Mexican American communities and individuals. A hard-hitting film, it reportedly was taken so seriously by certain gangs that Olmos and his crew often had to fear for their safety. Other films and television projects in which he has appeared include *A Burning Season* (1994), *A Million to Juan* (1994), *My Family/Mi Familia* (1995), *Selena* (1997), *In the Time of Butterflies* (2001), and the PBS drama *American Family* (2002). Edward James Olmos also directed *Walkout* (2006), an HBO film based on the real-life events that took place in 1968 when Mexican American high school students in the Los Angeles area staged walkouts from their schools to protest major inequities in their education. During these years, Olmos went through a divorce with Kaija Olmos after nineteen years of marriage. He married Lorraine Bracco in 1994 and became stepfather to her two daughters. As a result of these marriages, Olmos's blended family brought together Mexican, Swedish, Italian, British, and French ancestry. Olmos and Bracco have since divorced.

Edward James Olmos has become even more active as a spokesperson, organizer, and speaker for Latina/o community organizations and particularly as a champion for Latina/o media representation and media production in more recent years, illuminating the impact that one individual can have on the evolution of Hollywood Latinidad and on Latina/o lives and opportunity.

He is celebrated in another mural now, this one the genuine article. At the corner of Wilshire and Alvarado streets in Los Angeles, the building-high mural "Los Angeles Teachers" features teacher Jaime Escalante and Olmos dressed in character as Escalante. Painted in 1997 by artist Hector Ponce, the mural symbolizes how Olmos in fact has come to be viewed as a leader and teacher of Latina/os, other Angelenos, and Americans more generally, with a direct pedagogical function in addition to serving as a star icon. This appears to be a role the actor-producer continues to personally embrace. Among other efforts, he co-founded the Los Angeles Latino International Film Festival over a decade ago and became an organizer and the spokesperson for the Latino Book and Family Festival, which travels to cities throughout the Southwest, promotes Latina/o writers, and offers support to Latina/o communities and families on a variety of issues. Olmos also has recently lent his time and energy to such causes as protesting the bombing of Vieques Island in Puerto Rico and speaking out for the rights of Latina/o immigrants. Other recent projects, aside from his role on the *Battlestar Galactica* television series, include a bilingual drama based on Carlos Fuentes's *The Crystal Frontier,* about U.S.-Mexico border issues and their impact on individuals on each side of the border.

* * *

As mentioned earlier, Edward James Olmos is one of very few Mexican American actors to achieve star status in the realm of U.S. film or television. Although much of the progress achieved in Latina/o visibility and representation is due to the work of Mexican American activists, some of whom are now media producers (one industry insider jokingly referred to them as Hollywood's "Mexican mafia" during my research in Los Angeles), few Mexican American actors have been cast in lead roles and even fewer have been promoted in a manner that would encourage their stardom on a national or international level, making Olmos's stardom all the more important. Why have Mexican Americans remained largely unrepresented in this regard?

For one, this situation can be understood from a historically informed perspective on the internal colonization of Mexican Americans that continues to deny their presence or frames it in relation to "minority status," as Frances Aparicio and Cándida Jáquez note regarding the marginalization of Mexican American contributions to Latin and American musical styles.[62] Even while they constitute the majority of Latina/os, they are the most marginalized; it is a dynamic that bleeds through to social attitudes and beauty ideals such as can affect casting and promotional efforts. These dynamics are often less overt when it comes to film and television, however.

Typically they are manifest when Mexican American actors are not seen as embodying the preferred "Latin look," for example. Such standards favor a generic, hard-to-identify Latin appearance and European features over more indigenous, Mexicana features. As such it can be seen when producers and casting directors favor foreign-born Latina/os over Mexican American actors, even in the casting of Mexican American and Mexican roles. The casting of Paz Vega in *Spanglish* (2004) and Penelope Cruz in *All the Pretty Horses* (2000) are just two examples. As one Los Angeles talent agent noted in 2000, "Most of the new Latin actors are from Spain or Mexico . . . besides Catherine Zeta Jones!" Considering that Latin American media industries also tend to favor colonial (European) standards of beauty, these performers do not challenge Hollywood paradigms. In addition, as I was told in interviews with a Mexican American casting director, a Mexican American writer and acting trainer, and an Anglo-American agent who works largely with inexperienced Latina/o actors who find work as film extras, Mexican American acting hopefuls tend to vie for roles with an unequal hand to play, as they often have not had access to the acting training or theatrical experience of foreign-born or East Coast Latina/os. (A thought-provoking finding in my research is the fact that a number of Latina/o stars who hail from the East Coast had benefited from attending a performing arts–focused public high school in their youth. Such schools are part of the public school system in New York City but happen to be an anomaly in much of the Southwest, where the majority of Mexican Americans live.)

On the other hand—and this is where Edward James Olmos's busy resume makes perfect sense—Mexican American actors with darker skin and clearly indigenous features *have* at times experienced success with respect to getting cast in small, stereotypically Latina/o and ethnic roles in mainstream films. Where the all-too-visible glass ceiling exists for these actors is in subsequently being cast and promoted in lead roles and as potential stars. For example, Lupe Ontiveros, a talented Chicana from Texas, has had a busy career playing Latina mothers and maids, including roles in Latino-directed films such as *El Norte* (1983), *My Family/Mi Familia* (1995), and *Real Women Have Curves* (2002), and in films such as *As Good as It Gets* (2007). But, as Chris Holmlund notes, Ontiveros's talent as a performer is typically overlooked because she lacks what are seen as "marketable looks"; her short, stocky body, dark tan skin, and indigenous facial features do not lend themselves to the fantasy of the Latina love interest/sex object that has been constructed by Hollywood tradition.[63] Ontiveros thus is a busy working actor but has not been promoted as a Hollywood star.

It should be emphasized, however, that Mexican American actors, like all Latina/os, possess a diversity of skin tones and appearance that cannot be pigeonholed into one "look"; it is those with darker and more indigenous features that face particular obstacles when competing against other Latina/os for roles that go beyond the old standbys of criminals and servants. Constance Marie, who has appeared in many Latina/o-directed films and recently portrayed George Lopez's wife on *The George Lopez Show,* for example, likely has experienced more opportunity due to her olive skin and European phenotypic features. Gendered notions also have played into the varying opportunities experienced by Mexican American actors. Mexican American men such as Edward James Olmos, in contrast to their female counterparts, are typically offered a wider range of roles, which provides more avenues for stardom. Jacob Vargas, for example, has had the opportunity to showcase his acting abilities in diverse roles, with a résumé that includes *Mi Vida Loca* (1993), *Get Shorty* (1995), and *Traffic* (2000).

Edward James Olmos, similar to the few other Mexican American actors busy working in films and television, began his career playing Latino criminals and other background characters. What was unique about Olmos's career in the 1980s, however, is that he also had the opportunity to portray Mexican American and Latino heroes of a wide variety. He imbued these roles with a humanity and spirit that caught the eye of critics and audiences, in addition to portraying small roles in highly successful mainstream films and television series, and together these developments set the stage for his future stardom. In this regard, Edward James Olmos clearly benefited from the trend of Latino feature filmmaking. Perhaps just as important, the pedagogical role that the star took on through his promotion aided in the process of breaking through the obstructions, ideological and industry-specific, that have traditionally deflected opportunities for Mexican American actors. In journalists' discussion of "Hispanic Hollywood" of the 1980s, he was framed as a self-sacrificing community leader. As such, he could symbolically reassure the (presumed white) American public that Latina/o film production—and Latina/o activism more generally—would work within and not against U.S. social institutions. Radical or not, however, Edward James Olmos has been a central figure in the ongoing development and promotion of Latina/o feature film production and Latina/o stardom, and in challenging Hollywood paradigms, to a degree that goes far above and beyond what chroniclers of the "Decade of the Hispanic" might have predicted. It will be essential to continue to study his successes, given his unique image and role, both in Hollywood and "Latinowood."

6

Crossing Over the Latina Body

Jennifer Lopez and the
1990s "Latin Wave"

It was a handful of photographs that appeared in *Entertainment Weekly* a decade ago that inspired the research that ultimately became this book. On October 9, 1998, then up-and-coming actress Jennifer Lopez headlined the week's cover story, on industry "divas." While that wasn't so unusual, the photographs that accompanied the story were. The cover photo showed Lopez wearing only a pair of black tights and a satisfied smile, posed with her back to the camera. It was apparently meant to showcase, well, her rear end. The photo inside was in the same vein, covering two pages and set up like a centerfold; Lopez's backside filled most of the right-hand page. The headline superimposed on top, "From here to DIVANITY," with the Y curved like a voluptuous woman, reiterated that Lopez had arrived as a celebrated, or at least heavily hyped, Hollywood body.[1]

This was just one example of the massive number of promotional texts surrounding Nuyorican (New York–born Puerto Rican) performer Jennifer Lopez in 1998 and 1999 that focused on her supposed prodigious backside. In the fall of 1998 in particular, dozens of newspapers, entertainment magazines, and entertainment news programs around the country and the globe reported the "news" of Lopez's voluptuous rear end and lack of desire to change it. Multitudes of newspaper columnists wrote about the aforementioned *Entertainment Weekly* story and photos and what they described as the new, public obsession with Lopez's rear end. Christopher Goodwin, writing for the Style section of London's *Sunday Times,* for example, praised "Jennifer Lopez's bottom, her backside, her butt, her rear, her rump, her posterior, her gorgeously proud buttocks, her truly magnificent, outstanding booty."[2] And television notables were not to be left out of the fray. Jay Leno, after waxing poetic on the virtues of the Lopez derrière, twirled the actress when she arrived on the stage of his late-night talk show so that his live and television audiences could get an eyeful. *Saturday Night Live* even spoofed Lopez when guest host Lucy Lawless portrayed her with a gargantuan rear end and ego in a skit during an October 1998 episode.[3]

What I found most striking about this discourse was that it was happening at the same time that Jennifer Lopez was obviously rising in status in Hollywood. The actress—in these few years before she launched her profitable sidelines as a singer, designer, and media producer, in other words before she became "J.Lo"—was already well on her way to becoming a recognized actress. Lopez had scored a success, with Latina/o audiences and many critics, in the title role of *Selena* (1997), a biopic based on the life of the late, beloved singer of Tejano music, and was about to be seen in a starring role in *Out of Sight* (1998), directed by A-list director Steven Soderbergh and co-starring George Clooney. As a result, she was being recognized in a variety of ways as an up-and-coming star. One of the showiest promotions she received was her inclusion with other young actresses on the cover (albeit in the less visible inside fold) of *Vanity Fair*'s April 1997 Hollywood issue. She also became the first Latina to earn over a million dollars with her reported $2 million salary in *Out of Sight*.[4] Thus, this "booty brouhaha" was a major element of Jennifer Lopez's introduction to the public as a potential star on a national and global scale.

I also found the dynamics by which Lopez and other Latina/o performers were promoted in discussions of a "Latin Wave" entering the mainstream culture in the late 1990s important to explore and critique. As noted in the Introduction of this book, hints of ambivalence could easily be discerned in this marketing. For instance, Latina/o performers often were referred to as "crossover" stars, even if they grew up in the United States and didn't speak fluent Spanish. In discourse that echoed Rita Moreno's "barefoot" years, they also were often labeled in a manner which insinuated that, as Latina/os, they were innately sexy, fiery, and/or irresistible.

Audience reception reveals an even greater complexity regarding the promotion of Jennifer Lopez as a potential star, moreover. In relation to Latina/o reception, the undue attention to Lopez's body needs to be understood beyond the reiteration of spitfire publicity. From the perspective of Latina/o audiences, for Lopez, a *Puertorriqueña* with a curvy body, to declare as beautiful and to unashamedly display her well-endowed posterior could be viewed as proud and positive—a revolutionary act posing a challenge to Anglo beauty ideals typically reflected and perpetuated in Hollywood-driven media images.[5] This moment in Latina star promotion thus needs to be considered from a variety of perspectives to understand its varied impact.

A number of interesting questions about contemporary Latina/o stardom can be raised regarding Lopez's rise to mainstream fame. Why should so much attention be paid to Jennifer Lopez's body and particularly her rear end in the English-language press in the late 1990s? Why has she been so successful, in settings in which Latinas often have not been offered opportunities? And if there was in fact a wave of Latino and Latina stars breaking on the beach of U.S. popular culture in these years, how did this come about and what is its impact on Hollywood Latinidad? With these questions in mind, in this chapter I explore Jennifer Lopez's career and the publicity she received as a window into shifts in Latina/o opportunity and status in Hollywood, the United States, and increasingly, in global media markets. Lopez's physical transformations and career developments since the 1990s raise new questions as well. In particular, I explore in my conclusions the centrality of upper-class associations and ethnic flexibility to Jennifer Lopez's more recent, multivalent star image.

Latina/os Coming into Their Own in 1990s Hollywood

The 1990s witnessed a continuation of New Hollywood shifts that amounted to increasing interest in casting and promoting a handful of African American and Latina/o actors as potential stars. The industry's discovery of the potential profits to be earned from the growing Latina/o audience, as noted in the previous chapter, encouraged media executives to give Latina/o-themed films and TV series greater opportunity. A growing openness toward Latina/o stardom can be attributed as well to the rise in bilingual and English-language Latina/o-oriented news outlets that promoted Latina/o performers.[6] Some of these magazines and other news outlets were founded in the late 1980s and were joined by others in the next decades; reports on Latina/o celebrities and Latina/o-oriented entertainment projects have figured heavily in their content.

In many ways, the mainstream media coverage of Tejano singer Selena's death in 1995 paved the way for a greater emphasis on Latina/o-oriented celebrity news in general in the late 1990s. One of the first Mexican American women to achieve widespread fame in U.S. popular culture—though with her death rather than her considerable achievements during her life—was Selena Quintanilla Pérez. Known simply as Selena to her fans, she became known to the mass public following her slaying at the hands of a former employee. She was (and is) dearly beloved by many Mexican Americans and other Latina/os, especially girls who looked up to her; her untimely death naturally brought about an intense desire to hear her music, and to read and talk about her. Shortly after her death, *People Weekly* put Selena on their cover in the Southwest.[7] The run of four hundred thousand copies promptly sold out, as did a subsequent tribute issue of one million copies. This served as strong testimony to the size and profitability of the Latina/o audience, prompting the launch of *People en Español,* which since has seen competition from English-language (*Latin Style, Latin Girl, Moderna*), bilingual (*Latina, Estylo*), and Spanish-language magazines such as *Cristina,* all of which devote much of their content to Latina/o performers.[8] This outlet for star promotion has greatly assisted in launching the careers of contemporary stars, including Jennifer Lopez. The increased record sales of and media attention given to Tejano music after Selena's death also gave momentum to the marketing of other Latin music, Latina/o performers, and Latina/o-themed film projects in the late 1990s, particularly as music and film increasingly were viewed as marketing tools for one other. The success of Ricky Martin's self-titled English-language album in the summer of 1999 was a watershed moment in this respect. The simultaneous success of Martin, Lopez, Cristina Aguilera, and other Latina/o performers helped prompt the discussion of a "Latin Wave" in U.S. entertainment in 1998 and 1999.

Directly related to the "Latin Wave" label also was the news that the Latina/o population was growing rapidly; it was projected that by 2000 they would comprise 12.5 percent of the nation's population, surpassing African Americans as the nation's largest nonwhite group.[9] By the 1990s, Latina/os also were beginning to be viewed as an important political bloc and consumer market. The growing and lucrative Latina/o market had a collective $380 million buying power in 2000, a 66 percent increase since 1990, and the proclivity of Latina/os for going to the movies and watching television was now noted in studies, while advertising agencies and trade journals such as *Variety* had begun tracking the Latina/o audience and its media habits.[10]

Latino actors and actresses also were benefiting in the 1990s from working with talent managers and producers who specialized in the career management and promotion of nonwhite performers. This new breed of cultural brokers has included such professionals as manager-producer Eric Gold, producers Kenneth "Babyface" Edmonds and Tracy E. Edmonds, and Benny Medina, Jennifer Lopez's former manager. These agents, managers, producers, and publicists have become respected players in the industry and are often

African American or Latina/o themselves. Professionals such as Medina, who formerly was a music producer and has, in addition to Lopez, managed the careers of such performers as Will Smith, Jada Pinkett Smith, and Vivica A. Fox, increasingly have experience and connections in multiple entertainment realms and a sense of how to effectively and synergistically market nonwhite stars to both white audiences and audiences of color.

Progress in the realms of advertising and talent and media development has not resulted in the end of social problems experienced by Mexican Americans, Puerto Ricans, and other U.S. Latina/o groups, however. In fact, poverty was slightly higher among Latina/os in 2000 than in 1970, while such problems as unemployment and high school dropout rates continue to be major concerns.[11] As Martha Menchaca documents, the continuing abandonment of many city neighborhoods by middle-class whites, increasing ethnic segregation of schools, and unabated influx of Latina/o immigrants to the United States has contributed to an entrenched "system of social apartness" that reinforces the economic inequities that many Latina/os face.[12] Latina/os also face continued negative attitudes in the public consciousness. Mexican Americans and Mexican immigrants, in discourses that echo those of the 1930s, again have been accused of stealing jobs by public pundits such as Lou Dobbs. Both a reflection of and catalyst in such scapegoating, the news media and politicians have focused heavily on reinforcing and policing the U.S.-Mexico border in recent years, while American culture is being policed in proposed or passed legislation in many states that denies services to undocumented immigrants and instates "English-only" policies in schools and other social institutions. Considering these facts, contemporary Latina/o stardom such as exemplified by Jennifer Lopez's career trajectory is all the more remarkable.

Lopez's Early Career and the Construction of Latina Authenticity

To many it may have appeared that Lopez burst on the scene overnight, attended by immediate discussion of her body. Her fame actually was the result of years of hard work as a dancer, such as in her years as a Fly Girl for Fox's *In Living Color,* and in small but memorable roles in a wide variety of television series and films. For several years, she was promoted primarily to Latina/o and African American niche markets, before she had major opportunities for broader exposure and stardom.

According to interviews, Jennifer Lopez had a middle-class upbringing in the Castle Hill neighborhood of the Bronx, New York. She was born on July

24, 1970, to Puerto Rican parents—Guadalupe, a kindergarten teacher, and David, a computer technician—the second of three daughters. Similar to the performer who Lopez credits with being one of her primary influences, Rita Moreno, Lopez aspired to a career in dance and theater from an early age. Lopez similarly began taking dance lessons at the age of five and acted in her first film role in *My Little Girl* (1986) at the age of sixteen. After her high school graduation in 1987, what followed were lean years of doing musical theater in New York and in touring dance ensembles.

The rise of African American–oriented television programming, in the form of the new Fox network, offered the young performer an early opportunity. Lopez got her first break in 1991, when she beat out over two thousand hopefuls to become one of the Fly Girls, the house dancers on Fox TV's Afrocentric sketch comedy series *In Living Color* (1990–94). As publicity photographs and the episodes themselves reveal, Lopez dressed very much the home girl as a dancer in the ensemble, sporting in one photo, for example, a dark red mouth, big earrings, and tough-girl attitude. Her body type has been cited by series choreographer Rosie Perez as one of the reasons why she was selected, as Jennifer Lopez's curvaceous, bottom-heavy body was seen as potentially attractive to viewers. Her body type also arguably contributed to the view that she was a "real" Latina and thus fitting for a show targeting the "urban" demographic.[13]

As a Fly Girl for two seasons, Lopez gained important exposure; she was soon appearing as a dancer in music videos such as Janet Jackson's 1992 "That's the Way Love Goes." Lopez next secured a recurring role in the 1994 series *South Central,* a hard-hitting Fox dramedy about a working-class African American mother and her three children in working-class Los Angeles, as well as roles on the night-time soaps *Second Chances* (1993–94) and *Hotel Malibu* (1994). Lopez also had acquired Eric Gold of Gold-Miller Company as her personal manager. Gold had helped produce *In Living Color* and also managed the careers of the four Wayans brothers, Jim Carrey, and director Gregory Nava, making him one of the new cultural brokers previously discussed. His cadre of clients also underscores the ability of agents to "package" multiethnic projects, including the director, actors, and other key personnel, by the 1990s. Together, these developments led to Lopez securing a number of small film roles. She portrayed a young, Depression-era Mexican immigrant in Gregory Nava's Mexican American family saga *My Family/Mi Familia* (1995); a Puerto Rican cop who catches the fancy of her co-workers, played by Wesley Snipes and Woody Harrelson, in *Money Train* (1995); a femme fatale of Apache descent in Oliver Stone's neo-noir *U-Turn* (1997); and a sweet Latina school teacher to Robin Williams's adult child in *Jack* (1996).

The most notable of these roles was that of Maria Sanchez in Gregory Nava's *My Family/Mi Familia,* a young Mexican mother who survives hardships in the Depression-era United States, including a forced deportation to and difficult journey back from Mexico. Lopez's promotion at this point in her career appeared to emphasize talent and cultural authenticity; Gold/Miller publicized Lopez's Best Supporting Actress nomination by the Independent Spirit Awards with a full-page ad in *Variety* that featured Lopez in her Depression-era costume as Maria Sanchez.[14] In an interview with reporter Alisa Valdes of the *Boston Globe,* Lopez's authenticity also was legitimized through a focus on her family. In describing them, Lopez stated, "We were a lot like the family in the movie. You know, all the passion and the things that immigrant Latino families go through."[15]

While *My Family/Mi Familia* offered Lopez a role of complexity, compelling emotion, and agency, in contrast she was treated as an accessory character in *Jack,* as a gutsy but otherwise one-dimensional love interest in her turn as a Latina cop in *Money Train,* and as a prototypical, sexually inviting femme fatale in Oliver Stone's *U-Turn.* Lopez received positive attention in reviews for all of these films, however. For example, reviewers of *Money Train,* even though they generally panned the film, declared that Lopez displayed "sexy spirit" and "wit and grace" in her role.[16] Moreover, the film grossed a respectable $35.4 million. *Jack* grossed $58.6 million, and so was helpful for Lopez's career even though it did little to showcase her acting. Lopez and her management team were planning for her to achieve greater stardom, however. Anticipating obstacles Latinas had encountered in Hollywood in the past and proactively working to undermine them was one aspect of her career strategy. In particular, Lopez wanted to avoid being typecast. According to Lopez, quoted in *Latina* in June 2001: "From the beginning I realized that as a Latin woman I was going to have certain obstacles to overcome that maybe other actresses wouldn't. So I always made very specific choices not to get pigeonholed, not to ever let anybody say, 'She can't do that.' Even from the first two choices [referring to *My Family/Mi Familia* and *Money Train*], I made sure that people couldn't say I did the same thing twice."[17] Her next film role, however, both capitalized squarely on her Latina heritage and was vital to her future stardom. Her role as Selena in Gregory Nava's 1997 film of the same name undoubtedly was extremely important to Jennifer Lopez's rise as a film star. The publicity for the film, primarily targeting Latina/os, also marked the beginning of the preoccupation with Lopez's body in her star promotion, although this Latina/o-oriented press coverage had a drastically different valence than the body-emphasizing coverage in the English-language press in the following year.

In a similar manner to the tribute articles that had eulogized Selena's life, news of the film production had been promoted in massive press coverage in both the English- and Spanish-language press. Responding to a heavily hyped, national casting call for the actress who would play the adult Selena, Jennifer Lopez beat out a purported twenty-two thousand other women vying for the role. She also received her first million-dollar paycheck, while the newly established Latina/o-oriented print media offered Lopez her first major star publicity, when *Latina* magazine put her on their inaugural cover in February 1997, right before *Selena* was released to theaters.

In portraying Selena, Lopez filled the shoes of a Latina heroine of mythic, even saintlike proportions to many in the Mexican American community. The film's promotional materials in turn capitalized on Lopez's uncanny resemblance to the late Tejano star when in costume and makeup. True to the role, Lopez looks decidedly bottom-heavy as Selena in the film. Even so, there was an initial backlash among Mexican Americans in response to the casting of a Puerto Rican actress in the role. To circumvent it, one promotional strategy apparently was to establish Lopez's legitimacy as a Latina and *Puertorriqueña* and thus her appropriateness for the role. Interviews in the Latina/o-oriented print media, on Spanish-language talk shows, and with Latina/o reporters in the mainstream press thus focused heavily on such topics as Lopez's family, Puerto Rican heritage, and ability to speak Spanish, though somewhat broken Spanish. Many interviews also turned to discussion of the fact that she didn't use any padding to play the singer, who often had worn body-hugging stage costumes. Frances Negrón-Mutaner describes how Lopez's appearances on Spanish-language talk shows often would progress: "[T]here came a moment during the interview when the question had to be posed to Jennifer Lopez: 'Todo eso es tuyo?' (Is that body for real?) In other words, is that big butt yours or is it prosthetic? . . . Jennifer Lopez smiled as if she had been waiting a long time for this moment. She stood up, gave a 360 degree turn, patted her butt, and triumphantly sat down. 'Todo es mío.' It's all mine."[18] A similar exchange took place in the January 1, 1997 issue of *People in Español*. "Is that butt yours, or is it padded?" Lopez was asked. She laughed, and again said, "Todo es mío [It's all mine]."[19]

Negrón-Mutaner's interpretation of Lopez's "need to speak" about her rear end during the *Selena* publicity is that Lopez was claiming power not previously ascribed to Latina role models in the media through declaring and in fact physically demonstrating to the public her pride in the size of her rear.[20] While I agree with this analysis in relation to the Latina/o-oriented media, it doesn't fully explain Lopez's publicity in the English-language media in

Jennifer Lopez as Tejana singer Selena in Gregory Nava's *Selena* (1997).

1998. Throughout the *Selena* publicity, discussion of Lopez's curves took a wholesome tack and was paired with visual images of the Girl-Next-Door variety; along these lines, the above-mentioned *People en Español* article is accompanied by a photo of Lopez wearing a demure outfit and expression. This was a far cry from the almost raunchy sexiness that pervades much of the later interpretation of Lopez's body in the English-language media, as is discussed further below.

Lopez was lauded even before the film was released for her intelligent portrayal of Selena, particularly in capturing the late singer's warm and charismatic performance style. Reviews, in turn, were overwhelmingly positive. Critics described the actress as "vibrant" and "electrifying" in the role, while *Rolling Stone* began its review with "Jennifer Lopez excels as Selena."[21] Her performance also garnered her a Golden Globe nomination for Best Actress. As *Selena* producer Moctesuma Esparza has noted, the financial success of the film would prove to be a boon to future Latina/o-oriented projects. It grossed almost $12 million its opening weekend and eventually earned over $35 million in domestic box office alone, from mostly Latina/o audiences. While this was nowhere near the $54.2 million grossed by *La Bamba* in 1987, it was enough to highlight the continuing potential of the Latina/o moviegoing audience and to launch Lopez's career. Having incarnated Selena on the big screen, Lopez was embraced in the Spanish-language broadcast and print media as a reigning Latina star. Publicity for Lopez in the English-language media after this splash was low-key, however. A distinctly bifurcated publicity strategy to target Latina/o and non-Latino audiences appears to have begun in Lopez's promotion at this point in her career. In the few interviews and other coverage that Lopez garnered in the English-language press, Lopez's ethnicity tends to be downplayed and her Bronx roots emphasized. Lopez's Latin heritage and family, on the other hand, were the primary focus of her coverage in the Spanish-language media.

Lopez appeared in two other films in 1997, *Blood and Wine* and *Anaconda*, though both were overshadowed by her success in *Selena*. In *Blood and Wine*, Lopez played Gabriela, a Cuban immigrant nanny and the girlfriend of Alex, a wine dealer turned jewel thief played by Jack Nicholson. While some critics overlooked Lopez's performance, John Anderson of the *Los Angeles Times* praised her ability to fill the shoes of a complicated femme fatale.[22] Lopez's role in *Anaconda*, meanwhile, distinctly challenged old Latin spitfire myths. In this film, a smart B-film send-up, Lopez starred as a resourceful documentary filmmaker, Terri Flores, who, along with her film crew, must face a killer anaconda and equally deadly human villain in the Amazonian jungle. Terri Flores was unique as a professional, "take charge Latina."[23] The role played to traditional expectations through exploiting Lopez's beauty but offered surprising twists in scenes, such as the one in which Terri gets the better of the story's villain (Jon Voight) by deliberately performing the harlot role. Ultimately, *Anaconda* made a healthy profit, grossing almost $70 million. As a thriller that showcased an animatronic snake, it was not taken particularly seriously, however. In contrast, Lopez's next role, in Steven Soderbergh's *Out of Sight* (1998), and the star promotion efforts generated around the time of its release, would be instrumental in Lopez's increasing stardom.

Crossing Over the Latina Body: Jennifer Lopez and Mainstream Stardom

In the next stage of Lopez's career, a concerted effort was made to market the actress to non-Latino audiences through various publicity tactics, many of which paralleled the marketing of Latina performers in earlier decades. As mentioned previously, an emphasis on Lopez's body and especially her rear end was the overriding feature of this promotion. The inherent contradictions of this star promotion strategy provided an ongoing ideological tension to her publicity and also ultimately assisted in Lopez becoming a mainstream star in this period.

Lopez's rising status in 1997 was announced in the $2 million paycheck negotiated for her next role, that of a police officer opposite George Clooney's thief in the Jersey Films production *Out of Sight*. *Variety* announced that Cynthia Shelton-Drake of UTA, then Lopez's agent, had originally asked for $5 million for Lopez, however.[24] Despite this testament to Lopez's less than stellar status in the mainstream film industry, her stardom was unquestionable in the Latina/o press. Lopez appeared on her second cover of *Latina*, a vision of understated elegance in a satin dress and with her hair pulled back schoolmarm fashion, in February 1998. And while she did not win the Golden Globe for *Selena,* she was awarded Best Actress in a Film at the 1998 American Latino Media (ALMA) Awards, held annually by the Latina/o advocacy group, the National Council of La Raza, for her performance. From my position in the audience that night, it was clear that she was the star in the room around whom there was the most buzz.

Lopez had no intention of settling for this, however. As she stated in numerous interviews, she was interested in pursuing her career as far as it could go, and this likely played a part in her switch to new management. In 1998, she changed agents, from Shelton-Drake at UTA to Jeff Berg, the president of ICM and thus its most highly visible agent. She also switched from personal manager Eric Gold of Gold-Miller to Benny Medina of Handprint Entertainment, notable as mentioned previously for managing the careers of such stars as Will Smith and Sean Combs. The fruit of these strategies began to be evident in Lopez's publicity in early 1998, a few months before the release of *Out of Sight*. In this period, Jennifer Lopez made several moves that re-kindled discussion about her body, this time in the mainstream media. In an interview for *Movieline* (notably, the annual Sex issue) in February 1998, Lopez candidly discussed, seemingly without prompting, her curvy body and its uniqueness among the ranks of Hollywood actresses. Asked what nickname she might like to be called by the press, she declared: "The first thing that came to my head was the 'Butt' Girl because that separates me from everyone else. I love my body. I really, really dig my curves. It's all me and men love it. . . . So many girls here are so thin—in fact nobody else in Hollywood really has my type of body. My husband calls it 'La Guitarra,' like the shape of a guitar, which I love because that was always my ideal woman growing up. So call me the 'Guitar Girl!'"[25]

Lopez appeared on the magazine's cover in a front-view Jessica Rabbit pose, wearing nothing but a white fur stole wrapped strategically around her body, a first step in the construction of a star image that emphasized extraordinary sex appeal. She also was quoted in the article pointedly criticizing several actors and actresses, including Gwyneth Paltrow, Winona Ryder, and Wesley Snipes, marking the beginning of the construction of Lopez as an outspoken diva, which appears uncannily like a 1990s version of the spitfire.

Lopez also contributed in her public appearances in this period to the eventual obsession with her body in press discourse. At awards shows in early 1998, Lopez appeared in slinky dresses that made her back and rump a focal point; these dresses garnered a great deal of attention for Lopez. Reactions ranged from that of one Golden Globes reviewer, who blasted Lopez for wearing a dress that was "two sizes too small," to media reports, especially by male media professionals, that trumpeted Lopez's beauty and style in these back end–emphasizing outfits.[26] As one reviewer declared, "Best dressed [at the Oscars]: Jennifer Lopez. OK, so this is a man's perspective."[27]

The release of *Out of Sight* served to add more fuel to the fire of Jennifer Lopez's increasingly sexy and body-focused star image in the news media. There was seemingly endless attention in the celebrity publicity spheres of talk shows and entertainment magazines, not so much about Lopez's achievement in carving a niche for herself in the film industry, but to a seemingly trivial item: her butt. In this case, adeptly playing up tropes of the excessive and ir-resistible Latina body, both in the film and in public appearances, garnered Lopez a great deal of media attention.

Lopez's role and Steven Soderbergh's direction of the film likely assisted in playing this up. In *Out of Sight*, Lopez's embodiment of Federal Marshall Karen Cisco was seen as particular evidence of Lopez's beauty and sexual energy. The on-screen chemistry between Lopez and co-star George Clooney also was played up by Soderbergh to maximum effect; the camera lingers on Lopez's body and briefly on her rear end in a few scenes, while the lighting and use of close-ups emphasize both Lopez and Clooney's attractiveness and the sexual tension in the film. As a result, while Lopez's portrayal in the film was seen by critics as having substance as well as style, many reviewers also made mention of her sexy body or general sensuality in *Out of Sight,* describing her as, among other things, "scandalously sensual" and a "smoldering femme fatale" who wielded "Hispanic pocket dynamism" and "sexily slinky powers."[28] Adding fuel to this discourse, Lopez appeared at the premiere in a dress that "caused a near riot," according to Jeryl Brunner of *In/Style* magazine, and willingly spoke with reporters about her body, seemingly without prompting.[29] As noted at the beginning of this chapter, this led to what was apparently a media-driven obsession. In the fall of 1998, dozens of newspapers and magazines scrambled to run their own "booty story," writing about the media coverage by other sources or simply reprinting stories that had been released to news wires.

Subsequently, the publicity born from this period admires, obsesses on, and ruminates on Lopez's backside. Was this emphasis the result of the entrenchment of notions of the sexualized Latina body in U.S. popular culture? No doubt in part, though the overwhelming volume of stories of this nature would appear to be a deliberate move on the part of Lopez and her management team as well. This period of publicity, which effectively marketed Lopez as a Latina "crossing over" into the traditionally white star system, in fact was extremely contradictory. In this discourse Lopez was simultaneously marked as a "real" Latina breaking into the ranks of the hegemonically white star system, stereotyped as a fetishized Latina spitfire, *and* established herself as an effective promoter in constructing a profitable star image and brand around which a franchise could be built.

First, it cannot be denied that Lopez was sexualized in this publicity and categorized under a familiar spitfire label. The tendency of reporters to dwell exclusively on Lopez's body underscores a continued process of racialization, demarcating Latina/os as in possession of "more body," emotion, and sexual passion than their white counterparts, that can accompany Latina/o star promotion even in the present day. Along these lines, despite the generally positive discussion of Lopez's acting abilities, it wasn't easy to focus on her talent when most of what we saw of her was her backside. Lopez was not constructed as a victim in this discourse, however. Far from being uncomfortable, she appeared to leap at opportunities to express her bodily and (to a lesser extent) ethnic pride. For example, Lopez continuously stated that she felt no need to change her body in order to attain success as a Hollywood actress.

"I don't know what it is with everyone," Lopez said in *The (Singapore) Straits Times*. She continued: "I guess I'm a little hippy. Latinas and black women have a certain body type. We're curvy. It's in the history books. I didn't start a revolution. But I don't mind if the big-butted women in the world are a little happier because of a few cameramen's obsession with my behind."[30] In discussion of her aspirations for her acting career, Lopez demonstrated a strong desire to avoid being pigeonholed as a Latina, describing herself as an "actress who is Latin—not a Latin actress as in one who just does Latin roles."[31] But when it came to her non-normative body by Hollywood standards in this media moment, Lopez made no excuses. In this regard, Jennifer Lopez can be seen both as empowered and as an empowering role model for young women and in particular for young Latinas in this moment. In the process, she and her management team also took in hand how her body would be interpreted by the mainstream media, making what easily could have been considered a detriment into a trademark and positive selling point.

Furthermore, this publicity served as a reminder of the tensions inherent in U.S. beauty standards and the possibility that these standards were broadening, at least with respect to curvaceous rear ends. Given that Lopez's appearance was described in the media as beautiful as well as nontraditional in its voluptuousness, it appears that Lopez posed a challenge in this regard simply by unapologetically being herself. Journalist Donna Britt encapsulated the cultural shifts that the Lopez obsession underscored in her playful description of Lopez as having "a big ole cross-over butt."[32] Ripple effects in fact were soon felt. For example, Jean Godfrey-June, the beauty/fitness director of *Elle* magazine, trumpeted in November 1998, "Thanks to Jennifer Lopez, butts are back."[33]

Perhaps most important to Jennifer Lopez's future career, in this period she also was effectively marketed as a profitable media commodity and unique and videogenic star with broad appeal to diverse audiences. It was helpful that the "booty news" was visual and succinct and thus easily disseminated in various media forms—increasingly important in the convergent media environment. Whether audience members or media representatives admired or derided her, through the glaring emphasis on her body, Lopez became a topic of casual conversation and a household name, and thus a lucrative star commodity.

The "Latin Wave" and the Ambivalence of Crossover Stardom

As mentioned above, Lopez was also publicized prominently in news stories in this period that pronounced the increasing Latina/o visibility in the media industries, politics, and other aspects of U.S. social life, in a parallel to the media coverage that announced the rise of "Hispanic Hollywood" a decade earlier. Such articles made heavy use of the term "crossover" in describing the success of Lopez and other Latina/o performers, to the extent that it is important to explore.

First, what exactly is meant by crossover, or crossover stardom? While it is defined most simply as the process of becoming popular with a new audience, with respect to film stars the term has often been used to refer to nonwhite and particularly Latina/o performers who succeed in becoming popular with white audiences. According to scholars such as Reebee Garofalo and Steve Perry, the term actually originated in the music industry, used by marketing professionals in the 1950s to refer to then-revolutionary rock 'n' roll musical acts.[34] This entailed the sale of music with African American roots and by African American musical performers to white audiences. As such, it was initially an insider term used by producers and promoters, meant to emphasize the potential or demonstrated appeal of a particular performer. Notably, the first usages of the term to describe Latina/o actors and Latina/o-oriented films that I found in my research were in the late 1980s, in coverage of the new Latina/o-themed films. Since that time the popular usage of the term increased, reaching a peak during the news coverage of the more recent "Latin Wave" of 1998–99. At this time it was used to celebrate, but particularly to sell, a number of Latina/o performers simultaneously.

It should be pointed out that despite the presumably positive connotations of crossover stardom, "crossover" is a term avoided by many Latina/os working both behind and in front of the camera. In interviews that I conducted with Latina/o media professionals while doing research for this book, those who used it were typically producers who used the term to describe for non-Latina/o media professionals the potential of Latina/o-themed projects and Latina/o stars to appeal to a wide and profitable audience. For media professionals who didn't like the term, many stressed that it only emphasized barriers to Latina/o access and success in the media industries. Naturally, there are political implications of a U.S. performer being described in this manner; in the case of Latina/o crossover stardom such a promotional thrust can be said to position Latina/os as outsiders, as merely the exotic flavor of the month, to an American mainstream constructed as white.

In interpreting such promotional angles utilized in the selling of Latina/o actors and musical artists as potential stars, it also is important to consider anti-Latina/o and anti-immigration rhetoric centered on the U.S.-Mexico border. As Coco Fusco asserts, anti-immigration rhetoric can be understood "as a symptom of the fear that the Southwest might become part of Mexico, as it once was."[35] Formulations of crossover stardom similarly construct and maintain figurative borders, in this case which insist that Latina/os' "natural" place remains outside the Hollywood industries and that Latina/o stardom is thus unusual and new.

What deserves closer scrutiny, moreover, is the entrenched notion that the mainstream media audience is white; such a conceptualization arguably no longer applies, considering that nonwhites now comprise over 30 percent of the U.S. population and the numbers of mixed-race families and individuals also are on the rise. Consideration of the increasing creolization of the contemporary U.S. audience begs the question, what were "crossover" stars really crossing over to?

J.Lo: The Americanizing of a Latina Star

Jennifer Lopez proved that her image was far from static, however, as she was very quick to shake off both the "crossover" label and the sensational discourses that had been part of her promotion in 1998. Both her appearance and star image were soon to evolve, along a trajectory that has entailed a gradual but steady gaining of symbolic capital for the star. Lopez first underwent a dramatic physical transformation, which entailed dropping a reported two dress sizes.[36] Lopez's debut CD, *On the 6,* was released in June 1999 (not coincidentally, just a week after the release of Ricky Martin's *Livin' La Vida Loca*). It was accompanied by a body-emphasizing music video for the single "If You Had My Love" in heavy rotation on MTV. Photographs of a newly svelte Lopez were showcased in the packaging of the CD and in her print publicity at the time. Music critics panned Lopez's weak voice, although this did not affect album sales.[37]

Lopez's new look garnered as much media attention as had the blitz on her body in her earlier, softer state. Despite Lopez's proud assertions a year earlier that she liked her body the way it was, subtle aesthetic changes to Lopez's appearance included a slimmed-down body, possible cosmetic surgery to her nose and jawline, and blonde highlights—notably, often the main target of critics who declared she was whitening her appearance. News reports speculated on how Lopez had made the changes. "Her incredible shrinking booty is this year's greatest mystery this side of *The Blair Witch Project*," *Vanity Fair* declared in December 1999, while *Parade* newspaper supplement reported that Lopez had toned her body through an intense exercise regimen.[38]

Since that time, Lopez has typically maintained a lean, extremely fit (though still curvaceous) body, which has proven to be the ultimate marketing tool.

It can be viewed as a strategic business move, as the hegemonic ideal of Hollywood beauty has become leaner over the decades and particularly since the 1980s.[39] Lopez also began to employ a retinue of fashion stylists, personal trainers, and hair and makeup artists and became known for wearing trendy designer fashions and daring outfits. For example, at the 2000 Grammy Awards, Lopez wore a gravity-defying, plunging green Donatella Versace dress that perhaps was "the most talked about outfit in recent memory," according to one journalist.[40] For her efforts, her photos were on constant display in celebrity and fashion magazines. She and her stylists also received recognition via Lopez's earning of a number of celebrity fashion awards in 2000 and 2001. Just as Madonna had undergone a "gradual physical makeover from fleshy 'virgin' to lean machine" and effectively marketed herself as a rising star in the 1980s, so Jennifer Lopez's makeover from fleshy Latina to lean and expensively groomed icon arguably assisted in selling her to a broader audience and cemented her Hollywood star status.[41]

Another characteristic of Lopez's publicity in this period was that there was a great deal of it; after 1999, everything about her life seemed to be considered fodder for the celebrity gossip mills. Topics included a rumor that she insured her body for $1 billion (which Lopez later denied), stories of Lopez's supposed diva-like tantrums and demands, and discussion of her controversial photographs on magazine covers. Lopez also was romantically linked to a variety of men over the next few years, including her first husband, Ojani Noa, singer Marc Anthony, Sony Music executive Tommy Mottola, Sean "Puffy" Combs, and second husband Cris Judd. The subject of much tabloid gossip was her "are-they-or-aren't-they" dating relationship and eventual breakup from Combs, a popular rap singer and head of his own hip-hop entertainment and talent management company, Bad Boy Entertainment. Combs's skirmishes with the law, and the end of their relationship, announced officially in February 2001, also tallied a great deal of media coverage. In particular, a well-publicized incident in December 1999, in which the couple were questioned for hours at a Manhattan police station after a gun was found in Combs's vehicle following a bar shooting, arguably pointed to the dangers for Lopez of becoming too "urban" (in other words, racialized) through her personal connections and career choices. Efforts were subsequently made to disassociate Lopez from the incident, and later, from Sean Combs, despite his obvious status and success in the hip-hop entertainment and fashion worlds.

With respect to her film career, Jennifer Lopez further cemented her status as a star with a role she took in the futuristic psychological thriller *The Cell* in

2000. Focused on the tormented dreamscape of a sadistic killer, whose mind Lopez's character can enter through the use of a special machine, the film was downbeat but nonetheless allowed Lopez to be displayed in a wide variety of flamboyant costumes designed by Eiko Ishioka. The film was panned by critics as stronger on visuals than narrative, but Lopez again came out generally unscathed. The release of Lopez's second album, *J.Lo,* the same week in January 2001 as her film *The Wedding Planner* further demonstrated Lopez's potential as a driving force for synergistic profit making. The releases were accompanied by a media blitz that among other things announced Lopez's new nickname, "J.Lo," and emphasized her well-groomed beauty and ethnic ambiguity. Interestingly, the new nickname highlighted her increasingly ethnic image in the realm of popular music even while it elided her last name, the main reminder of her Puerto Rican heritage. Such developments highlight how Lopez's publicity was taking on multiple and distinct tracks, as she catered in her career to audiences of differing ages, ethnic backgrounds, and genders.

While *J.Lo* quickly became the top-selling album not just in the United States but also in a number of other countries, *The Wedding Planner* offered Lopez a shot at uncharted territory: the romantic comedy, a genre through which notions of white American femininity have often been articulated and conversely in which Latinas have seldom been cast. The film tells the story of Mary Fiore, a dateless, overworked wedding planner, who meets the man of her dreams only to find she is planning his wedding. Director Adam Shankman originally envisioned Mary as Armenian but changed her to Italian when Lopez signed on.[42] Lopez thus plays a white character in the film, a role in which a "Debbie Reynolds" undoubtedly would have been cast in Rita Moreno's starlet era, to refer to Moreno's complaint about the color line she encountered in the 1950s. Critics, notably, did not call attention to Lopez's ethnicity in their reviews. Columbia Pictures also called no attention to ethnic differences in its promotional poster for the film. In the poster, Jennifer Lopez, bronzed and sporting long straight hair with blond highlights, reclines against co-star Matthew McConaughey. Both are smiling amiably, but the poses of the two actors imply truce as well as sexual tension. From these visuals and the referent of romantic comedies of past eras, moviegoers can surmise that the film will provide a screwball-style clash of gender, but not of race or ethnicity, followed by an ultimate, happy romantic ending. The film did respectable box office, earning over $60 million domestically.

In another example of strategically synergistic marketing, Lopez's next film, *Angel Eyes,* was released in April 2001, at the same time as the unveiling of her new clothing line. In partnership with Andy Hilfiger, brother of

Jennifer Lopez and co-star Matthew McConaughey in a promotional poster for *The Wedding Planner* (2001).

designer Tommy Hilfiger, Lopez was putting out a line of urban-influenced street wear, "J.Lo by Jennifer Lopez," with prices ranging from $22 to $850. Given the range of prices, fans of all incomes would be able to emulate Lopez through purchasing her clothes. Notable with respect to Latina beauty and body ideals as well was the wide range of sizes. "So from little to voluptuous, everybody gets to be sexy," Lopez announced at the unveiling.[43] (The clothing line, retired in 2007, was a lucrative moneymaker for Lopez, with a reported $375 million in revenues in 2004 alone.)

Angel Eyes offered Lopez another non-Latina, or rather, ethnically ambiguous role. In the film, a moody psychological romance, Lopez plays a New York police officer, Sharon Pogue, who falls for a mystery man with amnesia. While Lopez's Latina appearance as Pogue is explained through the character perhaps being of partial Latina/o descent (Brazilian Sonia Braga is shown in a photograph to be her deceased mother), the actor chosen to play her brother does not look similarly ethnic. Lopez herself sported stridently blond hair and a tan for her portrayal, calling attention to her performance of whiteness. Notably, both *The Wedding Planner* and *Angel Eyes* capitalized on Lopez's rising status in their promotion; many reviews included snippets of interviews with Lopez and accompanying photographs of the star. This appears to confirm a major feat that *Vanity Fair* declared in June 2001, that Jennifer Lopez had become a star of enough stature and synergy to "open" a movie.[44]

As Jennifer Lopez's music and film careers developed in tandem with her ancillary businesses, a phenomenon already touched upon became more pronounced, that of Lopez sporting diverging ethnic looks. More specifically, this phenomenon entailed a play on ethnicity in Lopez's public appearances, through her use of cosmetic bronzers, differing hairstyles and textures, and the wearing of radically diverse fashions rife with ethnic and class-related associations. The roster of stylists working with Lopez enabled her to engage in a turn-on-a-dime visual play, assisted by her light olive skin and quasi-European features. Just to name a few of the many looks she embodied in public appearances between 1999 and 2001, Lopez played the role of the Latina erotic object, literally bronzed and glistening, as she appeared as an angel on the cover of the magazine *Notorious* in September/October 1999; a "tanned" beach bum, as was the case when she appeared in California surfer girl attire at an appearance at the Teen Choice Awards 2001; a Puerto Rican home girl, in hip-hop-inspired performances on music videos promoting her *J.Lo* album; and an elegant Hollywood actress, as she appeared at the Oscars and other awards shows. At its most facile, this phenomenon can be interpreted simply as a smart promotional strategy that has multiply positioned Lopez as a synergistic star,[45] but it cannot be ignored that ethnic notions were alternately exploited and avoided in the process. In this regard, the particular looks that Lopez embodied ultimately were not as important as her ability to transform or "unmark" her Latina ethnicity. In a dynamic similar to the whitening impact of "racial cross-dressing" on Irish and Jewish American performers of blackface over a century ago such as Michael Rogin describes, Lopez asserted with these transformations her ability to rise above her racialized status as a Latina and in fact manipulate it as an accessory in the realm of media spectacle.[46] In the process, her ability to both benefit from being Latina and not be confined by it was emphasized.

Notably, however, Lopez had less luck in being perceived as "raceless" with respect to her personal life. The media attention that revolved around "Bennifer," the nickname given to the relationship she shared with actor Ben Affleck from 2002 until early 2004, ultimately turned sour. The backlash, according to one public relations expert, was due in part to the couple being perceived as staging many of their public appearances together to attract attention to their careers.[47] Was it also linked to the couple being perceived as bicultural or even biracial? It's difficult to argue definitively, but if there were such negative reactions to the pairing, they would stand in distinct contrast to the way Desi Arnaz and Lucille Ball were treated as a couple decades earlier. Perhaps not coincidentally, Arnaz and Ball's press coverage established them as a star couple genuinely in love, while this was not the case for Affleck and Lopez. If "love conquers all" in the public imagination, even allowing individuals to violate traditional taboos regarding bicultural or biracial romance, perhaps this is key. Interestingly, Lopez's marriage in 2004 to a fellow Puerto Rican, singer Marc Anthony, has appeared both of less interest and to be more acceptable to American audiences.

* * *

As a review of her early career illustrates, Jennifer Lopez benefited from the growing interest in the Latina/o audience and openness to Latina/o stardom in U.S. and global popular culture that has come about since the 1990s. Lopez also has proven herself as a performer, producer, and businesswoman on the basis of talent, drive, and broad audience appeal, as her many successes in various entertainment mediums attest. Named the ninth richest woman in entertainment by *Forbes* in 2007, she has clearly learned how to maximize her profit potential as a Latina through emphasis on versatility, ethnic and otherwise, in her multifaceted star image in the contemporary media environment.

Despite the many accomplishments of Jennifer Lopez, her career also highlights that some obstacles remain in Hollywood with respect to Latina opportunity for stardom. The tenor of Lopez's introduction to mainstream audiences in the late 1990s in particular demonstrates an unchanging paradigm of racialization through body-focused discourses that have long been associated with Hollywood Latinidad. Such constancy illustrates continuing tensions and ambivalence in the popular imagination toward Latina/os in the United States, particularly regarding their positioning in relation to unambivalently white Americans.

While the promotional texts and discourses surrounding Jennifer Lopez illustrate the continuing entrenchment of the sexualized presentation of the Latina star body, her multifaceted career choices have complicated this pattern. In particular, the body-emphasizing thrust of Lopez's publicity has been joined in recent years by new promotional approaches that foreground class privilege as a mediating element, in an interesting echo of how Dolores Del Rio was promoted to moviegoers in her silent film heyday. The evolution of "J.Lo" thus demonstrates how through a high-class image, as manifest in Lopez's case in an emphasis on high fashion, grooming, and Lopez's own business franchise, entrenched tropes of Hollywood racialization in fact can be nullified or even reversed for some Latina/os (at least those with light skin and European features). The backlash against "Bennifer," however, which both Jennifer Lopez and Ben Affleck experienced in the form of their films and other projects faring poorly while they were a public couple, hints at the consequences of overexposure and perhaps that Latina/o stars are not able to ever fully lose their racialized status.

In addition, it is also important to consider not only Lopez's ethnic and racial fluidity in the evolution of her star image, but that she has now played a number of white film characters without comment or criticism from reviewers. This contemporary industrial flexibility and neutral critical reaction stands in contrast to how Latina/os had been cast in Hollywood films since the 1930s. In this manner, Lopez's film performances have entailed an interesting shift in the racialized politics of casting as experienced by a Latina actress who also has been known to portray distinctly Latina characters. Further research could fruitfully explore in more depth the impact of Lopez starring in these roles, which challenges former Hollywood conventions.

Lopez's star construction also has become increasingly complex as she has risen to become a successful multimedia performer, producer, and businesswoman. A recent trend is her involvement once again in a number of Latina/o-focused projects, including roles in the 2006 films *El Cantante,* about Puerto Rican salsa singer Hector Lavoe, and *Bordertown*, in which Lopez portrays a Mexican American journalist investigating the real-life murders of hundreds of Mexican women working for transnational corporations' factories near the U.S. border over the past decade. Neither film was financially successful, however. Among other things, these roles can be seen as attempts on the part of Jennifer Lopez to re-establish her authenticity as a Latina, perhaps for personal but likely also for professional reasons, after the prior emphasis on ethnic and racial fluidity in her star image ultimately did not result in the substantial breadth of opportunities that she purportedly had been seeking as an actress.

Jennifer Lopez also has had a much lower profile with respect to her promotion; whether this is by choice (Lopez recently gave birth to twins after a widely publicized pregnancy), waning interest in Lopez as a star figure, or mere coincidence is not clear. It does appear that she had faced a downturn in popularity after the heavy, multimedia exposure the star experienced in earlier years, and perhaps as a result of aging out of some of the acting opportunities that she initially experienced.[48] Lopez also had shifted some of her attention to producing; through her production company, Nuyorican Productions, she produced the 2007 MTV reality series *Dancelife* and film *Feel the Noise,* about a Nuyorican rap hopeful who has to move to Puerto Rico. It may be that her influence will continue to be felt, but more extensively through her work in this regard than through her accomplishments as an actress. Given her considerable impact on Hollywood Latinidad since the 1990s, the future career of Jennifer Lopez will, regardless, be of major interest and importance.

7

Ethnic Ambiguity in the Era of *Dark Angels*

Jessica Alba and Mixed Latina/o Trends

In surveying Latina/o representation and stardom in the Hollywood media industries since the millennium, I'm cautiously optimistic. Latina/os are being featured in more nuanced and compelling roles, while more Latina/o actors and actresses are gaining the publicity and popularity that qualify them as full-fledged members of the Hollywood star system. Prime examples include America Ferrera, winner of multiple awards in 2007 for her role as the star of ABC's *Ugly Betty,* and Michael Peña, who has recently been cast in showy roles in such productions as *Crash* (2004), *Babel* (2006), and the HBO movie *Walkout* (2006).

The relationship of Latina/o stardom to imagined racial borders has become even more complicated in recent years, however. More specifically, while many successful Latina/o performers over the decades have been of mixed ethnic and racial heritage, it is now more likely that actors will highlight this *mestizaje* in their publicity. Actors such as Jessica Alba (who is of Mexican, French-Canadian, Danish, English, and Italian descent) and Freddie Prinze Jr. (who is Puerto Rican and German Hungarian on his late, famous father's side, and Irish, English, and Native American on his mother's) are just two members of this growing contingent; they are joined by such performers as Rosario Dawson (who is Puerto Rican, Afro-Cuban, Irish, and Native American), Salma Hayek (who is Lebanese and Mexican), Jimmy Smits (Puerto Rican and Surinamese), and Cameron Diaz (Cuban and German American).

That is not to say that there isn't a great deal of diversity among this contingent. Some stars of partial Latina/o descent foreground their Latin American ancestry (such as Rosario Dawson, who has always been forthcoming about her heritage), while others choose not to dwell on it in their publicity but are nevertheless "claimed" by the Latina/o-oriented entertainment news media and Latina/o fans (as was the case for Freddie Prinze Jr. for some years before he publicly embraced his Puerto Rican heritage). Respective of the many differences among what I term "mixed Latina/o" stars, to highlight that they have public images both as mixed race and as Latina/o, their careers have much to teach us about Hollywood Latinidad and racial categories more generally in the contemporary moment. Has something shifted in Latinowood, or in the industry's casting norms, that currently privileges actors of partial Latina/o heritage? And what are the implications of this phenomenon with respect to imagined racial borders and notions of what it means to be Latina/o in U.S. popular culture today?

In this chapter I consider these questions and speculate in particular on the impact of the increasing emphasis on *mestizaje,* which I define here strictly as racial hybridity, in Hollywood media productions on Latina/o opportunity and star promotion.[1] To do so, I analyze the public image and career of one of the most successful actresses of mixed Latina/o background today, Jessica Alba, and to a lesser extent that of her contemporary, Rosario Dawson. Alba and Dawson serve as apt case studies for this exploration, given that their multiracial heritage has often figured as a topic of discussion in their interviews with the press. Their careers and the promotional texts that have contributed to their public images, including critics' reviews, promotional materials, and interviews, thus provide rich texts for the study of discourses circulating on mixed-race and Latina/o identities in the mass media and U.S. social life today.

Jessica Alba got her start as a young teen in a variety of small film and television roles, and has since become a star of enough repute to play herself on HBO's satire of Hollywood stardom, *Entourage* (2004–). Interestingly, Alba's breakout role, and the one that she is arguably best known for, was that of racially mixed and genetically enhanced Max Guevara in the science fiction television series *Dark Angel* (2000–2002). This character, a heroic warrior of the future with a Hispanic last name and the DNA of multiple individuals of diverse racial heritage, is part of the new wave of mixed-race characters that have become increasingly visible in Hollywood film and television texts in recent years.[2] Jessica Alba and *Dark Angel* thus offer a rich case study of mixed Latina/o stardom and representation. In Alba's career trajectory since the series end, she also has had an increasingly visible profile that sheds additional light on the treatment of a mixed Latina star in contemporary Hollywood.

To further explore these casting and promotional tendencies, I contrast

Alba's career and public image with that of her contemporary Rosario Dawson. Dawson, some might say, is seen as a more serious actress, as surveys of her films and film reviews bear out; she has acted in numerous well-received independent films and has worked for a greater number of critically acclaimed directors, including Spike Lee, Robert Rodriguez, and Oliver Stone. She does not appear to be considered for the same roles as Jessica Alba, however, when it comes to bigger budget, studio-driven films. In such films Dawson often has small roles amidst large ensemble casts, as was the case in *Alexander* (2005), *Sin City* (2005), and *Rent* (2005), or has been stuck in thankless best friend roles, as in *Down to You* (2000) and *Josie and the Pussycats* (2001). This is beginning to shift as Dawson is being cast in more female lead roles, however; her work in *Men in Black II* (2002) and *Clerks II* (2006) are cases in point. Quick distinctions between the two actresses also can be discerned with respect to physical appearance, as discussed in more detail below, but even more so with respect to public image, which in turn has influenced their casting opportunities. Dawson typically has played Latina and African American characters, while over the years Alba has been cast in a number of what presumably are white roles, the dynamics and the consequences of which I explore in more detail below. In particular, I interrogate how the actresses' public images have developed over the years and how they have been received by media gatekeepers such as critics and journalists. How has the mixed ancestry of each actress been treated in their press coverage, and what has been the impact of their evolving images on the casting opportunities that they have experienced? Through asking these questions, I aim to shed light on the boundaries of mixed-race and Latina identities as articulated in contemporary Hollywood media productions and star promotion, and to explore the racial valence of Hollywood Latinidad as articulated with respect to mixed Latina/o stars in the present moment.

Latina/os and the Trend for Ethnic Ambiguity

This is not to say that it is new for Latina/o stars to be of mixed racial heritage. As can be surmised from my discussion in the Introduction, given the privileging of fair skin and other European phenotypal features in Hollywood, Latina/o actors and actresses with some European ancestry have traditionally had an advantage with respect to being considered for lead roles, a paradigm that is only recently beginning to lose power. In more recent years, producers' casting of Spanish actors and actresses such as Antonio Banderas, Penelope Cruz, and Paz Vega in Latina/o roles is just one manifestation of this continuing preference. But while many Latina/o stars have been of mixed ancestry, stars of partial Latina/o descent often didn't admit to or didn't heavily publicize it prior to the 1990s, the decade in which mixed-race births boomed in this country. Those who chose not to "out" themselves as mixed race likely were hoping to avoid being typecast in ethnic roles, or alternately, wanted to maintain the careers that their "Latin look" enabled.[3] Mixed Latina/o actors and actresses of past eras include the late Anthony Quinn (who was Mexican and Irish), *Wonder Woman*'s Lynda Carter (who is half Mexican), and Raquel Welch (of half-Bolivian heritage). Notably, some previously "closeted" mixed Latina/o actors and actresses who have "come out" regarding their Latin heritage have found new acting opportunities as a result. Raquel Welch, born Jo Raquel Tejada, for example, was quickly cast in Latina film and television roles.[4]

The apparent vogue for mixed Latina/o stars follows the more general popularity in Hollywood and U.S. popular culture since the 1990s for ethnically ambiguous looks. Mixed-race actors and models in particular began to be centrally featured in the 1990s in advertising and media productions, alongside ethnically inflected and "multicultural" products and aesthetics.[5] These trends have been prompted, among other catalysts, by increasing ethnic diversity and cultural curiosity in this country. In the realm of Latina/o-oriented media outlets, this has translated to a focus on mixed Latina/o celebrities "getting back to their roots" through discussion of their ancestry and family in interviews and photo shoots that take place in their ancestors' country of origin. One example was *Latina* magazine's cover photo and story with model Christy Turlington, who is of partial Salvadoran descent, in January 1999, accompanied by the headline "*Nuestra* Christy returns to El Salvador." And with respect to the Hollywood media industries, it can be seen as dovetailing with film production companies and networks' increased aim to capture the Latina/o audience, along with other viewers of a variety of ethnic and racial backgrounds.

Within these new formations, Latina/o icons and images have been centrally featured. This is likely because of the Latina/o legacy of *mestizaje*: Latina/os, though acknowledged to varying degrees in the United States and Latin American countries as multiracial, are of widely mixed ethnic and racial descent with respect to indigenous and Spanish ancestry and heritage that can be traced to African and other origins. As Gregory Velasco y Trianosky notes, "the central racial and cultural reality of Latina/o life is that everyone is *mestizo*."[6] This legacy of hybrid ancestry, among other things, has historically been interpreted in the United States as reasoning for the racialization of and discrimination against Latina/os in legal policy and by social institutions. It comes as somewhat of a surprise, then, given this long history and statistics which indicate that the rate of Latina/o out-marriage is estimated at one in five marriages,[7] that scholarship on mixed race in the United States has often neglected to focus on mixed-race families or individuals of partial Latina/o descent.[8] In part this is because of continued confusion and debate regarding whether Latina/os are a race or an ethnic group—and thus, whether Latina/o-white relationships or individuals can be viewed as interracial.

Perhaps most important when it comes to the predominance of individuals of full or partial Latina/o descent among the new wave of multicultural figures in U.S. popular culture, some (though certainly not all) Latina/os possess an appearance similar to that of more clearly biracial or multiracial individuals in a U.S. racial context. As noted in this book's Introduction, citing Clara Rodríguez, the "look" historically popularized for Latina/os in Hollywood includes a light tan, *café au lait* complexion that falls between stereotypical norms of white and black skin tones, while some Latina/os also possess other phenotypal features that defy easy racial categorization.[9] An illustration of how this look can be construed for a trendy multiracial appearance: In 2003, a *New York Times* article on the new vogue for racially ambiguous models and actors in the realms of fashion, advertising, and media, what it termed "Generation E.A. (Ethnically Ambiguous)," opened with the story of Leo Jiménez, a young model extremely popular with designers and club promoters because of his multiracial good looks. The model's "steeply raked cheekbones, dreadlocks, and jet-colored eyes" were the result not of being the child of biracial parents, however, as the article went on to reveal, but simply of being Colombian.[10] As Leo Jiménez aptly illustrates, Latina/os are already mixed race, and as such have at times become trendy in the midst of the vogue for the multiracial figure.

Performers of Latina/o and other racial ancestry such as Jessica Alba and Rosario Dawson thus have at times been pulled into the wave of popular interest, gaining acting and promotional opportunities in the midst of what Danzy Senna has termed the "Mulatto Millennium,"[11] at least in part because of their racially or ethnically ambiguous appearance. Among their contemporaries are countless lesser-known actors and actresses who, like Leo Jiménez, are being cast in minor, nonspeaking, and extra roles to help flesh out the concertedly multicultural film and television story worlds set in both present and future settings. Examples include crowd scenes in *The Fast and the Furious* (2001) and the films of the futuristic *Matrix* trilogy (1999–2003). As such they are possibly portraying Latina/os, but just as likely are meant to be interpreted as Filipino, Samoan, half-African American, or Asian, or simply light-skinned "ethnic" types. While it could be argued that this amounts to increased casting opportunities for Latina/o actors and actresses and thus should be interpreted as a progressive development, it is important to examine what happens to Latina/o representation in the process. To begin to explore these dynamics, the case studies of Jessica Alba and Rosario Dawson illuminate the cinematic construction of Latinidad in relation to the careers and public images of two contemporary actresses of partial Latina/o descent.

Jessica Alba and Max Guevara: Mixed Latina/o Icons?

According to biographies of Jessica Alba, the actress was born in 1981 in Pomona, California. With an ambiguous ethnic appearance, she has related to interviewers that her mother is of Danish, French Canadian, English, and Italian descent, while her father is Mexican American. Notably with respect to her Mexican heritage, Alba's father, Mark Alba, has been described in drastically diverse ways by the news media, some of which clearly seem to attempt to avoid the label of Mexican American. He was described by *Marie Claire* magazine as "Mexican-Indian and Spanish," for example.[12] At the other extreme, he was described as "dark Mexican" in a 2005 *Rolling Stone* interview with Alba.[13] Such odd treatment of Jessica Alba's paternal heritage likely reflects the historical colonization and related denigration of Mexican Americans in the United States, as Rafael Pérez-Torres and Angharad Valdivia argue regarding the privileging of other Latina/o origin groups in sociopolitical spheres and popular culture.[14] As the lack of Mexican American stars aside from Edward James Olmos illustrates, anti-Mexican sentiment has in fact contributed to difficulties that many Mexican American actors face in Hollywood casting scenarios.

Alba was fairly young when she began performing; reports state that she was twelve when she began acting classes. She got her first, minor film role a year later in the children's comedy *Camp Nowhere* (1994); other roles followed in commercials and children's television series such as Nickelodeon's *The Secret World of Alex Mack* (1994–98), on which she appeared in 1994, and *Flipper* (1995–2000), on which she had a recurring role from 1995 to 1997. A survey of her work in these years reveals that she likely benefited from the newly multicultural ethos and casting of Nickelodeon, Disney, and other children's media producers, trends that Angharad Valdivia documents.[15]

Jessica Alba at a public appearance in recent years.

Ambiguously ethnic roles in which the young actress appeared during these years include her role as Maya on *Flipper* and as tomboy Samantha Swoboda in the children's techno-geek action film *P.U.N.K.S.* (1999).

With regard to star promotion, the publicity that Alba received was negligible at this stage in her career. While critics at times made mention of Alba as attractive, as they did in reviews of the teen horror-comedy, *Idle Hands* (1999), in which she played a Girl-Next-Door type, none of the publicity that could be found for Alba from these years mentioned ethnicity.[16] Apparently it was considered prudent to promote the young actress merely as an "American" teen, even while she found much of her opportunity in nonwhite roles. Perhaps another reason for this lack of ethnic specificity was due to a perceived lack of attention on the part of young viewers to performers' racial identities. Advertising firms were finding in 1990s studies that this was often the case, and media producers likely were taking notice.[17] According to this research, it did not seem to matter to the same degree for Jessica Alba's similarly aged fans as it did for their parents whether she was white, Latina, mixed, or all of the above.

At the age of eighteen, Jessica Alba's career took a dramatic turn. She was given her first major role when she was cast by *Dark Angel* executive producers James Cameron and Charles H. Eglee to play Max Guevara, a genetically enhanced (or, in *Dark Angel*-speak, transgenic) female in a dystopic future. Max is an escaped X-5, a multiracial warrior engineered in a laboratory, who ultimately becomes a reluctant hero. Over one thousand young women reportedly were considered in the producers' search for an actress with an appearance and stage presence suitable to portray Max. In this search, a multiracial look was clearly part of the producers' vision. "If you're really going to assemble the best of humanity, why not cross the whole genetic spectrum?" Eglee asserted in an interview with *Entertainment Weekly* in 2000. "We wanted someone with a transgenic look."[18] Casting director Robert Ulrich explained that the series was cast to support the multiracial aesthetic they were aiming to create. "It was in the future when everyone was going to be mixed and hopefully mixed in together. And obviously that was a very important part to casting the character of Max. And I think that was one of the most wonderful things about Jessica, because it's hard to tell what exactly Jessica's ethnic background is."[19] (Interestingly, Geneva Locke, who plays the young Max in flashbacks to the experiences of the X-5's as children, is not Latina but rather of Chinese and Irish descent.)

After the series debuted in the fall of 2000, Alba was quickly noticed by viewers and especially by young male fans. News stories about the series make note of the boom in Jessica Alba–dedicated websites and other signs of the young actress's increasing popularity, even though *Dark Angel* did only moderately well in the ratings in its two seasons and was panned by some reviewers. For instance, at the culmination of the 2000–2001 season, Jessica Alba was awarded a 2001 Teen Choice Award and the 2001 *TV Guide* Award for Breakout Star of the Year. She also began to get offers to star in films and other projects.

An interesting question can be posed regarding the impact of Alba, as a mixed Latina star, rising to stardom in the portrayal of a mixed-race and part-Latina character. Max Guevara is not so neatly categorized, however, as her backstory complicates how she can be read with respect to racial or ethnic identity. She is clearly identified as mixed race in the storyline; for example, she admits in the pilot episode that she was genetically engineered with DNA from multiple, distinctly different individuals. As Max jokingly describes herself, in her design she was given "the head of a lion, body of a goat. . . . Your basic hodgepodge." One could argue that the character is also coded as Latina according to Hollywood traditions of racial marking, with Alba's olive complexion and dark brunette hair and makeup in the role contributing to this construction. This proves difficult to sustain, however, given that Max does not identify as Latina in the narrative. She never, for instance, questions the origin of her seemingly Hispanic last name, while the series producers reveal in commentary that accompanies the season 1 DVD set that her first name is short for the ethnically generic "Maximum." We also learn early in season 1 that Max's mother, who by appearance in flashback could be Latina, was not her biological mother but rather a surrogate.

And while Max has DNA that can be traced back to multiple different individuals, and the story premise foregrounds that she is undeniably multiracial, the series does not explore mixed-race identity on more than a metaphoric level. Perhaps most important in this regard is the fact that Max's genetic mélange was manufactured in a laboratory and thus is removed from any connection to ethnic history or communities. Max also is characterized as so mixed that any one possible identity is nullified. "With my DNA, I'm pretty much a blood relative to everybody who's been anybody, ever. Winston Churchill . . . Einstein . . . Pocahontas," she shares with her compatriot and love interest Logan Cale in a season 1 episode.[20] Max's racial identity rather is one of affiliation, demonstrated in her sense of responsibility to her "family" of similarly engineered X-5s. Her X-5 brothers and sisters, a virtual United Colors of Benetton corps of genetically manufactured supersoldiers, while providing a visible metaphor for multiracial identity, also symbolize the elision of race. Max Guevara is the most developed case in point; in her case, Latina/o culture, history, and community were effaced in her creation.

Notably, despite Max Guevara's ambiguous but clearly mixed-race status, early publicity for the series seldom made mention of Jessica Alba's multiethnic roots. While readers today are likely used to hearing of Alba's "smoky multicultural looks" and heritage of "ethnic mélange," little mention was made in the articles that heralded the debut of *Dark Angel* of Alba's mixed ancestry.[21] The first publicity for the series in *Entertainment Weekly*, for example, described only Alba's beauty (more specifically, her "mouth-agape beauty and swollen lips").[22] Other journalists chose to focus on *Dark Angel*'s similarity to other sexy and hard-fighting female characters on television, such as Buffy of *Buffy the Vampire Slayer*.[23] When Alba's ancestry was mentioned, it was at times reported incorrectly, often with her Mexican heritage downplayed or left out entirely. For instance, in a 2001 *Entertainment Weekly* article, journalist Benjamin Svetkey described her as "a genetics experiment all her own. Part Spanish, part Danish, part Canadian, and part Italian."[24]

The Latina/o-oriented press was quick to notice the actress and to trumpet her arrival as a new Latina star, however. This is unsurprising, given that the casting of a Latina, whether of full or partial descent, as the lead in a network television series was almost unprecedented in 2000. Alba and the *Dark Angel* series were mentioned in news outlets such as *Latina, Hispanic, People en Español*, and *Latin Heat* industry trade journal, with Alba touted as a rising star. Alba later was awarded a 2001 ALMA (American Latina/o Media Arts) Award by the National Council of La Raza as Breakthrough Star of the Year. This was followed by a second ALMA Award in 2002, this time for Outstanding Actress in a Television Series. It would appear that Alba was fully embraced as a Latina actress within Latina/o-oriented media circles, even while she was increasingly promoted in the mainstream press as mixed race. Schisms could occasionally be noted in relation to this dual promotional strategy, such as in coverage in the Latina/o-oriented media that chided the actress for not embracing her Mexican ancestry more fully. For instance, a news item reported by *Latina* magazine in the spring of 2006 described her as "Mexican-American Alba (you can keep denying it, mi'ja, but we know the truth!)."[25]

Notably, in the period in which *Dark Angel* was broadcast, multiraciality was garnering a great deal of attention in popular culture. Films such as *The Fast and the Furious* (2001) and *The Scorpion King* (2001) were being released, while their mixed-race stars, Vin Diesel and Dwayne "The Rock" Johnson, respectively, were prompting entertainment news media coverage of what Valdivia has termed the rising "ethnification" of popular culture.[26]

By 2001, news coverage of Jessica Alba often focused on her diverse ethnic background, now usually more correctly described. One especially blatant example was *Entertainment Weekly*'s quiz on its EW.com website, titled "What Nationalities Are in Jessica Alba's Ancestry?" Given *Dark Angel*'s lower ratings in 2001–2, Alba appeared to be receiving attention in part simply because she appealed to many fans. What would become of Alba's career and public image when she no longer was cast in a role that placed multiraciality at its crux, however?

Jessica Alba's career has taken new turns in the years since *Dark Angel* was cancelled in 2002. While the actress has appeared in a handful of films since, a survey of these films reveals that producers and casting directors were at least initially unsure of how to cast the actress outside of futuristic and/or fantastic settings. This is not to say that they may not have had high expectations with respect to her ethnic versatility—as long as the characters she was portraying were not white. For example, in 2003, Alba portrayed both a native Iban woman in 1930s Malaysia in the period drama *The Sleeping Dictionary* and a brash Puerto Rican dancer from the Bronx in the urban dance drama *Honey*. Unfortunately, Alba appears out of her element in both roles, particularly with respect to her attempt to proximate believable accents for her characters.[27] While *Honey* earned some respectable early box office and did fairly well in DVD sales, *The Sleeping Dictionary* was never released in theaters; both films were panned by critics.

Alba fared better with respect to storylines set in more fantastic surroundings. Two of her more recent roles involved portraying comic book figures. These were the superhero Sue Storm/Invisible Girl in *Fantastic Four* (2005) and a sweet stripper in Frank Miller and Robert Rodriguez's *Sin City* (2005). Controversy initially arose among comic book fans over the casting of Alba as the historically Nordic and blonde Sue Storm, which she supposedly muted when she appeared in dyed blonde hair and impressed fans in the film. *Sin City*'s Nancy Carruthers, as portrayed by Alba, also appears to be (ambiguously) white. Similarly, Alba was cast opposite Paul Walker in the deep-sea-diving thriller *Into the Blue* (2005), in a case of color-blind casting that had the actress don various bikinis and allowed her to utilize her scuba diving skills.

In the meantime, Jessica Alba has been consistently lauded in the press for her beauty and even more so for her perceived sexiness, in a manner that echoes Latina star promotion of past decades. To list a handful of her recent accolades in this regard, Alba was named one of *Teen People*'s "25 Hottest Stars Under 25" in 2005, while her performance in *Sin City* was awarded

Sexiest Performance by the MTV Movie Awards. In 2006, she also topped *Playboy's* Hottest Celebrities list. This celebration of Alba's body has accompanied her rising status as an actress. A recent illustration of this trend in Jessica Alba's career: In June 2006, she was named "Must Girl of the Summer" by *Entertainment Weekly,* appearing on its cover and headlining its 2006 "It List." In its story on the star, the magazine declared Alba to be "on the brink of Hollywood domination"; at the time she had five film releases scheduled for 2007.[28]

Notably, as Alba has become increasingly successful as a Hollywood actress and visible as a public figure, she has spoken more candidly about her heritage, in a manner that implies both association and disassociation with her Mexican American heritage. For instance, asked by *iF Magazine* how it felt to be viewed as the "face of Latino industry [in Hollywood]," she responded, "I'm proud of it. I grew up in California and my great grandparents are from Mexico on my dad's side. I'm half Mexican and the other half is French and Danish. My dad is proud of my family name and they are all very proud of me. The more racially diverse mainstream movies can be and mainstream Hollywood can be, this is for the better. Latin, Black, Asian, Middle-eastern, anything to change it up is great. There was before an idea of what an American movie star had to be or what criteria you had to fit in to be a leading lady or man and it's changing. And I'm glad to be part of this group of people who are ethnically diverse."[29] Her expressions of Latina pride have been tempered in relation to other statements she has made in interviews, however. Aside from being of mixed racial heritage, she apparently grew up in a family in which the Mexican American members, particularly her grandfather, had decided to stop speaking Spanish in order to better assimilate to Euro-American culture. As she told journalist Allison Glock, "I never really belonged anywhere. . . . I wasn't white. I was shunned by the Latin community for not being Latin enough."[30] Perhaps because of the complexity of Alba's relationship with Mexican American culture, her discussions with interviewers in recent years have addressed elements of Latina identity that go beyond appearance, such as language and cultural habits. For instance, Alba has made mention of how her life has been impacted by not being given the opportunity to learn Spanish when she was growing up, and that she had begun taking lessons to learn it. Her ambivalent connection to Latina/o culture and acts of retro-acculturation point to the complexity of "Latinidades" experienced by many acculturated young Latina/os today, arguably making her a potential icon for contemporary identity.

A Less Trendy Ambiguity: The Case of Rosario Dawson

Alba's off-white, vaguely Latina appearance and the advantages it affords her as a Hollywood actress become more apparent when her opportunities and promotions are compared with that of her peer, Rosario Dawson. As noted previously, while Dawson has had a busy career and is also widely praised as attractive, she has experienced very different acting opportunities. We can surmise that this is in part because the two actresses have made different career choices. Arguably, however, this is also because Dawson's more markedly ethnic appearance and urban image have resulted in a star image racialized as nonwhite and thus in media industry perceptions that her marketability to white filmgoers is not as broad as Alba's.

A comparison of the actresses' promotional texts and filmographies reveals the influence of a performer's appearance, associations with differing regions (Alba with California, Dawson with New York City), and early career choices on critics' and journalists' ultimate construction of a Latina/o star's image with respect to race. This is particularly noticeable in the case of mixed-race actors, who may be racialized in star promotion in a manner that in fact differs from their actual racial makeup and/or identity. For example, Halle Berry is interpreted by journalists as African American even when she brings her Euro-American mother with her to the Oscars, Cameron Diaz is perceived and promoted as unambiguously white, and Salma Hayek simply as Latina, even while their mixed racial heritage, which belies this simplicity, is known to much of the public. Mixed race is increasingly an identity category available to stars, but one that is unstable when it comes to its impact on their careers.

In this regard, Jessica Alba's initial lack of ethnic self-labeling in her career and her light tan, not brown, skin and girlish image have contributed to the perception that she is ethnically ambiguous of the degree most preferred by Hollywood producers and casting directors in casting lead roles. Like Jennifer Lopez, Alba has achieved what Diane Negra has referred to as an "off-white" image.[31] Dawson, in contrast, has somewhat darker skin and dark hair that does not look as natural when dyed blonde (a look that Alba has recently been favoring), a more womanly and urban image, and has been associated with her mixed heritage since she began her acting career. Given Hollywood's ongoing, unwritten racial paradigms of casting, which still often dictate a color line between what are categorized as whiteness and nonwhiteness, it comes as no surprise that she has typically been cast only as Latinas, Latin Americans, and ambiguous ethnic types, and in one case, as Persian (in *Alexander*). She also has been much less likely than Jessica Alba to be cast in what are viewed as white roles. On the other hand, Dawson has received opportunities to portray the romantic partners of characters played by African American actors, including Will Smith in *Men in Black II* (2002) and Eddie Murphy in *The Adventures of Pluto Nash* (2002)—a casting paradigm that can be seen as a holdover from classical Hollywood's reluctance to portray mixed couples on screen. The rise of male actors of color who are seen as "having box office" and thus as able to headline a film has in this regard been a boon to Rosario Dawson's career.

Dawson also is viewed as more "urban" than Alba, which arguably has contributed to this racialization of her public image. A preponderance of Dawson's films have been set in New York City, beginning with *Kids,* and subsequently including such films as *He Got Game* (1998), *Light It Up* (1999), *Sidewalks of New York* (2001), *25th Hour* (2002), and *Rent* (2005). In these films, her major costars have often been other actors of color. Such was the case in *Light It Up,* a drama about New York City high school students in a standoff with police in an effort to force improvements at their school; Dawson plays a brainy student who is convinced to take part. In addition, the story that is often repeated about Dawson's entrée as an actress is that *Kids* director Larry Clark "discovered" Dawson on her Lower East Side tenement stoop when she was fifteen.[32] This and the predominance of New York–centric roles that Dawson has portrayed since have contributed to a public image that is strongly rooted in the city and its polyglot, distinctly nonwhite cultures. Common associations of Nuyorican and Afro-Cuban cultures with African American culture in the United States also have likely had an impact in this regard.[33]

It is important to note that the differing racialization of Alba's and Dawson's public images has taken place not only in Hollywood, but also in the Latina/o and African American–oriented news media and by ethnic advocacy groups that monitor media representation. More specifically, and in fact not surprisingly, Alba and Dawson have been embraced by their overlapping ethnic communities, but to different degrees. A review of their mention in Latina/o-oriented magazines and nominations for awards such as the National Council of La Raza's annual ALMA Awards supports the impression that, while both have been touted at various times as Latina stars, Jessica Alba appears to have received more attention from the U.S. Latina/o-oriented press and especially from Latina/o advocacy groups. On the other hand, Dawson has been additionally "claimed" by and lauded for her acting by African American–oriented media outlets such as *Essence* and *Jet* magazines and groups such as the NAACP, which has honored her at its annual Image Awards ceremony.[34]

Rosario Dawson in one of the roles that contributed to her urban, ethnic image. She starred with Raymond Usher (*left*) and Robert Ri'chard in the urban teen drama *Light It Up* (1999). Edmonds / Fox 2000 / The Kobal Collection.

Over the years, Dawson has received positive reviews from film critics (she has been described, among other things, as a "rising starlet" and "a lovely and appealing screen presence").[35] She was recently part of the ensemble cast of *A Guide to Recognizing Your Saints,* which was awarded a Special Jury Prize for best ensemble performance at the Sundance Film Festival 2006. Her "diverse as downtown" image has likely affected how she is viewed by Hollywood producers, who appear to still often be guided by white-centric norms, however.[36] Interestingly, the few directors that have cast her as a romantic lead opposite a white male have in fact been New Yorkers. They include Edward Burns, who cast Dawson in both *Sidewalks of New York* and *Ash Wednesday* (2002), and Spike Lee, who cast Dawson opposite Edward Norton in *25th Hour.*

It is worth exploring that Alba's *mestizaje* appears more desirable than Dawson's not only to Hollywood producers but to Latina/o organizations and media outlets, which underscores the vagaries of Latinidad as defined within Latina/o communities themselves. What factors determine whether a star of partial Latino ancestry will be embraced by U.S. Latina/o audiences? Notably, differing types of racial ambiguity are not embraced equally. As Gregory Velazco y Trianosky argues, while *mestizaje* is very much a part of Latina/o and Latin American history, it still is not necessarily acknowledged or celebrated.[37] Vicki L. Ruiz has also noted that "color judgments" are common among Mexican Americans and Mexicans, while Ian Haney Lopez has documented how a desire to be seen legally as white has at times led Mexican Americans to decry their indigenous heritage and to distance themselves from African Americans.[38] Indigenous and African ancestry often continues to be denied and denigrated in casual talk and actions (as when children are dubbed with nicknames such as La Negra, for instance), while fair skin is typically celebrated. Similar patterns at times can be discerned in the U.S. Latina/o media when it comes to coverage of mixed Latina/o stars, and Latina/o actors cast in African American roles have seldom received accolades from Latina/o organizations. Arguably for mixed Latina stars their approximation of the expected "Latin look" is still a necessity—but the more they can play with whiteness within these parameters, the better.

An illustration of the importance of perceived assimilability to whiteness for being viewed as a bankable Hollywood actress is evident in the career of Jessica Alba, who is currently constructed as the millennial Girl Next Door. The complexity of this construction should be acknowledged, however. Her public image arguably is coming full circle as she is seen simultaneously as mixed race *and* as the average U.S. American girl. As she noted to *Entertainment Weekly* in June 2006 in response to her popularity, "People today, especially this next generation of kids, they don't look like middle America anymore. They're not all blond and blue-eyed. They're more ethnically mixed. Today, the girl next door looks more like me."[39] This can be viewed as a strategic move in the development of her public image, but also as a sign of an increased broadening of ethnic notions in the popular imagination. Moreover, it is paying off. Alba appears to be following in the path set by Jennifer Lopez as she is beginning to be cast in a number of non-ethnically specified roles in upcoming films, a definite shift from how she was cast a few years ago. Her 2007 films included the medical drama *Awake*, the romantic comedy *Good Luck Chuck*, the Ten Commandments-inspired satire *The Ten*, and the comedy *Bill*, in addition to the *Fantastic Four* sequel, *4: Rise of the Silver Surfer*.

Mestizaje versus Hollywood Latinidad: A Final Word

> Both in the mainstream and at the high end of the marketplace,
> what is perceived as good, desirable, successful is often a face
> whose heritage is hard to pin down.
>
> —Ron Berger, chief executive, RSCG MVBMS Partners advertising
> firm, as quoted in Ruth La Ferla, "Generation E.A.," *New York
> Times* (December 28, 2003): section 9, page 1, paragraph 4

In exploring Jessica Alba and Rosario Dawson's evolving careers and public images, it becomes clear that in many ways Max Guevara's ambiguous but deracialized identity serves as an apt metaphor for how the actress who portrayed her was initially sold to the U.S. American public, and how Rosario Dawson, running up against what we might call the "one-drop rule of racialized casting," has not and likely will not any time soon be given this opportunity on the big-budget film playing field. More recently, Alba has begun to complicate her image, however, as she identifies publicly as mixed race as opposed to simply Latina and shares more information about her struggles as an individual and as an actress of partial Mexican American descent. A mixed Latina star's embracing of *mestizaje* in this manner can in fact challenge Hollywood's imagined constructions of Latinidad and the nation's distinct denial of ethnic and racial hybridity through racialization, offering a transgressive potential such as Gloria Anzaldúa describes in her exhortations to Chicanas to embrace the racial ambiguity of their ancestry.[40]

But while her stardom thus complicates Latina visibility in Hollywood story worlds and promotional realms, Alba notably has had many doors open to her that are still not available to other Latinas, in large part because of her off-white appearance and image. As Ron Berger, chief executive of advertising firm and trend research company Euro RSCG MVBMS Partners, notes in the quote above, the most desirable look for many advertisers and media producers today is one that is hard to pinpoint with respect to race and ethnicity—that is, as long as some of that heritage appears to be European or European American, as the success of such mixed-race, non-Latino actors and performers as Keanu Reeves, Vin Diesel, and Jennifer Beals also highlight. From this perspective, is Alba's success reflective in any shape or form of a rising status of Latina/os in the United States or in Hollywood with respect to casting opportunities? Not necessarily, considering that in this process Latinidad is often nullified, construed merely as a hint of ethnic possibility that is seldom made meaningful. Latina/o representation can in fact be in danger of being submerged and homogenized in star promotion that whitens and denies Latina/o, African, and indigenous ancestry and appearance while exalting the multiethnic. Acknowledgment of the diverse range of real-life Latin looks—which run the gamut from indigenous and dark-skinned African phenotypic features to the look of "*güeros*" of more European appearance, as Clara Rodríguez's discussion of Hollywood's "Latin look" underscores—and thus the fallacy of positing one racialized category for Latina/os, is what is at stake.

On the other hand, while ambiguity and approximation of whiteness can result in increased opportunity in contemporary films and television, Latinidad as constructed by Hollywood still rests on notions of distinctive elements and traits, a conundrum with which actors have to contend. We Latina/os also typically expect Latina/o stars to embody our own notions of Latina/o appearance (despite the fact that Latina/os can have widely varying skin tones and features). Given these expectations, if mixed Latina/o stars are not viewed as embodying a clearly Latina/o look, they typically won't be cast in Latina/o roles.

The tensions inherent in these dynamics of contemporary stardom undoubtedly will continue to be felt as the Latina/o population grows and notions of Latinidad take on more valences in the Hollywood media industries and in the wide variety of Latina/o communities in this country. As José Itzigsohn notes, "The continuous growth in the number and diversity of Latino populations, the increasingly multiethnic character of Latino urban populations, and the surge in Latino political organizations during the 1990s confront us with new and different situations."[41] In this regard, the multicultural wave of media stardom needs to be viewed critically, particularly with respect to how it has the potential both to spur and to halt progress toward increasingly diverse and dimensional Latina/o images, both on screen and as represented in the star system. Responsibility in this regard lies with Latina/o communities and media outlets as well. As Gloria Anzaldúa also emphasized in her discussion of the empowering potential of what she termed "*Mestiza* consciousness," the challenge for Chicana/o communities who wish to empower their members is to embrace indigenous and other histories that traditionally have been erased.[42] Mixed Latina stars such as Jessica Alba and Rosario Dawson serve as important totems in this regard, as their future careers and public images will reveal a great deal about the racial borders that affect Latina/os and whether they are typically transgressed.

Notes

Introduction. Latina and Latino Stars in U.S. Eyes

1. I use the gender-inclusive term "Latina/o" and the gender-specific "Latina" and "Latino" throughout this book to refer to men and women in the United States of Latin American heritage. This is with the caveat that such a pan-Latino label encompasses a wide range of diverse communities. More specific labels (e.g., Mexican American, Puerto Rican) are utilized when referring to Latino groups of specific national heritage. I also use "Chicana/o" to refer to Mexican Americans specifically during the peak of Chicana/o activism and when this label was and is utilized as an expression of ethnic self-pride by people of Mexican American descent.

2. "The Latino Explosion" issue, *Newsweek* (September 9, 1999). Mireya Navarro, John Leland, and Veronica Chambers, "Generation Ñ," *New York* (July 12, 1999).

3. Charles Ramírez Berg, *Latino Images in Film: Stereotypes, Subversion, and Resistance* (Austin: University of Texas Press, 2002), 66–86.

4. Richard Dyer, *Heavenly Bodies: Film Stars and Society* (Hampshire, UK: MacMillan, 1986).

5. In this assumption, I build on important foundational scholarship that has documented the impact of stardom with respect to racialization. This work includes but is not limited to Dyer, *Heavenly Bodies,* and idem, *White* (London: Routledge, 1997); Diane Negra, *Off-White Stardom: American Culture and Ethnic Female Stardom* (London: Routledge, 2001); Ana M. López, "Are All Latins from Manhattan? Hollywood, Ethnography, and Cultural Colonialism," in *Unspeakable Images: Ethnicity and the American Cinema,* ed. Lester D. Friedman (Urbana: University of Illinois Press, 1991), 404–24; and Angharad Valdivia, "Latinas as Radical Hybrid: Transnationally Gendered Traces in Mainstream Media," *Global Media Journal* 3, no. 4 (Spring 2004). Online: http://lass.calumet.purdue.edu/cca/gmj/sp04/gmj-sp04–valdivia.htm.

6. Frances Aparicio and Susan Chávez-Silverman, eds., *Tropicalizations: Transcultural Representations of Latinidad* (Hanover, N.H.: Dartmouth College Press, 1997), 15–16.

7. López, "Are All Latins from Manhattan?" 404.

8. See, for example, Dyer, *White;* George Lipsitz, *The Possessive Investment in Whiteness: How White People Profit from Identity Politics* (Philadelphia: Temple University Press, 2006); Ella Shohat and Robert Stam, *Unthinking Eurocentrism: Multiculturalism and the Media* (London: Routledge, 1994).

9. Alberto Sandoval-Sánchez, *José, Can You See? Latinos On and Off Broadway* (Madison: University of Wisconsin Press, 1999), 8.

10. For further discussion, see Dyer, *White.*

11. See, for example, Negra, *Off-White Hollywood;* Michael Rogin, *Blackface, White Noise: Jewish Immigrants in the Hollywood Melting Pot* (Berkeley: University of California Press, 1996); and Linda Mizejewski, *Ziegfeld Girl: Image and Icon in Culture and Cinema* (Durham, N.C.: Duke University Press, 1999).

12. Michael Omi and Howard Winant, *Racial Formation in the United States: From the 1960s to the 1980s* (New York: Routledge and Kegan Paul, 1986).

13. Neil Foley, "Straddling the Color Line: The Legal Construction of Hispanic Identity in Texas," in *Not Just Black and White: Historical and Contemporary Perspectives on Immigration, Race, and Ethnicity in the United States,* ed. Nancy Foner and George M. Fredrickson (New York: Russell Sage Foundation, 2004), 353.

14. For instance, Latina/os have been categorized on the U.S. census in widely divergent ways over the decades. Mexican Americans, in particular, have shifted from being categorized as a nonwhite race in 1930 to being categorized as an ethnic group that could be of white or other racial status today. See Ian Haney López, *White by Law: The Legal Construction of Race* (New York: NYU Press, 2006), 82. "Hispanic/Latino" is currently defined on the census as an ethnic group (of white, black, indigenous, or other racial status), rather than a distinct race. For further discussion of the complex history of the racial categorization of Latina/os, see Clara Rodríguez, *Changing Race: Latinos, the Census, and the History of Ethnicity* (New York: NYU Press, 2000), and Martha Menchaca, *Recovering History, Constructing Race: The Indian, Black and White Roots of Mexican Americans* (Austin: University of Texas Press, 2002).

15. Examples of such studies include Albert Bandura, *Social Foundations of Thought and Action: A Social Cognitive Theory* (Englewood Cliffs, N.J.: PrenticeHall, 1986), and George A. Comstock and Hae-Jung Paik, *Television and the American Child* (San Diego: Academic, 1991). A more recent study conducted by research and advocacy organization Children Now also found that "across all races, children are more likely to associate positive characteristics with White characters and negative characteristics with minority characters." Children Now, *A Different World: Children's Perceptions of Race and Class in Media* (Oakland, Calif.: Children Now, 1998), 112. Children Now also has conducted many other surveys of television representation and its impact

on children of various ethnic backgrounds; see the Children Now web site at www
.childrennow.org to access to its many reports on these studies.

16. Christine Gledhill, Introduction, in *Stardom: Industry of Desire,* ed. Christine
Gledhill (London: Routledge, 1991), xiv.

17. Allison R. Hoffman and Chon A. Noriega, *Looking for Latino Regulars on Prime-
Time Television: The Fall 2004 Season,* CSRC Research Report, 4 (Los Angeles: UCLA
Chicano Studies Research Center, December 2004).

18. It is said that James Baldwin first used the term to describe Sidney Poitier in
1968. Kobena Mercer's "Black Art and the Burden of Representation," *Third Text*
(Spring 1990), also provided a seminal description.

19. U.S. Bureau of the Census, *Population Projections of the United States by Age,
Sex, Race, and Hispanic Origin: 1995 to 2050* (Washington, D.C.: U.S. Department
of Commerce, 1996). Available online in pdf format: http://www.census.gov/prod/
www/abs/popula.html#popest.

20. "Latinowood" is a term I first heard used by Bel Hernandez, editor and publisher of *Latin Heat* trade journal, when I interned for the journal as a part of my
research in Los Angeles. A regular "LatinoWood, U.S.A." column in the journal
reports on production deals and other breaking news. Online: http://www.latinheat
.com/index.php.

21. See, for example, Ramírez Berg, *Latino Images in Film;* López, "Are All Latins
from Manhattan?"; Chon A. Noriega, Introduction, *Chicanos and Film: Representa-
tion and Resistance,* ed. Chon A. Noriega (Minneapolis: University of Minnesota
Press, 1992), xi–xxvi; Clara E. Rodríguez, Introduction, in *Latin Looks: Images of Lati-
nas and Latinos in the U.S. Media,* ed. Clara E. Rodríguez (Boulder, Colo.: Westview
Press, 1997), 80–84, and *Heroes, Lovers, and Others: The Story of Latinos in Hollywood*
(Washington, D.C.: Smithsonian, 1994); Angharad Valdivia, *A Latina in the Land of
Hollywood and Other Essays on Media Culture* (Tucson: University of Arizona Press,
2000), and multiple recent essays; and Gary Keller, *Hispanics in Hollywood Film: An
Overview and Handbook* (Tempe, Ariz.: Bilingual Review Press, 1994).

22. Antonio Ríos-Bustamante, "Latino Participation in the Hollywood Film Industry,
1911–1945," in *Chicanos and Film: Representation and Resistance,* ed. Chon A. Noriega
(Minneapolis: University of Minnesota Press, 1992), 18–28; Clara Rodríguez, "Visual
Retrospective: Latino Film Stars," in *Latin Looks: Images of Latinas and Latinos in the
U.S. Media,* ed. Clara E. Rodríguez (Boulder, Colo.: Westview Press, 1997), 80–84.

23. Rodríguez, Introduction, *Latin Looks,* 4.

24. Rosaura Sánchez notes also the intricate relationship between cultural racialization and the discrimination that has been experienced by Mexican Americans. As
she asserts, "The racism suffered has always been intersected by ethnocentrism, clas-
sicism, linguistic oppression, and judicial prejudice." Sánchez, *Telling Identities: The
Californio Testimonios* (Minneapolis: University of Minnesota Press, 1995), 285.

25. Alicia Rodríguez-Estrada, "Dolores Del Rio and Lupe Velez: Images On and Off

the Screen: 1925–1944," in *Writing the Range: Race, Class and Culture in the Women's West*, ed. Elizabeth Jameson and Susan Armitage (Norman: University of Oklahoma Press, 1997), 475–92.

26. Angharad Valdivia, "Is Penélope to J.Lo as Culture Is to Nature? Eurocentric Approaches to 'Latin' Beauties," in *From Bananas to Buttocks: The Latina Body in Popular Film and Culture*, ed. Myra Mendible (Austin: University of Texas Press, 2007), 129–48.

27. Dyer, *White*, 19.

28. Joanne Hershfield, *The Invention of Dolores Del Rio* (Minneapolis: University of Minnesota Press, 2000), xi.

29. See, for example, Richard Dyer's analysis of the star promotion of African American musical artist and film star Paul Robeson in *Heavenly Bodies*; Diane Negra's analysis of the establishment of "off-white" images for classical and contemporary film stars of ethnic origins seen as assimilable to whiteness in *Off-White Hollywood*; Shari Roberts on the construction of Carmen Miranda's star image in "'The Lady in the Tutti Frutti Hat': Carmen Miranda, a Spectacle of Ethnicity," *Cinema Journal* 32, no. 3 (Spring 1993): 3–23; and Chris Holmlund's discussion of the inclusion of elements of excess in the racialization of film stars' images in *Impossible Bodies: Femininity and Masculinity at the Movies* (London: Routledge, 2002).

30. Shohat and Stam, *Unthinking Eurocentrism*, 138

31. Frances Aparicio and Susana Chávez-Silverman, Introduction, *Tropicalizations*.

32. *Entertainment Weekly* (November 24, 2000).

33. A dynamic that was recalled to my attention by Sandy Varga, former advertising manager of *Latin Heat* trade journal, when I was conducting research in Los Angeles.

34. According to the study, in 1998 Latina/o members of SAG (Screen Actors Guild) comprised only 4.3 percent of total SAG membership, and worked on average only 2.9 percent of actors' workdays. They also were more often cast in supporting rather than lead roles in comparison to white and African American actors. Harry P. Pachon et al., *Missing in Action: Latinos in and out of Hollywood* (Los Angeles: The Tomás Rivera Policy Institute, 1999). Online: http://www.trpi.org/update/media.html.

35. Gill Branston, *Cinema and Cultural Modernity* (Buckingham, UK: Open University Press, 2000), 115. See also Reba L. Chaisson, *For Entertainment Purposes Only? An Analysis of the Struggle to Control Filmic Representation* (Lanham, Mass.: Lexington, 2000), and Barry King, "Articulating Stardom," in *Stardom: Industry of Desire*, ed. Christine Gledhill (London: Routledge, 1991).

36. Sarah Berry, "Hollywood Exoticism: Cosmetics and Color in the 1930s," in *Hollywood Goes Shopping*, ed. David Desser and Garth S. Jowett (Minneapolis: University of Minnesota Press, 2000), 110.

37. Ramírez Berg, *Latino Images in Film*, 42.

38. Ibid., 66–86.

39. Valdivia, *A Latina in the Land of Hollywood*, 243.

40. Jose E. Limón, "Stereotyping and Chicano Resistance: An Historical Dimension," reprinted in *Chicanos and Film: Representation and Resistance*, ed. Chon A. Noriega (Minneapolis: University of Minnesota Press, 1992), 3–17.

41. Ella Shohat, "Ethnicities-in-Relation: Toward a Multicultural Reading of American Cinema," in *Unspeakable Images: Ethnicity and the American Cinema*, ed. Lester D. Friedman (Urbana: University of Illinois Press, 1991), 215–50.

42. Joshua Gamson, *Claims to Fame: Celebrity in Contemporary America* (Berkeley: University of California Press), 1994.

Chapter 1. Latin Lovers and American Accents: Dolores Del Rio and Hollywood's Transition to Sound

Some material in this chapter previously appeared in print in my articles "Dolores Del Rio, the First 'Latin Invasion,' and Hollywood's Transition to Sound," *Aztlán: A Journal of Chicano Studies* 30, no. 1 (Spring 2005): 55–85; and "When Dolores Del Rio Became Latina: Latina/o Stardom in Hollywood's Transition to Sound," in *Latina/o Communication Studies Today*, ed. Angharad N. Valdivia (New York: Peter Lang, 2008), 27–50.

1. "The Latin Invasion," *Photoplay* (June 1927), 59.

2. Ibid.

3. See Joanne Hershfield, *The Invention of Dolores Del Rio* (Minneapolis: University of Minnesota Press, 2000), and Ana M. López, "From Hollywood and Back: Dolores Del Rio, A Trans(National Star)," *Studies in Latin American Popular Culture* 17 (1998): 5–32.

4. Colin Shindler, *Hollywood in Crisis: Cinema and American Society, 1929–1939* (London: Routledge, 1999).

5. Cary McWilliams, *Southern California: An Island on the Land* (Santa Barbara, Calif.: Peregrine Smith, 1946); John R. Chávez, *The Lost Land: The Chicano Image in the Southwest* (Albuquerque: University of New Mexico Press, 1995), 85–97.

6. John Storm Roberts, *The Latin Tinge: The Impact of Latin American Music on the United States*, 2nd edition (New York: Oxford University Press, 1999).

7. Alexander Walker, *The Shattered Silents: How the Talkies Came to Stay* (New York: William Morrow & Co., 1979); Richard Kozarski, *An Evening's Entertainment: The Age of the Silent Feature Picture, 1915–1928* (New York: Scribner, 1990); Robert Sklar, *Movie-made America: A Cultural History of the Movies*, revised edition (New York: Vintage Books, 1994).

8. Sklar, *Movie-made America*, 100.

9. Allen R. Ellenberger, *Ramon Novarro* (Jefferson, N.C.: McFarland & Company, 1999), 70.

10. Gaylyn Studlar, *This Mad Masquerade: Stardom and Masculinity in the Jazz Age* (New York: Columbia University Press, 1996), 153.

11. Matthew Bernstein, Introduction, in *Visions of the East: Orientalism in Film,* ed. Matthew Bernstein and Gaylyn Studlar (New Brunswick, N.J.: Rutgers University Press, 1997), 6.

12. Ramon Novarro was born José Ramón Gil Samaniego in Durango, Mexico, where his younger second cousin, Dolores Asúnsolo (later Dolores Del Rio), also was born.

13. Studlar, *This Mad Masquerade,* 178.

14. "Americanization" programs, which began in earnest after World War I, aimed to forcefully encourage Mexican Americans to assimilate to Euro-American customs and culture, particularly through a focus on Mexican American homemakers, as Vicki Ruiz notes in *From Out of the Shadows: Mexican Woman in Twentieth Century America* (New York: Oxford University Press, 1999), 33–50. See also George J. Sánchez, *Becoming Mexican American: Ethnicity, Culture and Identity in Chicano Los Angeles, 1900–1945* (New York: Oxford University Press, 1993), for discussion of Americanization programs in Los Angeles. This was a separate issue from that of school segregation; throughout the Southwest, Mexican American children were often forced to attend substandard "Mexican schools" throughout the first half of the twentieth century. See Richard R. Valencia, Martha Menchaca, and Rubén Donato, "Segregation, Desegregation, and Integration of Chicano Students: Old and New Realities," in *Chicano School Failure: Past, Present, and Future,* ed. Richard R. Valencia (London: Routledge, 1991), 70–113.

15. Kathy Peiss, *Hope in a Jar: The Making of America's Beauty Culture* (New York: Metropolitan Books, 1998), 149.

16. Bridget Byrne, "Dolores Del Rio," *San Francisco Chronicle* (November 20–27, 1981).

17. Larry Carr, *More Fabulous Faces: The Evolution and Metamorphosis of Dolores Del Rio, Myrna Loy, Carol Lombard, Bette Davis, and Katharine Hepburn* (Garden City, N.Y.: Doubleday, 1979), 42.

18. "Pals First," *Variety* (August 26, 1926), 18.

19. Fred, "What Price Glory?" *Variety* (December 1, 1926), 12.

20. Walker, *The Shattered Silents,* 149.

21. Ivan St. John, "Daughter of the Dons," *Photoplay* (June 27, 1926), 66.

22. Harry D. Wilson, "Official biography of Dolores Del Rio" (1927), 6. Dolores Del Rio biography file, Margaret Herrick Library, Academy of Motion Picture Arts and Sciences, Los Angeles.

23. St. John, "Daughter of the Dons," 66.

24. Carr, *More Fabulous Faces,* 5.

25. Ibid.

26. Charles Eckert, "The Carole Lombard in Macy's Window," in *Stardom: Industry of Desire,* ed. Christine Gledhill (London: Routledge, 1991), 33.

27. Eric Braun, "Queen of Mexico," *Films and Filming* 18, no. 10 (July 1972): 35.

28. "Resurrection," *Variety* (December 1, 1926).

29. Sid., "The Loves of Carmen," *Variety* (September 28, 1927), 53.

30. "The Loves of Carmen," *Photoplay* (July 1927), 69.

31. Walker, *The Shattered Silents*, 49–62.

32. *Scribners*, April 1929. Cited in Donald Crafton, *The Talkies: American Cinema's Transition to Sound, 1926–1931* (New York: Charles Scribner's Sons, 1997), 450.

33. Ethan Mordden, *The Hollywood Studios: House Style in the Golden Age of the Movies* (New York: Alfred A. Knopf, 1988); Benjamin B. Hampton, *History of the American Film Industry: From Its Beginnings to 1931* (New York: Dover, 1970).

34. Ana M. López, "Are All Latins from Manhattan? Hollywood, Ethnography, and Cultural Colonialism," in *Unspeakable Images: Ethnicity and the American Cinema*, ed. Lester D. Friedman (Urbana: University of Illinois Press, 1991).

35. Curtis Marez, "Subaltern Soundtracks: Mexican Immigrants and the Making of Hollywood Cinema," *Aztlán: The Journal of Chicano Studies* 29, no. 1 (Fall 2004): 59.

36. Mordden, *The Hollywood Studios*, 175.

37. Sánchez, *Becoming Mexican American*, 213.

38. Rudolfo Acuña, *Occupied America: A History of Chicanos*, 4th edition (New York: Addison Wesley Longman, 2000), 216.

39. Nicholás Kanellos, *A History of Hispanic Theater in the United States: Origins to 1940* (Austin: University of Texas Press, 1990), 42–43.

40. Tino Balio, *Grand Design: Hollywood as a Modern Business Enterprise, 1930–1939* (New York: Charles Scribner's Sons, 1993), 13–15.

41. Carlos E. Cortés, "Chicanas in Film," in *Latin Looks: Images of Latinas and Latinos in the U.S. Media*, ed. Clara E. Rodríguez (Boulder, Colo.: Westview Press, 1997), 121–41.

42. Walker, *The Shattered Silents*, 209.

43. DeWitt Bodeen, *From Hollywood: The Careers of 15 Great American Stars* (South Brunswick, N.J.: A. S. Barnes and Company, 1976), 284.

44. Ellenberger, *Ramon Novarro*, 182.

45. Walker, *The Shattered Silents*, 1, 211.

46. Hershfield, *The Invention of Dolores Del Rio*, 15.

47. "Ramona," *Photoplay* (March 1928), 52.

48. Walker, *The Shattered Silents*, 82.

49. "Evangeline," *Vanity Fair* (September 1929), 77.

50. "Evangeline," *Film Daily* (August 4, 1929), 8. "Evangeline," *Variety* (July 31, 1929), 17.

51. "The Bad One," *Variety* (June 18, 1930), 37.

52. Bodeen, *From Hollywood*, 285–86.

53. Walker, *The Shattered Silents*, 203.

54. Rush., "Girl of the Rio," *Photoplay* (January 12, 1932), 15.

55. Ellenberger, *Ramon Novarro*, 226.

56. "Most Perfect," *Photoplay* (February 1933), 74.

57. Berg, *Latino Images in Film*, 76.

58. "Dolores Del Rio," *Film Weekly* (July 1972), 456.

59. David Ragin, *Movie Stars of the '30s* (Englewood Cliffs, N.J.: Prentice Hall, 1985), 46.

60. "I Live For Love," *Variety* (October 23, 1935).

61. Braun, "Queen of Mexico," 34–37.

62. George Hadley-Garcia, *Hispanic Hollywood* (New York: Carol Publishing Group, 1990), 5.

63. Sánchez, *Becoming Mexican American*, 226.

Chapter 2. The Good Neighbor on Prime Time: Desi Arnaz and *I Love Lucy*

1. Desi Arnaz died of lung cancer on December 2, 1986. He was sixty-nine.

2. As Ana M. López notes, Carmen Miranda was seen as embodying the balance that Hollywood was looking for—the Latin exotic who was so exaggerated as to be safe and thus palatable for American audiences. "Are All Latins from Manhattan? Hollywood, Ethnography, and Cultural Colonialism," in *Unspeakable Images: Ethnicity and the American Cinema*, ed. Lester D. Friedman (Urbana: University of Illinois Press, 1991), 404–24.

3. As Catherine Benamou describes, Good Neighbor films typically involved the "essentialization or conflation of different genres and national sources of Latin American music" among other problematic aspects of "Good Neighbor propaganda." *It's All True: Orson Welles's Pan-American Odyssey* (Berkeley: University of California Press, 2007), 201, 202.

4. Gustavo Pérez-Firmat, *Life on the Hyphen: The Cuban American Way* (Austin: University of Texas Press, 1994), 5. In his autobiography, *A Book*, Desi Arnaz himself notes that the major lesson he learned while performing as a young man in Xavier Cugat's band was how to successfully perform Cuban music for American audiences. Arnaz, *A Book* (New York: William Morrow, 1976).

5. Susan Murray, *Hitch Your Antenna to the Stars! Early Television and Broadcast Stardom* (New York: Routledge, 2005), 25–26, 50–52.

6. The series also spawned a number of other series and films starring Desi Arnaz and his then-wife Lucille Ball. These included the films *The Long, Long Trailer* (1954) and *Forever, Darling* (1956), and the television series *The Lucy and Desi Comedy Hour* (1957–60).

7. Pérez-Firmat, *Life on the Hyphen*; Alberto Sandoval-Sánchez, *José, Can You See? Latinos On and Off Broadway* (Madison: University of Wisconsin Press, 1999); Murray, *Hitch Your Antenna to the Stars;* Thomas Schatz, "I Love Lucy, Desilu, and the Rise of Network TV," in *Making Television: Authorship and the Production Process,* ed.

Robert J. Thompson and Gary Burns (New York: Praeger, 1990); Mary Desjardins, "Lucy and Desi: TV's First Family in the 1950s and the 1990s," in *Television, History, and American Culture,* ed. Mary Haralovich and Lauren Rabinovitz (Durham, N.C.: Duke University Press, 1999), 56–74; Caren Kaplan, "The 'Good Neighbor' Policy Meets the 'Feminine Mystique': The Geopolitics of the Domestic Sitcom." Paper presented at the Console-ing Passions conference, University of California–Los Angeles, April 1993.

8. Arnaz's music, including these songs, can be sampled on *The Best of Desi Arnaz: The Mambo King* (1992), among other recordings.

9. Arnaz, *A Book,* 111.

10. Ibid., 43.

11. As Pérez-Firmat notes, a *vivo* is a person who "lives and prospers by the virtue of his wit, his *viveza.* What the *vivo* lacks in formal education or native talent, he makes up for in plain smarts.... Throughout his career Desi repeatedly showed these qualities.... The other side of the *vivo* is that he tends to be a *vividor,* a *bon vivant,* and by all accounts Desi was certainly an inveterate *vividor,* one major reason for the collapse of his marriage." *Life on the Hyphen,* 52–53.

12. See Max Salazar, *Mambo Kingdom: Latin Music in New York* (New York: Schirmer Trade Books, 2002), 6–8; and John Storm Roberts, *The Latin Tinge: The Impact of Latin American Music on the United States,* 2nd edition (New York: Oxford University Press, 1999), 76–99.

13. Arnaz, *A Book* 50.

14. Malcolm Johnson, *New York Sun* (August 5, 1939).

15. Arnaz, *A Book,* 77.

16. Sandoval-Sánchez, *José, Can You See?* 46–47; Pérez-Firmat, *Life on the Hyphen,* 53–54.

17. Pérez-Firmat, *Life on the Hyphen,* 54.

18. Walt., "Too Many Girls," *Variety* (October 4, 1940), para. 4. Reprinted in *Variety Film Reviews 1938–1942,* volume 6 (New York: Garland Publishing, 1983), October 9, 1940, n.p.

19. Bosley Crowther, "Too Many Girls," *New York Times* (December 21, 1940), 43.

20. Mitch Tuchman, "Program Notes." *RKO Years,* August 13, 1940, n.p.

21. The headline in both the *Los Angeles Times* (December 1, 1940) and *Hollywood Citizen-News* (November 30, 1940).

22. "Navy Comes Through," *Variety* (October 14, 1942).

23. Arnaz, *A Book,* 134–35.

24. Ian Haney López, *Racism on Trial: The Chicano Fight for Justice* (Cambridge, Mass.: Belknap Press, 2003), 76.

25. Further discussion of discrimination experienced by Mexican Americans in the 1940s and '50s can be found in Rudolfo Acuña, *Occupied America: A History of Chicanos,* 4th edition (New York: Addison Wesley Longman, 2000), 263–327, and

Lorena Oropeza, ¡*Raza Sí! ¡Guerra No! Chicano Protest and Patriotism during the Viet Nam War Era* (Berkeley: University of California Press, 2005), 11–46.

26. For a thorough discussion of this history, see Rudolfo Acuña, *A Community Under Siege: A Chronicle of Chicanos East of the Los Angeles River, 1945–1975* (Los Angeles: University of California Press, 1984).

27. Chon A. Noriega, "Internal 'Others': Hollywood Narrative 'about' Mexican-Americans," in *Mediating Two Worlds: Cinematic Encounters in the Americas,* ed. John King, Ana M. López, and Manuel Alvarado (London: BFI, 1993), 52–66.

28. An estimated 500,000 Mexican Americans ultimately served for the United States during World War II. Richard Santillan, "Saving Private José: Midwestern Mexican American Men During World War II." California State Polytechnic–Pomona (Fall 2001). Unpublished manuscript, online: http://www.csupomona.edu/~jis/2001/Santillan .pdf.

29. "Bataan," *Hollywood Reporter* (May 26, 1943).

30. Arnaz, *A Book,* 160–61.

31. Pérez-Firmat claims that Arnaz made over $100,000 annually. *Life on the Hyphen,* 52.

32. "Lucille Ball Sues Sgt. Desi Arnaz for Divorce," *Los Angeles Times* (September 8, 1944).

33. Murray, *Hitch Your Antenna to the Stars,* 141.

34. See George Lipsitz, "The Meaning of Memory: Family, Class and Ethnicity in Early Network Television," reprinted in his book *Time Passages: Collective Memory and American Popular Culture* (Minneapolis: University of Minnesota Press, 1990), 39–75, for an astute analysis of the early ethnic comedies and how consumerism and assimilation factored in as major elements in their storylines.

35. Jess Oppenheimer, with Gregg Oppenheimer and Lucille Ball, *Laughs, Luck . . . and Lucy: How I Came to Create the Most Popular Sitcom of All Time* (Syracuse, N.Y.: Syracuse University Press, 1999), 132–34.

36. Murray, *Hitch Your Antenna to the Stars,* 134–35.

37. As reported by multiple scholars and other sources, including Mary Desjardins. Dejardins, "Lucy and Desi: Sexuality, Ethnicity, and TV's First Family," in *Television, History, and American Culture: Feminist Critical Essays,* ed. Mary Beth Haralovich and Lauren Rabinovitz (Durham, N.C.: Duke University Press, 1999), 58.

38. Martha P. Nochimson, *Screen Couple Chemistry: The Power of 2* (Austin: University of Texas Press, 2002), 19.

39. This was not the pilot that Arnaz and Ball had kinescoped as their "tryout" for CBS, however. The pilot was never broadcast, but is now available on the commercial DVD set of *I Love Lucy*'s first season episodes.

40. "I Love Lucy," *Variety* (October 17, 1952). Reprinted in *Variety Television Reviews 1951–1953,* volume 4 (New York: Garland Publishing, 1953), n.p.

41. Quoted in Coyne Steven Sanders and Tom Gilbert, *Desilu: The Story of Lucille Ball and Desi Arnaz* (New York: Quill/William Morrow, 1993), 47.

42. *Los Angeles Examiner* (April 6, 1952).

43. Sanders and Gilbert, *Desilu: The Story of Lucille Ball and Desi Arnaz,* 52.

44. Ibid., 41.

45. Lucille Ball actually gave birth to their son, Desi Jr., a few weeks later, on January 19, 1953.

46. Desjardins, "Lucy and Desi: TV's First Family in the 1950s and the 1990s," 56–74.

47. Sanders and Gilbert, *Desilu: The Story of Lucille Ball and Desi Arnaz,* 81.

48. Examples include the news articles "Arnaz Says TV Is Force for Good," *Los Angeles Mirror News* (May 23, 1958), and "The Biggest Man in Hollywood," *Chicago Tribune* (November 30, 1958).

49. Larry Walters, "The Biggest Man in Hollywood," *Chicago Tribune* (November 30, 1958), 13, 15.

50. Frederick Christian, "Lucille Ball's Serious Life with Desi Arnaz," *Cosmopolitan* (January 1960).

51. Quoted in Sanders and Gilbert, *Desilu: The Story of Lucille Ball and Desi Arnaz,* 198.

52. Ibid., 197.

53. This episode can be found on the DVD set *Saturday Night Live: The Complete First Season* (Universal Studios, 2006).

54. Arnaz, *A Book,* 319.

Chapter 3. A Fight for "Dignity and Integrity": Rita Moreno in Hollywood's Postwar Era

1. Charles Ramírez Berg, *Latino Images in Film: Stereotypes, Subversion, and Resistance* (Austin: University of Texas Press, 2002), 70–71.

2. Latina/o actors who have won the Academy Award include Jose Ferrer, who won the Best Actor award for *Cyrano de Bergerac* (1949); Anthony Quinn, who won two Academy Awards as Best Supporting Actor in his lifetime, for his roles in *Viva Zapata!* (1952) and *Lust for Life* (1956); Mercedes Ruehl, who won the award for Best Supporting Actress for *The Fisher King* (1991); and Benicio Del Toro, who was named Best Supporting Actor for *Traffic* (2000). Latina/os who have been nominated include Katy Jurado, who was nominated for Best Supporting Actress for *High Noon* in 1952; Anthony Quinn, who was nominated for Best Actor for *Wild Is the Wind* (1957) and *Zorba the Greek* (1964); Salma Hayek, nominated for *Frida* (2002); and Adriana Barraza (who is Mexican) for *Babel* (2006).

3. Moreno's two Emmy wins were for performances on episodes of *The Muppet Show* in 1977 and *The Rockford Files* in 1978. In addition, she won a Grammy Award for her work on an album of *Electric Company* songs in 1972. Finally, her Tony win was for her performance in the role of Googie Gomez in the Broadway play *The Ritz* in 1975.

4. Rita Moreno, interview with Susan Racho for *The Bronze Screen: 100 Years of the Latin Image in American Cinema*, 2000. Transcript of video footage, shared with the author by Susan Racho.

5. Quoted in Neil Hickey, "What Ever Became of Hollywood's Most Famous Spitfire?" *TV Guide* (December 2, 1970), 20.

6. See Sarah Banet-Weiser, *The Most Beautiful Girl in the World* (Berkeley: University of California Press, 1999), for further discussion of how race and national identity have been articulated in U.S. beauty pageants in the last century.

7. Colleen Ballerino Cohen, Richard Wilk, and Beverly Stoeltje, "Introduction: Beauty Queens on the Global Stage," in *Beauty Queens on the Global Stage: Gender, Contests, and Power*, ed. Colleen Ballerino Cohen, Richard Wilk, and Beverly Stoeltje (New York: Routledge, 1996), 4.

8. Shari Roberts, "'The Lady in the Tutti-Frutti Hat': Carmen Miranda, a Spectacle of Ethnicity," *Cinema Journal* 32, no. 3 (Spring 1993): 3–23, 4.

9. Rachel Rubin and Jeffrey Melnick, *Immigration and American Popular Culture: An Introduction* (New York: NYU Press, 2007), 104. They cite Steven Bender, *Greasers and Gringos: Latinos, Law and the American Imagination* (New York: NYU Press, 2003), xiv, 9.

10. For further discussion of these dynamics, see Laura Briggs, *Reproducing Empire: Race, Sex, Science and U.S. Imperialism in Puerto Rico* (Berkeley: University of California Press, 2002).

11. For further discussion of how Puerto Rican nationalists were treated by the U.S. news media, see José Ramón Sánchez, *Boriqua Power: A Political History of Puerto Ricans in the United States* (New York: NYU Press, 2007).

12. See the historical essays compiled in *Historical Perspectives on Puerto Rican Survival in the U.S.*, ed. Clara E. Rodríguez and Virginia Sanchez Korrol (Princeton, N.J.: Markus Wiener Publishers, 1996), for further discussion of the history of Puerto Ricans on the island and in the New York City region.

13. Susan Suntree, *Rita Moreno* (New York: Chelsea House, 1993), 33.

14. Ally Acker, *Reel Women: Pioneers of the Cinema 1896 to the Present* (New York: Continuum, 1991), 114.

15. Thomas Schatz, *Boom and Bust: American Cinema in the 1940s* (Berkeley: University of California Press, 1997).

16. Reported in *Motion Picture Herald* (July 17, 1948), 8; *Variety* (August 11, 1948), 5.

17. It is not clarified in the storyline, but Dolores is presumably Mexican American, given her devotion to the Virgin of Guadalupe and other references in the storyline.

18. "Rita Moreno Gets Contract," *Los Angeles Examiner* (December 26, 1949).

19. "Film Contract Approved for Rita Moreno," *Los Angeles Times* (December 26, 1949).

20. Ramírez Berg, *Latino Images in Film*, 71. For further discussion of how ethnic

American stars have been constructed as excessive, see Diane Negra, *Off-White Hollywood: American Culture and Ethnic Female Stardom* (London: Routledge, 2001).

21. "Toast of New Orleans," *Variety* (August 8, 1950); Phillip K. Scheuer, "Toast of New Orleans," *Los Angeles Times* (October 14, 1950).

22. Twentieth Century-Fox Publicity Department, "Biography Notes: Rita Moreno," 1954.

23. Robert Sklar, *Movie-made America: A Social History of American Movies* (New York: Random House, 1975), 282.

24. Charles Ramírez Berg, "Bordertown, the Assimilation Narrative, and the Chicano Social Problem Film," in *Chicanos and Film: Representation and Resistance,* ed. Chon A. Noriega (Minneapolis: University of Minnesota Press, 1992), 29–46; Chon A. Noriega, "Internal 'Others': Hollywood Narrative 'about' Mexican-Americans," in *Mediating Two Worlds: Cinematic Encounters in the Americas,* ed. John King, Ana M. López, and Manuel Alvarado (London: BFI, 1993), 52–66.

25. Howard McClay, "Howard McClay," *Los Angeles Daily News* (October 9, 1952).

26. Phillip K. Scheuer, "Rita Moreno's Principal Aim Is to Be a Bullfighter," *Los Angeles Times* (October 26, 1952).

27. Bolger, a song-and-dance man with roots in Vaudeville and a long career in motion picture musicals, is perhaps best known for playing the Scarecrow in MGM's *The Wizard of Oz* in 1939. His ABC series was also known as *Where's Raymond?*

28. Negra, *Off-White Stardom,* 142–43.

29. Ella Shohat and Robert Stam, *Unthinking Eurocentrism: Multiculturalism and the Media* (London: Routledge, 1994), 138.

30. Arthur G. Pettit surveys this history of Mexican American female representation in early literature and film in *Images of the Mexican American in Fiction and Film* (College Station: Texas A & M University Press, 1980). For discussion of contemporary representations of the excessive Latina body, see Angharad Valdivia, "Is Penélope to J.Lo as Culture Is to Nature? Eurocentric Approaches to 'Latin' Beauties," in *From Bananas to Buttocks: The Latina Body in Popular Film and Culture,* ed. Myra Mendible (Austin: University of Texas Press, 2007), 129–48.

31. Antonia Castañeda, "The Political Economy of Nineteenth Century Stereotypes of Californians," in *Between Borders: Essays on Mexicana/Chicana History,* ed. Adelaida R. Del Castillo (Encino, Calif.: Floricanto, 1990), 113–26.

32. Harry Brand, "Biography–Rita Moreno," Twentieth Century-Fox, 1954. Rita Moreno biography file, Margaret Herrick Library, Academy of Motion Picture Arts and Sciences, Los Angeles.

33. "Rita Moreno Notes," Twentieth Century-Fox, 1956. Rita Moreno biography file, Margaret Herrick Library, Academy of Motion Picture Arts and Sciences, Los Angeles.

34. Harry Brand, "Biography–Rita Moreno."

35. "Untamed," *New York Post* (March 2, 1955).

36. Suntree, *Rita Moreno,* 56.

37. Rita Moreno biography files, Margaret Herrick Library, Academy of Motion Picture Arts and Sciences, Los Angeles.

38. Suntree, *Rita Moreno,* 55–56.

39. Louis Berg, "Rita the Cheetah," *This Week Magazine, Los Angeles Times* (February 13, 1955).

40. Acker, *Reel Women,* 114.

41. Ibid.

42. Moreno has commented that she had been given the opportunity to audition for the role of Maria in the theatrical version of *West Side Story,* which debuted in 1957 (it subsequently was played by Puerto Rican actress Chita Rivera), but decided not to, and that she was considered too old for the role by the time it was in production as a film.

43. "West Side Story," *Variety* (September 13, 1961).

44. Rubin and Melnick, *Immigration and American Popular Culture,* 91.

45. Briggs, *Reproducing Empire,* 2.

46. Similar sentiments have also been expressed by scholars Richie Pérez and Alberto Sandoval-Sánchez. Pérez, "From Assimilation to Annihilation: Puerto Rican Images in Films, in *Latin Looks: Images of Latinas and Latinos in the U.S. Media,* ed. Clara E. Rodríguez (Boulder, Colo.: Westview Press, 1997), 151; Sandoval-Sánchez, *José, Can You See? Latinos On and Off Broadway* (Madison: University of Wisconsin Press, 1999), 63.

47. Rita Moreno, Letter to the Editor, *Daily Variety* (July 30, 1962).

48. "Rita Moreno," *Puerto Rico Herald* (August 10, 2000). Online: http://www .puertorico-herald.org/issues/vol4n32/ProfileMoreno-en.html.

49. Neil Hickey, "What Ever Became of Hollywood's Most Famous Spitfire?" *TV Guide* (December 2, 1972): 20.

50. Shaun Considine, "A Latin from Manhattan Stars at Last," *New York Times* (March 30, 1975): 1.

51. Ibid., 5.

Chapter 4. The Burden of Playing Chico: Freddie Prinze and Latino Stardom in Television's Era of "Relevance"

1. Latino-oriented series in the 1980s included *Condo* (1983) and *AKA Pablo* (1984), featuring comedian Paul Rodriguez. Attempts in the 1990s then included *Common Law* (1996), starring comedian Greg Giraldo, and *Union Square* (1997–98), centered on actress Constance Marie. Neither of these series lasted longer than a season, however. Lack of adequate network promotion and commitment and a lack of Latino writers and producers were major pitfalls for these series. More recent shows that have been more successful include *Resurrection Blvd.* (2000–2002), *American Family* (2002–04), *The George Lopez Show,* and most successful of all, *Ugly Betty* (2006–).

2. There are incongruities with respect to how Prinze's paternal heritage has been described. While he described himself as half Hungarian, recent accounts indicate that Prinze's father was actually German but grew up in Hungary. His son, Freddie Prinze Jr. has stated this in interviews, as he did on a *Howard Stern Show* appearance in 2001. Online: http://www.freddieprinzejr.com/transcript_stern01.htm.

3. The work of Chon Noriega, *Shot in America: Television, the State, and the Rise of Chicano Cinema* (Minneapolis: University of Minnesota Press, 2000) and Greg Oguss, "'Whose Barrio Is It?' Chico and the Man and the Integrated Ghetto Shows of the 1970s," *Television & New Media* 6, no. 1 (2005): 3–21, are notable contributions in this regard.

4. See Peter Biskind, *Easy Riders, Raging Bulls: How the Sex-Drugs-and-Rock-N-Roll-Generation Saved Hollywood* (New York: Simon and Schuster, 1999), and David A. Cook, *Lost Illusions: American Cinema in the Shadow of Watergate and Vietnam (1970–1979)* (Berkeley: University of California Press, 2002).

5. Todd Gitlin, *Inside Prime Time* (New York: Pantheon, 1983), 203–20; Erik Barnouw, *Tube of Plenty: The Evolution of American Television* (Oxford, UK: Oxford University Press, 1975), 430–40.

6. For overviews of different aspects of Chicano activism in this period, see Lorena Oropeza, *¡Raza Sí! ¡Guerra No! Chicano Protest and Patriotism during the Viet Nam War Era* (Berkeley: University of California Press, 2005), and Ian Haney López, *Racism on Trial: The Chicano Fight for Justice* (Cambridge, Mass.: Belknap Press, 2003).

7. Neil Foley, "Straddling the Color Line: The Legal Construction of Hispanic Ethnicity in Texas," in *Not Just Black and White: Historical and Contemporary Perspectives on Immigration, Race, and Ethnicity in the United States,* ed. Nancy Foner and George M. Fredrickson (New York: Russell Sage Foundation, 2004), 353.

8. Noriega, *Shot in America,* 16.

9. Numerous studies in the last few decades have documented the under-representation of Latina/os on prime time since the 1950s, with S. Robert Lichter and Daniel R. Amundson's 1994 study providing an important foundation for this research. Lichter and Amundson, *Distorted Reality: Hispanic Characters in TV Entertainment* (Washington, D.C.: Center for Media and Public Affairs, 1994). The most recent study, of fall 2003 prime-time programming, found that Latina/os comprised 6 percent of prime-time characters while comprising about 13 percent of the U.S. population. Half of the Latina/o characters also appeared on just one network, ABC. Allison R. Hoffman and Chon A. Noriega, "Looking for Latino Regulars on Prime Time Television: The Fall 2004 Season," *CSRC Research Report* 4 (December 2004).

10. Kathryn C. Montgomery, *Target: Prime Time: Advocacy Groups and the Struggle over Entertainment Television* (New York: Oxford University Press, 1989), 56, 62.

11. Ibid., 51–62. In my Los Angeles research interviews, casting director Bob Morones, Nosotros president Jerry Velasco, writer and acting mentor Danny Mora, and *Latin Heat* editor-publisher Bel Hernandez (all actors in earlier years) also described

taking part in protests against the lack of Latina/o inclusion in network programming and being privy to meetings with network executives in the 1970s. Their memories of network response included groups being given small financial grants and being offered promises for future hires and programming that were not kept.

12. Similar awards are also now given out annually by such groups as the National Council of La Raza (NCLR) and the Imagen Foundation. NCLR's awards show, the American Latino Media Awards or ALMA Awards, is now the largest and most widely publicized; it is typically televised on one of the major networks each year.

13. Donald Bogle, *Brown Sugar: Eighty Years of America's Black Female Superstars* (Cambridge, Mass.: De Capo Press, 1990).

14. James Komack, The Wolper/Komack Company, Inc. "Now, Chico!" *Chico and the Man* script draft (August 13, 1976), 3. James Komack files, Wisconsin Center for Film and Television Research, University of Wisconsin–Madison.

15. Ibid., 2.

16. Jerry Buck, Associated Press, "The Chemistry Was Perfect," *Boston Globe* (August 18, 1974).

17. This claim was reported, for instance, in television critic Cecil Smith's syndicated news column, which appeared in such newspapers as the *Scrantonian* (as "'Chico, Man' Smash Hit") and the *TV Times* section of the *Los Angeles Times* (as "Chico and the Man: NBC's Controversial Hit") on November 10, 1974.

18. Montgomery, *Target: Prime Time*, 63.

19. NBC Program Test Report, *Chico and the Man*, March 1974. NBC Program Research department, internal memorandum.

20. NBC Program Test Report, *Chico and the Man*, "Second Thoughts" (September 13, 1974). NBC Program Research department, internal memorandum.

21. "'Chico and the Man' New TV Offering Next Season." UPI newswire article that ran in the Fort Wayne, Indiana *Journal-Gazette* (June 30, 1974).

22. Ibid.

23. Lee Winfrey, "TV News Gets Break in Equal Time Denial," *Philadelphia Enquirer* (September 30, 1974).

24. Cecil Smith, "'Chico, Man' Smash Hit." This syndicated column was located as a reprint in [Scranton, Pennsylvania] *Scrantonian* (November 10, 1974).

25. Freddie Prinze, *Looking Good!* Audio CD of Prinze's comedy act. Collectables Records, 2000.

26. Edwin Miller, "Call Me a Hungarican!" *Seventeen* (October 1974), 122.

27. Cited in "Prinze of Prime Time," *Time* (September 30, 1974). Online: http://aolsvc.timeforkids.kol.aol.com/time/magazine/article/0,9171,908804,00.html.

28. Daniel Bernardi, "Prinze, Freddie," *Museum of Broadcast Communications*. Online: http://www.museum/tv/archives/etv/P/htmlP/prinzefredd/prinzefredd.htm.

29. Cited in Marc Jacobson, "Freddie Prinze: Laughing Up From the Hood," *New York* (August 26, 1974), 42.

30. "Chico's Wild Ways!" *Sixteen* (March 1975), 3, 12.

31. Harry Waters, "Hot Hungarian," *Newsweek* (November 11, 1974), 74–75; "The Prinze of Prime Time," *Time* (September 30, 1974); Tom Burke, "The Undiluted South Bronx Truth about Freddie Prinze," *Rolling Stone* 179 (January 1975); Bill Davidson, "'Get Out of Here and Take Your Flies with You,' *TV Guide* (November 23, 1974), 25–27; Rosemary Edelman, "'Pobrito,' It Ain't Easy Being a Star," *TV Guide* (February 15, 1975); Edwin Miller, "Call Me a Hungarican!" *Seventeen,* 121–22; "Chico's Wild Ways!" *Sixteen,* 3, 12; "Freddie Prinze out the Window," *Playboy* (May 1974), 165.

32. Tobias letter, Hal Kanter files. Wisconsin Center for Film and Television Research, University of Wisconsin–Madison.

33. Vahac Mardirosian, "Chicano Educators Object: Under Fire: Chico and the Man." Op-ed piece, *Los Angeles Times* (October 4, 1974).

34. "Television and Radio: Mexican-Americans Hate 'Chico,'" [Columbus, Ohio] *Catholic Times* (October 18, 1974).

35. Cited in Frank Torrez, "Man in the Middle," *Los Angeles Herald-Examiner* (October 8, 1974).

36. "KNBC-TV License Challenged by Chicanos," *Brooklyn Belvedere Comet* (November 21, 1974).

37. Alicia Sandoval and Paul Macias, "'Chico and the Man': Some Chicanos Are Not Amused," *Los Angeles Times* (October 24, 1974).

38. David Winder, "Chicano Views Begin to Bend TV," *Christian Science Monitor* (November 20, 1974).

39. Davidson, "'Get Out of Here and Take Your Flies with You,'" 25–27.

40. These changes were revealed in the "Veterans" episode, which aired November 8, 1974.

41. This was in fact the norm on all of the "socially relevant" series of this era, but was increasingly criticized by ethnic media advocacy groups and others.

42. Torrez, "Man in the Middle."

43. Memorandum from Warren Murray to Robert Howard (December 5, 1974), NBC. *Chico and the Man* production files, Box 23, "Chicano Writers" folder. David L. Wolper Collection, USC Cinema and Television Library, University of Southern California, Los Angeles.

44. Ibid.

45. Cecil Smith, "'Chico, Man' Smash Hit."

46. Daniel Bernardi, "Prinze, Freddie," para. 4.

47. *TV Times,* supplement to the *Los Angeles Times* (November 10, 1974).

48. Greg Oguss, "Whose Barrio Is It?" 13.

49. Charles Ramírez Berg similarly writes about the transgressive potential of actually hiring Latinos to play Latino characters in film. *Latino Images in Film: Stereotypes, Subversion, and Resistance* (Austin: University of Texas Press, 2002), 83–85.

50. Oguss, "Whose Barrio Is It?" 2.

51. Ibid., 11.

52. NBC Memorandum. Recording of *Chico and the Man* Concept Meeting on May

10, 1976. Folder 9, Box 39, The David L. Wolper Collection, Cinematic Arts Library, University of Southern California–Los Angeles.

53. Noriega, *Shot in America*, 71.

54. Plot summary, *The Million Dollar Rip-off*. Internet Movie Database. Online: http://www.imdb.com/title/tt0074903/plotsummary.

55. In the recent study of prime-time representation by Allison R. Hoffman and Chon Noriega, it was found that fully half of Latina/o representation on the networks in Fall 2003 was in ABC programming. "Looking for Latino Regulars on Prime Time Television."

56. Chon A. Noriega, "The Numbers Game," *Jump Cut* 39, June 1994. Reprinted in *The Future of Latino Independent Media: A NALIP Sourcebook* (Los Angeles: UCLA Chicano Studies Resource Center, 2000).

Chapter 5. The Face of the "Decade": Edward James Olmos and Latino Films of the 1980s

1. I use the male-specific "Latino" here because these nationally distributed feature films were directed exclusively by men. Latina filmmakers, while they did exist, tended to produce shorter narrative films or documentary films outside the Hollywood system in this period, as Rosa Linda Fregoso notes. Fregoso, "Chicana Film Practices: 'Confronting the Many-headed Demon of Oppression,'" in *Chicanos and Film: Representation and Resistance,* ed. Chon A. Noriega (Minneapolis: University of Minnesota Press, 1992), 168–82.

2. For a thorough accounting of the marketing and distribution of many of these films, see Henry Puente, *The Promotion of U.S. Latino Films*. Dissertation, University of Texas at Austin, 2004.

3. See Ana M. López, "Greater Cuba," for discussion of the Cuban exile filmmakers and later generations of U.S. filmmakers of Cuban descent. In *The Ethnic Eye: Latino Media Arts,* ed. Chon A. Noriega and Ana M. López (Minneapolis: University of Minnesota Press, 1996), 38–58.

4. This title includes a play on the slang word *pocho,* which usually translates to "Americanized Mexican." While it is typically used as an insult, it has been embraced with tongue-in-cheek humor by some Mexican Americans.

5. Credited to "Dr. Rusty Filero and Dr. Yanomamez of the National Pochisimo Institute," apparently pseudonyms of Lalo Alcaraz. "The Pochteca Calendar of Raza Popular Culture," *San Francisco Bay Guardian* "Puro Pop" A&E Pullout (March 11–17, 1998), 1.

6. Among other major awards and nominations, Olmos has won an Emmy for his work on *Miami Vice;* two Golden Globes, for his work on *Miami Vice* and *The Burning Season;* and an Independent Spirit Award for Best Actor for *Stand and Deliver.* He also was nominated for an Academy Award for Best Actor for *Stand and Deliver* and for a Tony for his work on the theatrical version of *Zoot Suit.* He also has been

awarded multiple times for his acting and directing by the National Council of La Raza (NCLR)'s American Latino Media Awards, most recently for directing the HBO film *Walkout* in 2005 and for his work on *Battlestar Galactica*.

7. Puente, *The Promotion of U.S. Latino Films,* 101–2, 108–9.

8. Stephen Prince, *A New Pot of Gold: Hollywood under the Electronic Rainbow, 1980–1990* (New York: Charles Scribner's Sons, 2000), 172–74.

9. Chon A. Noriega documents the origins of Chicano independent cinema in *Shot in America: Television, the State, and the Rise of Chicano Cinema* (Minneapolis: University of Minnesota Press, 2000). See also Charles Ramírez Berg, *Latino Images in Film: Stereotypes, Subversion, and Resistance* (Austin: University of Texas Press, 2002), 185–89; and Lillian Jiménez, "From the Margin to the Center: Puerto Rican Cinema in New York," in *Latin Looks: Images of Latinas and Latinos in the U.S. Media,* ed. Clara E. Rodríguez (Boulder, Colo.: Westview Press, 1997), 188–99.

10. Jason C. Johansen, "Notes on Chicano Cinema," in *Chicanos and Film: Representation and Resistance,* ed. Chon A. Noriega (Minneapolis: University of Minnesota Press, 1992), 303.

11. See Noriega, *Shot in America,* for a well-researched history of these early films and their relationship to Chicano public affairs shows that were broadcast on public television stations, particularly in the cities with large Latina/o populations.

12. Aida Barrera, creator-producer of *Carrascolendas,* notes that this was the case for individuals who worked on the production in Austin, Texas, in the 1970s. See Barrera, *Looking for Carrascolendas: From a Child's World to Award-Winning Television* (Austin: University of Texas Press, 2001).

13. Puente, *The Promotion of U.S. Latino Films,* 148–53.

14. Arlene Dávila, *Latinos, Inc.: The Marketing and Making of a People* (Berkeley: University of California Press, 2001). Puente, *The Promotion of U.S. Latino Films,* 205.

15. Gary D. Keller, *Hispanics and United States Film: An Overview and Handbook* (Tempe, Ariz.: Bilingual Press, 1992), 151.

16. Guy D. Garcia, "Burning with Passion," *Time* (July 11, 1988), 56.

17. Ibid., 59.

18. Pachucos and pachucas were young Mexican American men and women who created their own subculture in the 1930s and 1940s. They wore the stylish zoot suits of the era, spoke a form of slang called Caló, and are generally considered the precursors of the Chicana/o activists of the 1960s. See A. Madrid Barela, "In Search of the Authentic Pachuco: An Interpretive Essay, Part I," *Aztlán: A Journal of Chicano Studies* 4, no. 1 (Spring 1973): 31–60, and Catherine Sue Ramírez, "Crimes of Fashion: The Pachuca and Chicana Style Politics," *Meridians* 2, no. 2 (2002): 1–35.

19. For further discussion of the trial and the climate toward Mexican Americans in Los Angeles in this period, see Eduardo Obregón Pagán, *Murder at the Sleepy Lagoon: Zoot Suits, Race, and Riot in Wartime L.A.* (Chapel Hill: University of North Carolina Press, 2006).

20. Based on Henry Leyvas, the actual chief defendant in the Sleepy Lagoon trial.

21. Yolanda Broyles-Gonzalez, *El Teatro Campesino: Theater in the Chicano Movement* (Austin: University of Texas Press, 1994), 189.

22. Ibid., 189–95. The negative reaction of East Coast critics was first noted by Jorge Huerta in *Chicano Theater: Themes and Forms* (Ypsilanti, Mich.: Bilingual Review Press, 1982).

23. The Broadway version of *Zoot Suit* received positive reviews from the *Wall Street Journal, Variety,* and *Newsweek,* among other news outlets.

24. Broyles-Gonzalez, *El Teatro Campesino,* 204–205.

25. "*Zoot Suit,*" *Variety* (September 30, 1981); Vincent Canby, *New York Times* (January 22, 1982), Section C, Weekend Desk, 10.

26. "Movie Review: 'Zoot Suit': The Play Is the Thing." *Los Angeles Times* (September 30, 1981), 4.

27. Puente, *The Promotion of U.S. Latino Films,* 120–25, 153.

28. Quoted by Chris Chase, "At the Movies," *New York Times* (January 29, 1982): Section C, 17.

29. Pat Hilton, "Edward James Olmos," *Drama-logue* (June 18–24, 1987), 15.

30. Cited in Louis Carrillo, *Edward James Olmos* (Austin, Tex.: Raintree Steck-Vaughn Publishers, 1997), 29.

31. Christine Geraghty, "Re-examining Stardom," in *Reinventing Film Studies,* ed. Christine Gledhill and Linda Williams (London: Hodder Arnold, 2000), 183–201.

32. A corrido is a Mexican American ballad, which traditionally related the story of legendary figures and current events. For more information about the history of corrido and the "Ballad of Gregorio Cortez" in particular, see Américo Paredes, *"With His Pistol in His Hand": A Border Ballad and Its Hero* (Austin: University of Texas Press, 1970).

33. Guy D. Garcia, "Burning with Passion," *Time* (July 11, 1988), 59.

34. Rosa Linda Fregoso, *The Bronze Screen: Chicana and Chicano Film Culture* (Minneapolis: University of Minnesota Press, 1993).

35. Tina Daniell, *Hollywood Reporter* (October 7, 1983), 29.

36. Gus D. Garcia notes, based on an interview with Edward James Olmos, that it was a five-year process. Garcia, "Burning with Passion." Other journalists have written that Olmos spent one or two years promoting the film around the Southwest.

37. Pat Aufderheide, "An Actor Turns Activist," *Mother Jones* (November 1983), 60.

38. Cited in Alan Weisman, "The Hollywood Route," *Los Angeles Times Magazine* (March 27, 1988).

39. "'Stand' delivers a memorable lesson," *USA Today* (March 11, 1988). Jack Krull with Jennifer Foote, "To Señor, With Love, Brains and Ganas," *Newsweek* (March 14, 1988), 62.

40. Krull with Jennifer Foote, "To Señor, With Love, Brains and Ganas," 62.

41. "Teacher's Pet," *Los Angeles Weekly* (March 3–11, 1988), 39.

42. Cited in Hilton, "Edward James Olmos," 14–15.

43. Ibid.

44. Jason C. Johansen, "Hispanic Market: Hit or a Miss?" *Los Angeles Times* (April 21, 1981), Sunday Calendar, 4.

45. Ibid.

46. Ibid.

47. José Itzigsohn posits that the government's adoption of the term Hispanic was a "result of the visibility acquired by Chicanos and Chicanas and Puerto Ricans during the civil rights struggles." Itzigsohn, "The Formation of Latino and Latina Panethnic Identities," in *Not Just Black and White: Historical and Contemporary Perspectives on Immigration, Race, and Ethnicity in the United States,* ed. Nancy Foner and George M. Fredrickson (New York: Russell Sage Foundation, 2004), 199. The problematic dynamics inherent in the term have been aptly documented by José Calderón, "'Hispanic' and 'Latino': The Viability of Categories for Panethnic Unity," *Latin American Perspectives* 19 (Fall 1992): 37–44; and Suzanne Oboler, *Ethnic Labels, Latino Lives* (Minneapolis: University of Minnesota Press, 1995).

48. Jennifer Foote, "Hispanic Hollywood: 'La Bamba' heralds a new Latin beat on celluloid," *Newsweek* (August 17, 1987), 66.

49. Ibid., 151.

50. Richard Lacayo, "A Surging New Spirit," *Time* (July 11, 1988), 46.

51. Kathleen Newman, "Latino Sacrifice in the Discourse of Citizenship: Acting Against the Mainstream, 1985–1988," in *Chicanos and Film: Representation and Resistance,* ed. Chon A. Noriega (Minneapolis: University of Minnesota Press, 1992), 69.

52. Ibid., 67.

53. Victor Valle, "A Chicano Reporter in 'Hispanic Hollywood': Editorial Agendas and the Culture of Professional Journalism," in *Chicanos and Film: Representation and Resistance,* ed. Chon A. Noriega (Minneapolis: University of Minnesota Press), 270.

54. The one exception, Olmos's role as El Pachuco, arguably had little impact because *Zoot Suit* received considerably less attention in the national press than did *Stand and Deliver.*

55. Newman, "Latino Sacrifice in the Discourse of Citizenship," 67.

56. Ilene Goldman, "Crossing Invisible Borders: Ramón Menéndez's *Stand and Deliver,*" in *The Ethnic Eye: Latino Media Arts,* ed. Chon A. Noriega and Ana M. López (Minneapolis: University of Minnesota Press, 1996), 81–94.

57. Cited in Charlotte Wolter, "Edward James Olmos," *Hollywood Reporter* (January 23, 1989), 16.

58. Ibid.

59. Reba L. Chaisson, *For Entertainment Purposes Only? An Analysis of the Struggle to Control Filmic Representations* (Lanham, Mass.: Lexington, 2000), 38.

60. Table of Contents, *Time* (July 11, 1988), 3. The Olmos mural was painted by artist Joe L. Gomez.

61. Ricardo Romo, "Border Murals: Chicano Artifacts in Transition," *Aztlán: A Journal of Chicano Studies* 21, no. 1,2 (1992–96): 125–54.

62. Frances P. Aparicio and Cándida F. Jáquez, Introduction, in *Musical Migrations: Transnationalism and Cultural Hybridity in Latina/o America,* ed. Frances Aparicio, Cándida Jáquez, and Maria Elena Cepeda (New York: Palgrave Macmillan, 2003), 9.

63. Chris Holmlund, *Impossible Bodies: Femininity and Masculinity at the Movies* (London: Routledge, 2002), 122.

Chapter 6. Crossing Over the Latina Body: Jennifer Lopez and the 1990s "Latin Wave"

Some material in this chapter previously appeared in print in my article "The Hollywood Latina Body as Site of Social Struggle: Media Constructions of Stardom and Jennifer Lopez's 'Cross-over Butt,'" *Quarterly Review of Film and Video* 19, no. 1 (January 2002): 71–86.

1. Degan Pener, "From Here to DIVANITY," *Entertainment Weekly* (October 9, 1998), 28–31.

2. Christopher Goodwin, "Bum's the Word," *(London) Sunday Times* (September 20, 1998), Style, 6.

3. "A&E Biography: Sean 'Puffy' Combs," *Saturday Night Live,* NBC, aired October 17, 1998.

4. Brantley Bardin, "Woman of the Year: Jennifer Lopez," *Details* (December 1998), 141–45, 199.

5. For further examination of the reaction of Latina viewers to the discussion of Jennifer Lopez's body, see Katynka Z. Martínez, "Real Women and Their Curves: Letters to the Editor and a Magazine's Celebration of the 'Latina Body,'" in *Latina/o Communication Studies Today,* ed. Angharad Valdivia (New York: Peter Lang, 2008), 137–60.

6. For a history of Latina/o media outlets in the United States, see Federico Subervi-Vélez et al., "Mass Communication and Hispanics," in *Handbook of Hispanic Cultures in the United States: Sociology,* ed. Felix Padilla, general ed. Nicolás Kanellos and Claudio Esteva-Fabregat (Houston: Arte Publico, 1994), 304–57.

7. In the rest of the country a photo of the cast of *Friends* was used on the cover, on the assumption that Selena would be of interest to readers only in the Southwest.

8. América Rodriguez, *Making Latino News: Race, Language, Class* (Thousand Oaks, Calif.: Sage, 1999), 60–61.

9. "The Hispanic Population: A Census 2000 Brief" (Washington, D.C.: U.S. Census Bureau, U.S. Department of Commerce, May 2001).

10. As Arlene Dávila documents, the first Latino-owned advertising agencies were leading early Latino-oriented advertising. Interestingly, these agencies, owned predominantly by Caribbeans, initially promoted the employment of notions of pan-Latino identity that elided differences between national origin groups. Dávila, *Latinos, Inc.: The Making and Marketing of a People* (Berkeley: University of California Press,

2001). For more information on Latina/o media habits, see Harry P. Pachon et al., *Missing in Action: Latinos in and out of Hollywood* (Los Angeles: The Tomás Rivera Policy Institute, 1999). Online: http://www.trpi.org/update/media.html.

11. The proportion of Latina/os living in poverty rose from 21.5 percent in 1972 to 29.6 percent in 1982 (Bogue quoted in Rudolfo Acuña, *Occupied America: A History of Chicanos* [New York: Addison Wesley Longman, 2000], note 121, 409). In 1999, this proportion had fallen to 22.8 percent; in contrast, 7.7 percent of non-Hispanic whites lived in poverty. *The Hispanic Population in the United States: Population Characteristics, March 2000* (Washington, D.C.: U.S. Census Bureau, U.S. Department of Commerce, 2001). See *The Hispanic Population in the United States: Population Characteristics, March 2000* for further information about education attainment, employment, and other measures of the quality of Latina/o life in the United States today.

12. Martha Menchaca, *The Mexican Outsiders: A Community History of Marginalization and Discrimination in California* (Austin: University of Texas Press, 1995), 169.

13. Frances Aparacio, "Jennifer as Selena: Rethinking Latinidad in Media and Popular Culture," *Latino Studies* 1, no. 1 (2003): 90–105.

14. Advertisement, Gold/Miller, *Variety* (February 23, 1996).

15. Alisa Valdes, "Fly Girl Makes the Leap to Movies," *Boston Globe*, reprinted in *The Press-Telegram* (May 30, 1995), D4.

16. Richard Travers, "Money Train," *Rolling Stone* (November 1995); "Money Train," *San Francisco Examiner* (November 22, 1995).

17. Suzan Colón, "You Go, J.Lo," *Latina* (June 2001), 84.

18. Frances Negrón-Mutaner, "Jennifer's Butt," *Aztlán: A Journal of Chicano Studies*, 22.2 (Fall 1997): 186.

19. "Jennifer Lopez," *People en Español* (January 1, 1997), 89.

20. Negrón-Mutaner, "Jennifer's Butt," 186.

21. "Lopez Can't Lift *Selena* above the Ordinary," *San Francisco Chronicle* (March 21, 1997); Roger Ebert, *"Selena," Chicago Sun-Times* (March 21, 1997). *"Selena," Rolling Stone* (April 17, 1997).

22. John Anderson, "Blood and Wine," *Los Angeles Times* (February 21, 1997).

23. "Anaconda," *HBO Film Reviews* (November 22, 2000). Online: http://www .hbo.com/Filmreviews/reviews/anaconda.shtml.

24. "Lopez to Star in *Out of Sight,*" *Variety* (May 15, 1997). While Shelton-Drake had emphasized that Lopez was a rising star and could draw in Latina/o moviegoers, particularly given how well *Selena* and *Anaconda* had performed, she had not been able to convince the Jersey Films team to pay this amount. "What will the snake get for his next picture?" *Variety* quipped, commentary that appears to scoff at the thought of paying Lopez's asking price.

25. Stephen Rebello, "The WOW," *Movieline* (February 1998), 93.

26. Quoted by news anchor Susan Campos on the NBC television news program *Saturday Today* (March 21, 1998).

27. Dusty Saunders, "Great Moments on Oscar Night," *Rocky Mountain News* (March 24, 1998), 38A.

28. Stuart Kemp, "A New View of Death," [Glasgow, Scotland] *Herald* (December 3, 1998), 16; Jack Matthews, "The Robber Steals a Marshall's Heart," *Newsday* (June 26, 1998), B3; Quentin Curtis, "The Arts: Vision of Lowliness," *The Daily Telegraph*, London (November 27, 1998), 26; Ann Hornaday, "'Sight' for Sore Eyes," *Baltimore Sun* (June 26, 1998), 1E.

29. *In/Style* magazine, 184.

30. Kelvin Tong, "Curvy? Butt It's in the History Books," *The [Singapore] Straits Times* (July 9, 1998), 1, L7.

31. Sarah Gristwood, "Features: Mouth of the Border," *The Guardian*, London (November 20, 1998), 4.

32. Donna Britt, "It's Ethnic America through a Rear-View Mirror," *Newsday* (October 14, 1998), A41.

33. Jean Godfrey-June, Editor's Note, *Elle* (November 1998), 224.

34. Reebee Garofalo, "Culture versus Commerce: The Marketing of Black Popular Music," *Public Culture* 7 (1994): 275–87; Steve Perry, "Ain't No Mountain High Enough: The Politics of Crossover," *Facing the Music*, ed. Simon Frith (New York: Pantheon, 1988), 51–87.

35. Coco Fusco, *English Is Broken Here: Notes on Cultural Fusion in the Americas* (New York: New, 1995), 65.

36. As Katynka Z. Martínez notes, this transformation can be followed by simply comparing Lopez's covers of *Latina* magazine over this time span. "Real Women and Their Curves: Letters to the Editor and a Magazine's Celebration of the 'Latina Body,'" in *Latina/o Communication Studies Today*, ed. Angharad Valdivia (New York: Peter Lang, 2008), 153.

37. The album eventually went double platinum, with over two million sales, and garnered a number of hit singles.

38. "Jennifer Lopez," *Vanity Fair* (December 1999). "Ask Marilyn," *Parade*, date unavailable, 1999.

39. Scholars such as Susan Bordo and Rebecca Epstein theorize this new ideal for what Bordo terms the "slender body." Susan Bordo, *Unbearable Weight: Feminism, Western Culture, and the Body* (Berkeley: University of California Press, 1993). Rebecca Epstein, "Sharon Stone in a Gap Turtleneck," in *Hollywood Goes Shopping*, ed. David Desser and Garth S. Jowett (Minneapolis: University of Minnesota Press, 2000), 179–204. According to Bordo, such bodies are associated with discipline, self-control, success—and I would add "class," as in upper-class status. Given the strength of these norms, actresses now generally are expected to achieve a lean, hyper-controlled body.

40. "Starstruck: Jennifer Lopez," *Planet Out* (Mar. 21, 2001). Online: http://www.planetout.com/entertainment/starstruck/feature/package.html?sernum=145.

41. Epstein, "Sharon Stone in a Gap Turtleneck," 194.

42. Director's Commentary, *Wedding Planner* DVD.

43. Associated Press, "Jennifer Lopez Debuts Clothing Line" (April 26, 2001).

44. Ned Zeman, "Every Move She Makes," *Vanity Fair* (June 2001), 172.

45. As noted by Tara Lockhart, "Jennifer Lopez: The New Wave of Border Crossing," in *From Bananas to Buttocks: The Latina Body in Popular Film and Culture,* ed. Myra Mendible (Austin: University of Texas Press, 2007), 154.

46. Michael Rogin, *Blackface, White Noise: Jewish Immigrants in the Hollywood Melting Pot* (Berkeley: University of California Press, 1996), 4.

47. Richard Laermer, "The 'Lo' Blows: Learning From The Dull Buzz Around J.Lo And Ben," *RLM Public Relations Newsletter* (Nov. 3, 2003), para 6. Online: http://www.rlmpr.com/?pg=newsletter&id=75.

48. *People* magazine, for instance, asked, "Is there too much J.Lo?" in 2002, while Lopez was still engaged to Ben Affleck. Steven M. Silverman, "Overexposed? Is There Too Much J.Lo?" *People* (Dec. 9, 2002): headline. Online: http://www.people.com/people/article/0,,625069,00.html.

Chapter 7. Ethnic Ambiguity in the Era of *Dark Angels*: Jessica Alba and Mixed Latina/o Trends

Some material in this chapter previously appeared in print in my article "Mixed Race in Latinowood: Latino Stardom and Ethnic Ambiguity in the Era of *Dark Angels*," in *Mixed Race Hollywood,* ed. Mary Beltrán and Camilla Fojas (New York: NYU Press, 2008), 248–68.

1. As noted in more detail in this book's Introduction, race is understood here as socially (as opposed to biologically) and politically constructed but resulting in concrete consequences for individuals. In the United States racialization has taken place in relation to white-black and white-nonwhite binary paradigms, with "mixed race" individuals and families challenging these constructed racial divisions. I build in this conceptualization on the work of such scholars as Michael Omi and Howard Winant, and Rosaura Sánchez and Clara Rodríguez in relation to the racialization of Latina/os in particular. See Omi and Winant, *Racial Formation in the United States: From the 1960s to the 1990s* (New York: Routledge, 1994); Rosaura Sánchez, *Telling Identities: The Californio Testimonios* (Minneapolis: University of Minnesota Press, 1995); Clara Rodríguez: *Changing Race: Latinos, the Census and the History of Ethnicity* (New York: NYU Press, 2000).

2. For discussion of the new centrality of mixed-race actors and models in film, television, and popular culture, see Mary Beltrán and Camilla Fojas, Introduction, *Mixed Race Hollywood,* ed. Mary Beltrán and Camilla Fojas (New York: NYU Press, 2008), in addition to the essays in this collection; Marilyn Halter, *Shopping for Identity: The Marketing of Ethnicity* (New York: Schocken Books, 2000); Leon E. Wynter, *American Skin: Pop Culture, Big Business, and the End of White America* (New York: Crown, 2002); Danzy Senna, "The Mulatto Millennium," in *Half and Half,* ed. Clau-

dine O'Hearn (New York: Pantheon, 1998), 205–8; and Caroline A. Streeter, "The Hazards of Visibility: 'Biracial' Women, Media Images, and Narratives of Identity," in *New Faces in a Changing America: Multiracial Identity in the 21st Century,* ed. Loretta I. Winters and Herman L. DeBose (Thousand Oaks, Calif.: Sage, 2003), 301–22.

3. As noted in the Introduction, fair, blonde, and blue-eyed Latina/o actors typically are not considered for Latina/o roles; by Hollywood standards they do not have the preferred "Latin look." See Clara E. Rodríguez, Introduction, *Latin Looks: Images of Latinas and Latinos in the U.S. Media,* ed. Clara E. Rodríguez (Boulder, Colo.: Westview Press, 1997), 4. Such rules regarding the "type" of Latina/o who might be considered for lead roles are beginning to shift, but only slightly.

4. Since she began to publicly promote herself as half Bolivian, Welch was cast in the Latina/o-themed *Tortilla Soup* (2001) and a television series about a Mexican American family written and produced by Gregory Nava, *American Family* (2002).

5. For further discussion of these trends, see Halter, *Shopping for Identity;* and Beltrán and Fojas, Introduction, *Mixed Race Hollywood.*

6. Gregory Velasco y Trianosky, "Beyond Mestizaje: The Future of Race in America," in *New Faces in a Changing America: Multiracial Identity in the 21st Century,* ed. Loretta I. Winters and Herman L. DeBose (Thousand Oaks, Calif.: Sage, 2003), 176.

7. Figures from the 2000 Census cited by Franziska Castillo, "Is Your Family Interracial?" *Latina* (August 2007), 123.

8. Recently scholars such as Gregory Velasco y Trianosky, Angharad Valdivia, and George J. Sánchez have begun to remedy this gap through critical attention to Latinidad in relation to hybridity and/or mixed race; I build on their work here. See Velasco y Trianosky, "Beyond Mestizaje"; Valdivia, "Latinas as Radical Hybrid: Transnationally Gendered Traces in Mainstream Media," *Global Media Journal* 3, no. 4 (Spring 2004). Online: http://lass.calumet.purdue.edu/cca/gmj/sp04/gmj-sp04–valdivia.htm. Sánchez, "Y Tú Que? (Y2K): Latina/o History in the New Millennium," in *"Mixed Race" Studies: A Reader,* ed. Jayne Ifekwunigwe (London: Routledge Press, 2004), 276–82.

9. Clara E. Rodríguez, Introduction, *Latin Looks.*

10. Ruth La Ferla, "Generation E.A: Ethnically Ambiguous," *New York Times* (December 28, 2003), sec. 9, p. 1.

11. Danzy Senna, "The Mulatto Millennium," 205.

12. Dennis Hensley, *Marie Claire* (August 2005), para. 4. Online: http://magazines.ivillage.com/marieclaire/mind/celebinterview/ articles/0,,673522_673618–2,00.html.

13. Alba appears to be quoted in this article by Allison Glock, "The Body and Soul of Jessica Alba," *Rolling Stone* (June 30, 2005), 76–83, para. 6. The paragraph in which the quote appeared is not listed in the excerpted article on *Rolling Stones'* web pages, but the complete article can be found in its reprint version. See "Fantasy

Figure," *The (London) Guardian* (July 17, 2005). Online: http://film.guardian.co.uk/interview/interviewpages/0,,1530103,00.html.

14. Rafael Pérez-Torres, *Mestizaje: Critical Uses of Race in Chicano Culture* (Minneapolis: University of Minnesota Press, 2006); Valdivia, "Latinas as Radical Hybrid."

15. Angharad Valdivia, "Mixed Race on Disney Channel: From *Johnnie Tsunami* through *Lizzie McGuire* and Ending with the *Cheetah Girls*," in *Mixed Race Hollywood: Multiraciality in Film and Media Culture*, ed. Mary Beltrán and Camilla Fojas (New York: NYU Press, 2008).

16. Marc Savlov, "Idle Hands," *Austin Chronicle* (April 30, 1999). Online: http://www.austinchronicle.com/gbase/Calendar/Film?Film=oid%3a142862; Ron Wells, "Idle Hands," *Film Threat* (April 26, 1990). Online: http://www.filmthreat.com/index.php?section=reviews&Id=710.

17. For example, see BBDO New York, "TV Viewing Habits Differ in Black Households," *Minority Markets Alert* 7, no. 5 (May 1995), 2.

18. Eglee cited by Benjamin Svetkey, "The Terminatrix," *Entertainment Weekly* (March 16, 2001), para 14. Online: http://www.ew.com/ew/article/0,,280327_1,00.html.

19. *Dark Angel: Genesis.* 20th Century Fox, 2000. Featurette, *Dark Angel: The Complete First Season* DVD set.

20. *Dark Angel* Season 1, Episode 10: "Art Attack."

21. Benjamin Svetkey, "Jessica Alba Is Our Must Girl of the Summer," *Entertainment Weekly* (June 30, 2006), 45–51, para. 9, and Allison Glock, "The Body and Soul of Jessica Alba," para. 7.

22. Dan Snierson, "Back to the Future: EW Goes behind the Scenes at Fox's Latest Foray into Sci-fi Drama," *Entertainment Weekly* (Mar. 28, 2000), para. 3. Online: http://www.ew.com/ew/article/0,,85597,00.html.

23. For example, see Lewis Beale, "Attack of the Sexy Tough Women," *New York Daily News* (October 19, 2000), 52.

24. Benjamin Svetkey, "The Terminatrix," para. 12.

25. Latina.com, "Jessica Alba to host MTV Movie Awards," http://www.latina.com/latina/searchresults.jsp;jsessionid=2A538684F558A74579BCED3D09A6A9B8.

26. Valdivia, "Latinas as Radical Hybrid," para. 13.

27. Ella Shohat and Robert Stam's discussion of white centrism as reinforced in studio-era Hollywood through lack of attention to realistic language and accent of nonwhite characters, particularly those from regions deemed Third World, is still relevant when considering Alba's (lack of) verisimilitude in these roles. *Unthinking Eurocentrism: Multiculturalism and the Media* (New York: Routledge, 1994).

28. Svetkey, "Jessica Alba Is Our Must Girl of the Summer," 45–51.

29. Emanual Itier, "Exclusive Interview: Jessica Alba Is Very Visible in *Fantastic Four 2*," *iF Magazine* (June 18, 2007). Online: http://www.ifmagazine.com/feature.asp?article=2173.

30. Allison Glock, "The Body and Soul of Jessica Alba," para. 7.

31. Diane Negra, *Off-White Hollywood: American Culture and Ethnic Stardom* (London: Routledge, 2001).

32. This information has been confirmed by Dawson in multiple published interviews, including Logan Hill's "Avenue A-Lister" in *New York* (September 5, 2005).

33. See Juan Flores, "Qúe Assimilated, Brother, Yo Soy Assimilado: The Structuring of Puerto Rican Identity in the U.S.," in *Challenging Fronteras: Structuring Latina and Latina/o Lives in the U.S.,* ed. Mary Romero, Pierrette Hongdagnu-Sotelo, and Vilma Ortiz (New York: Routledge, 1997), 175–86.

34. Alba has been nominated three times for ALMA Awards, twice for *Dark Angel* and once for her role in *Sin City.* Rosario Dawson, in contrast, has received one ALMA Award nomination, for *Rent,* and has received nominations from the NAACP, Black Reel, and the Black Movie Awards for her performances in *Light It Up, Rent, 25th Hour,* and *Sin City.* In 2004, she was given the Rising Star Award at the American Black Film Festival.

35. "Love in the Time of Money," *The Hollywood Reporter* (January 14, 2002); Andrew O'Hehir, "Movie Reviews: *The Rundown,*" Salon.com (September 26, 2003). Online: http://www.salon.com.

36. Logan Hill, "Avenue A-Lister," *New York* (September 5, 2005).

37. Gregory Velasco y Trianosky, "Beyond *Mestizaje.*"

38. Vicki L. Ruiz, "Color Coded: Reflections at the Millennium," in *Decolonial Voices: Chicana and Chicano Cultural Studies in the 21st Century,* ed. Arturo J. Aldama and Naomi H. Quiñonez (Bloomington: Indiana University Press), 378; Ian Haney López, *Racism on Trial: The Chicano Fight for Justice* (Cambridge, Mass.: Belknap Press, 2003), 76–79.

39. Svetkey, "Jessica Alba Is Our Must Girl of the Summer," para. 8.

40. Gloria Anzaldúa, *Borderlands/La Frontera: The New Mestiza, Second Edition* (San Francisco: Aunt Lute Books, 1999), 99–122.

41. José Itzigsohn, "The Formation of Latino and Latina Panethnic Identities," in *Not Just Black and White: Historical and Contemporary Perspectives on Immigration, Race, and Ethnicity in the United States,* ed. Nancy Foner and George M. Fredrickson (New York: Russell Sage Foundation, 2004), 200.

42. Anzaldúa, *Borderlands/La Frontera,* 99–122.

Index

Page numbers in italics refer to illustrations.

ambivalence toward Latina/os in the United States, 42, 75, 85, 152; as evidenced in media representation, 2, 72, *73*, 85, 152; expressed about Latino films by film studios, 123; expressed by the U.S. news media, 123–26
American Family, 127, 186n1
American Indian actors, 118
"Americanization" programs and U.S. Latina/os, 21, 178n14
American Playhouse, 119
Amundson, Daniel R., 187n9
Anaconda, 140–41, 195n24
Andrade, Ray, 93–94, 100, 101
Angel Eyes, 148–49
Anzaldúa, Gloria, 170–71
Aparicio, Frances: and Cándida Jáquez, 128; and Susan Chávez Silverman, 3, 10
archival research, 13
Arnaz, Desi, 4, 14, 63, 68; assimilation of, as U.S. star, 60–61, 169; critical reception of, 46, 48, 50, 55; and *I Love Lucy*, 40, 51–61, 65; marriage of, to Lucille Ball, 46–48, 50–54, 59, 60–61; as musician and band leader, 40, 43, 44–45, 50, 53, 54, 63; name change of, 50; nightclub act of, with Lucille Ball, 52; 1940s theater and film career of, 40, 45–51, 68; pan-Latino "translation artist," 41, 43, 63, 180n4; in relation to Cuban American identity, 40, 43; as television executive, 40, 53, 58–59, 60, 183n48; as *vividor*, 181n11; youth of, 44
assimilation: and Desi Arnaz, 60–61; as focus of some U.S. Latina/os, 49; in relation to marriage to an unambiguously white American, 56
audience reception: and Latina reaction to discussion of Jennifer Lopez's body in the mainstream media, 194n5
authenticity, perceived: as standard for Latina/o performers, 43–44, 60; trope of, in Latina/o star promotion, 136, 137

baby boom: children of, as young adults, 89; impact of, 21, 51
Bad One, The, 34
Baldwin, James, 7
Ball, Lucille, 14, 46–48, 50–54, 59, 60–61
Ballad of Gregorio Cortez, The, 15, 109, 113, 118, 119–20; original corrido, 119, 192n32

Bamba, La, 108, 113, 122, 123, 140
Banderas, Antonio, 9
bandido/cholo roles, 2, 12
Barrera, Aida, 191n12
Bataan, 49–50, 60
Battlestar Galactica, 128
beauty norms: broadening of, 144, 169–70; and Latinas, 22, 62, 66, 132–33, 143–44; and Mexican American actors, 128–30; and national beauty pageants, 184nn6–7; and Edward James Olmos, 125; and privileging of Latin Americans among Latina/os, 129. *See also* Eurocentric standards of attractiveness; whitening
Beltrán, Mary, 197n2, 198n5
Benamou, Catherine, 180n3
Berg, Charles Ramírez. *See* Ramírez Berg, Charles
Bernstein, Matthew, 20
Berry, Sarah, 11
bifurcation of Latina/o actors' opportunity: based on appearance, 7–9, 156, 166
biracial and bicultural star couples: Desi Arnaz and Lucille Ball, 47–48, 52, 61; Jennifer Lopez and romantic partners, 147, 151, 152
Bird of Paradise, 35
black-white binary: and U.S. notions of race, 5–6
Bladerunner, 114, 116, 118
blockbuster films: impact of, on stardom, 111
blond hair: as signifier of "whiteness," 66, 166, 198n3
Bodeen, DeWitt, 29
body, the: and counter-hegemonic potential, 132–33, 143–44; differing valence of, in English-language and Latino-oriented press, 136, 138–39; emphasized in Latina star promotion, 10, 85, 138, 185n30; and Hollywood standards, 7–9; and Latinas in 1930s films, 39; in Jennifer Lopez's career, 16, 132–33, 136–39, 142–44, 152; in Rita Moreno's career, 62–63, 74–75, 78, 83, 85; slender and controlled, 146–147, 196n39
body type: and perceived Latina authenticity, 136
"booty brouhaha": and Jennifer Lopez, 131–32, 143–44
Born in East L.A., 108, 113
brand: contemporary stars as, 143

culture, 159, 185n30; as veterans, 49. *See also* Latina/os
Mexican cinema, 38
Mexican Spitfire film series, 27, 66
Mexico: actors from, 21
MGM (Metro Goldwyn Mayer), 49, 68–70
Miami Vice, 109, 120
Milnick, Jeffrey, 66–67, 79
Miranda, Carmen, 10, 27, 41, 48, 55, 67, 90, 180n2
miscegenation: as banned in Production Code, 28–29
Miss America pageant, 66
mixed race: and Jessica Alba, 159–65, 168–71; and Rosario Dawson, 166–68, 170–71; as emphasized in *Dark Angel*, 161–64; and Latina/o actors, 4, 16, 71, 113, 154–77; and Freddie Prinze, 86, 96, 98, 187n2; and racialization based on appearance, 166; vogue for, in contemporary media, 157–58, 163, 197n2
Money Train, 136, 137
Montalban, Ricardo, 50, 71, 91
Montgomery, Kathryn, 93
Moreno, Antonio, 21, 27
Moreno, Rita, 4, 10, 14–15, 62–65, 67–85; contract of, with MGM, 68–70; contract of, with Twentieth Century-Fox, 75–77; critical reception of, 70, 74, 79, 83; post-studio career of, 71–74; recent career of, 84; and *The Ritz*, 82, 83–84; upbringing of, and years as a child performer, 67–68; and *West Side Story*, 78–80
multicultural ethos: in contemporary children's television programming, 159, 161
Muni, Paul, 12
mural art: and Chicana/o and Puerto Rican activism, 108–9, 110, 126–27, 193n61
Murray, Susan, 42, 43
music: as element of Hollywood Latinidad, 27, 41, 43, 84
My Family/Mi Familia, 136–37

NAACP, 167
nationality: impact of, on opportunity for Latina/o actors, 8–9, 78, 113, 129
Nava, Gregory, 113, 136–37
Navy Comes Through, The, 48, 50
NBC (National Broadcasting Company), 52, 86–87, 93, 106

NCLR (National Council of La Raza), 163, 167, 188n12
Negra, Diane, 74, 166
networks, television: notions of, about Latina/os as potential series stars, 15, 52, 89, 92, 93–94; response of, to Chicana/o media advocates, 90–91, 93–94, 187–88n11
New Hollywood shifts: impact of, 111, 125, 133–35
Newman, Kathleen, 124–26, 193n51
Night of the Following Day, 81
1920s era: attitudes toward Mexicans in, 23, 24; social interests of, 9, 19
1930s era: interests of filmgoing audiences in, 27, 28; social interests of, as evidenced in Hollywood films, 26–27; social interests of, as evidenced in social institutions and "Americanization" programs, 178n14
1940s and '50s era: impact of social shifts on film industry and film genres in, 41, 66; popular television programming in, 52; racial politics of casting in, 63, 75, 84–85; rise of consumerism and home ownership for white Americans in, 51–52, 66; status of Mexican Americans and other U.S. Latina/os in, 49, 181–82n25
1960s and '70s era: perceived attitudes of television viewers in, 103; social shifts in, 88–91, 98
1980s era: continued economic disparities between Latina/os and non-Hispanic whites in, 127; rising visibility of Latina/os in popular culture in, 108–9, 111, 122
1990s and 2000s era: social shifts in, 1–2, 133–35, 140, 144–46
Nochimson, Martha, 53
Noriega, Chon A., 7, 49, 71, 88, 187n3, 187n9, 190n55; on Chicano cinema, 112, 191n9, 191n11; on *Chico and the Man*, 90, 105
Norte, El, 15, 108, 113, 122
Nosotros (actors' advocacy group), 13, 91
Novarro, Ramon, 18, 21, 27–28, 30, 35

Oboler, Suzanne, 193n47
"off-whiteness": in relation to star image, 74, 166
Oguss, Greg, 88, 103, 104–5, 187n3
Olmos, Edward James, 4, 15, 108–11, 113, 114–30; awards received by, 109, 116, 190–91n6; central role of, in Latina/o

Suberví-Vélez, Federico, 194n6
Summer and Smoke, 80
Suntree, Susan, 62
Súper, El, 108
symbolic annihilation, 12
"synergistic" star couple: Desi Arnaz and
 Lucille Ball as example of, 53, 56–58, 60
synergy: as element of star and media promotion, 134, 135

talent: recognition of, as overriding promotional element, 118–19, 120, 124
talent managers and agents: as cultural brokers, 134–35, 136, 141–42; and Jennifer Lopez, 141; and Rita Moreno, 70–71; rising
 importance of, in post-studio era, 70
Teatro Campesino, El, 192n21
television: as forum for a film's premiere,
 119; impact of, in the United States, 41, 42,
 51–52, 66; and new formation of stardom,
 42; opportunities for Latina/o actors
 and performers in, 4, 86, 105–6, 186n1;
 produced by Latina/os, 4, 14, 40, 58–59,
 191n11
television programming: bilingual children's
 programming, 112; "ethnic" situation
 comedies, prior to mid-1950s, 52, 182n34;
 featuring nonwhite stars, 111; Latina/o
 public affairs shows, 112; and Latina/o
 representation, 107, 163, 175n17, 187n9;
 Latina/o-themed, 133; "socially relevant"
 situation comedies of 1970s, 3, 89, 111–12.
 See also *Chico and the Man; I Love Lucy*
theater: as providing more opportunity for
 Latina/o actors, 78, 81
tie-ins: and star image, 42, 76
Toast of New Orleans, 69–70
Tomás Rivera Policy Institute, 11
Tony Award: and Rita Moreno, 116, 191n6
Too Many Girls: film (1940), 45–46, 47; theatrical version (1939), 45
Tovar, Lupita, 27
training, theatrical: impact of, on actors' opportunities, 69, 129
transitional moments in Latina/o media
 representation and stardom, 3
transition from silent to sound film, 2, 4,
 26–32; impact of, on film industry, 26–27;
 and radio broadcast by United Artists actors, 31–32

Treaty of Guadalupe Hidalgo: life for Mexican Americans afterward, 75
Treviño, Jesus, 112
tropicalism: as reinforcing hegemonic notions; 10; as utilized in star promotion,
 9–10, 15, 74–75
Twentieth Century-Fox, 37, 48, 75–77, 122
typecasting: attempts to avoid, 136, 144

Ugly Betty, 2, 63, 107
Union Square, 186n1
United Artists: and Dolores Del Rio, 18,
 31–32, 34; and Rita Moreno, 68, 75
Universal Pictures, 116
Untamed, 77
"urban" audience: sought by Fox Television, 136
urban image, impact of: on Rosario Dawson, 167, 168; on Jennifer Lopez, 147
U.S. audience: perceived as white, 146
U.S.-centric ideology: and Hollywood films,
 41, 65–66

Vagabond King, The, 77
Valderrama, Wilmer, 17
Valdez, Luis, 112, 113, 115
Valdivia, Angharad, 7, 9, 159, 163, 198n8
Valentino, Rudolph, 20
Valle, Victor, 125
Vargas, Jacob, 130
Vega, Paz, 129
Velasco y Trianosky, Gregory, 157, 169,
 198n8
Vélez, Lupe, 8, 18, 21, 25, 27

Walker, Alexander, 20, 26
Warner Bros., 36, 122
wave of interest in Latina/o performers and
 culture, 9, 17, 108–9, 111; in 1920s, 17–22,
 38; in 1980s, 108–9, 123–24; in 1990s, 132,
 133–35, 144–46
Wedding Planner, The, 148; promotional
 poster, *149*
Welch, Raquel, 16, 157, 198n4
West Side Story, 11, 15, 63, 77–80, 186n42
What Price Glory?, 18, 24
whiteness: and casting of Latina/o actors,
 7–8, 38, 48, 63, 66 (*see also* Spanish ancestry); and casting paradigms, 7–8, 26–27,
 38, 175n22; as federal racial designation,

MARY C. BELTRÁN is an assistant professor of Communication Arts and Chicana/o and Latina/o Studies at the University of Wisconsin–Madison. She is the co-editor, with Camilla Fojas, of *Mixed Race Hollywood*.

The University of Illinois Press
is a founding member of the
Association of American University Presses.

Composed in 10.5/13 Adobe Minion Pro
with Frutiger and Bauer Bodoni display
by Jim Proefrock
at the University of Illinois Press
Manufactured by Cushing-Malloy, Inc.

University of Illinois Press
1325 South Oak Street
Champaign, IL 61820-6903
www.press.uillinois.edu